IF THE CAP FITS

IF THE CAP FITS

by

Colin Bateman

Tony Williams Publications

Published in Great Britain by Tony Williams Publications.

Designed and Typeset by Interface 0395 68681

Cover Design by Bob Bickerton

Printed and bound in Great Britain by R. Booth (Bookbinder) Ltd., Mabe, Penryn, Cornwall

Distributed by Little Red Witch Books 0823 490080

ISBN 1-869833-21-X

INTRODUCTION

THE problem has been what to leave out. All 267 of the cricketers to have played for England since the last War have, by the very process of collecting that famous dark blue cap, reached the top of their sport. In some cases, however, the cap has fitted a sight more snugly than in others. They are all fine players in their own right and all have stories to tell of their climb to the top, their time at the summit and their slide down the other side. You could, in fact, write a book about each of them.

These pages attempt to reveal some of the extraordinary characters nurtured in this summer game of ours. No other sport, surely, attracts such a diversity of performers: the player thrown off a tour and out of the game because he spoke to a newspaper; the player who tore up a cheque from his former England captain in anger; the best fast bowler in the country who spent his winters down the pit because his face did not fit; the player who cancelled his wedding to play for England; the player who turned up for a Test clutching a hoax telegram. And why did Colin Cowdrey's name provoke such a mixed response, why did Jim Laker resent Peter May, Geoff Boycott resent Mike Denness and Joe Hardstaff resent Gubby Allen? You will find the answers here.

I hope these pages will capture the joy and tragedy, the beauty and the beast of cricket. What I have discovered in my research is that nothing is new in the game: selectors have always had their favourites, players have always suffered shabby treatment, some have been picked because of who they knew not how they played, others have been ignored because of their tone of voice and independence of spirit. Disciplining players for what the Establishment sees as breaches of protocol is as old as the game itself.

The book is not a statistician's delight. It is not meant to be. It is deliberately light on the clutter of figures, but the relevant details are all here. The text is subjective and I have picked out 50 players for major profiles. These are not the most capped players nor the best. They are my selection of the 50 most significant Test players of the past 50 years. You are certain to disagree with some of the choices. Another 50 cricketers receive lengthy analysis but every player is profiled. I hope you enjoy the photographs, there is at least one of every player. The pictures are a fascinating mix, some have never been published before and they are as important as the text. After the players' section comes a brief guide to the 33 captains of England since the War with their records. There is also a 'Championship Table' of the counties who have provided the most men for national service.

The players are listed in alphabetical order wherever possible, although slight variations are made for presentation purposes. All statistics are correct to May 1 1993.

Colin Bateman
May 1993

ACKNOWLEDGEMENTS

I WOULD like to thank the following for sharing with me their memories, knowledge and opinions. Without their assistance this book would not have been possible.

David Allen, Dennis Amiss, Keith Andrew, Bob Appleyard, Trevor Bailey, Jack Bannister, Alec Bedser, Brian Bolus, David Brown, Alan Butcher, Donald Carr, Denis Compton, Nick Cook, Mike Denness, Godfrey Evans, Duncan Fearnley, David Foot, Pat Gibson, Tom Graveney, Joe Hardstaff, Michael Hill, David Hughes, Ray Illingworth, Alan Knott, Ken Lawrence, Peter Lever, David Llewellyn, David Lloyd, Arnold Long, Malcolm Lorimer, Brian Luckhurst, Peter May, Geoff Miller, Arthur Milton, Mike Murray, Peter Parfitt, Jim Parks, Pat Pocock, Geoff Pullar, Andy Radd, Peter Richardson, Mike Selvey, Phil Sharpe, Alan Smith, Mike Smith, John Snow, Brian Statham, David Steele, Micky Stewart, Raman Subba Row, Bob Taylor, Ivo Tennant, Fred Titmus, Mike Turner, Peter Walker, David Warner, Alan Wharton, Roy Wilkinson, Guy Willatt and Peter Wynne-Thomas. Thanks also to Bob Thomas for use of his picture library, and to Colorsport.

Above all, however, I would like to thank Brenda for her unflagging encouragement and patience.

Dedicated to the Three Musketeers.

TCCB

THE Publishers and Editor are pleased that **The Test and County Cricket Board** have accepted 'If The Cap Fits' as an official T.C.C.B. publication and thank them for their kind advice and support in the promotion of this book.

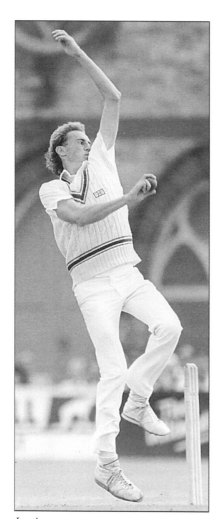

Jon Agnew

DAVID ALLEN
Gloucestershire 39 Tests 1960-66

DAVID Allen has become used to being a quiz question. When Colin Cowdrey went out to bat against the 1963 West Indians at Lord's with his broken arm in plaster, who was the other batsman? It was Allen, who protected Cowdrey and took the strike to save the Test. It is an injustice that such a fine slow bowler should always be associated with one of his displays as a doughty tail-ender. Allen, the Bristol boy with the soft vowels and the countryside amble to the wicket, was a constant member of the Test side for five years. Once Jim Laker had departed the scene, Allen had to contend with competition from fellow off-spinners Fred Titmus and Ray Illingworth, who were both better batsmen. And if any of the trio fell below par, Allen's Gloucestershire colleague John Mortimore was pushing for the off-spinner's role.

Yet Allen's subtle variations and accuracy made him a regular choice at home and an automatic selection for tours. In six winters he completed the set of all the Test-playing countries. He could bowl all day if the captain switched him on — and he often did. In India and Pakistan in 1961-62, he bowled an incredible 482 overs in the Test series alone. Today most spinners would be pleased to bowl so many in a championship season.

Allen's outwardly relaxed manner disguised the effort that went into his craft but some captains were suspicious, and towards the end of his 20 summers at Bristol his relationship with skipper Tony Brown, with whom he had grown up on a cricket field, became strained. Allen even found himself left out of his own benefit match. He is still a regular visitor to the Nevil Road ground and works in the drinks trade.

D.A. ALLEN born 29.10.35 (Horfield, Bristol). Tests 39 runs 918 average 25.50 wickets 122 average 30.97

JON AGNEW
Leicestershire 3 Tests 1984-85

TALL, lean but with deceptive pace when everything was in correct working order, Jon Agnew grew so frustrated with England's selection policy that his decision to give up playing at 30 to pursue a media career was made that much easier. His fleeting taste of Test cricket should have been added to in 1987 and '88 when he was the most consistent fast bowler in the country, taking 194 wickets, but in 1989, when England were desperate for pace bowlers, his omission amounted to wanton neglect by a regime which questioned his desire. Now making regular Test appearances as the BBC cricket correspondent.

J.P. AGNEW born 4.4.60 (Macclesfield, Cheshire). Tests 3 runs 10 average 10 wickets 4 average 93.25

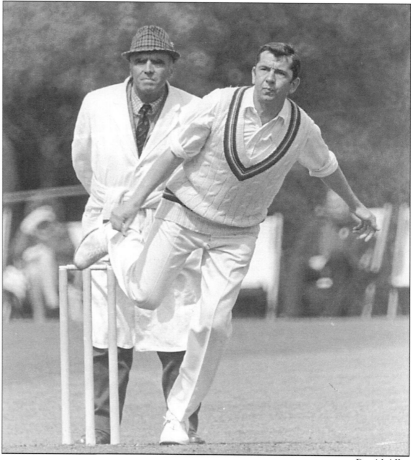

David Allen

SIR GEORGE 'GUBBY' ALLEN
Middlesex 25 Tests 1930-48

HE **WAS** not one of the greatest cricketers, but Gubby Allen has been the most influential figure in the game this century. For 60 years he was a revered figure in the corridors of power at Lord's, where he had a private entrance made for him from his garden, which backed on to the famous old ground. When he knew death was close late in 1989, he asked to be taken from hospital to his home so he could die within sight of the red-brick pavilion and the stand named after him.

George Oswald Browning Allen loved cricket but did not live for it. He had a colourful life that, like many England captains', began overseas. Allen was born in Australia but his father brought the family to England when he was six so the children could have an English education. He went to Cambridge but was playing for Middlesex irregularly from the age of 18.

He was a charging fast bowler with an excellent action and a hard-hitting middle-order batsman, but while he was with Middlesex over a 30 year span, he played only 146 matches. He had to work for a living in the City, turning out for Middlesex when he could spare the time. Even Saturday mornings were occupied by his job with Debenhams and often he would be named in the team but not be able to get away from work until after midday. It was on one such occasion that he turned up late, took the field and proceeded to take all 10 Lancashire wickets for 40 runs.

On his second England appearance, batting at No. 9, he scored 122 in New Zealand's inaugural Test. His partnership that day of 246 with Les Ames is still a world record for the eighth wicket. He was part of the 1932-33 'Bodyline' tour of Australia from which he emerged as England's White Knight as he took no part in Douglas Jardine's leg-side short-pitched fast bowling tactics which caused uproar. There are two versions of events: one is that Allen refused to have anything

to do with such dastardly tactics; the other, which several of his team-mates have voiced, is that he was not accurate enough and so bowled to an orthodox field. Whatever, the MCC saw him as the man to restore relations with Australia and groomed him as skipper for the return visit four years later.

Allen was already well versed in the workings of the MCC committee — then the most powerful body in cricket — having been elected a member at the tender age of 27. He had friends, notably Sir Pelham

Warner, in the right places and impressed with his strong, eloquent opinions. The 1936-37 tour of Australia as captain was the highlight of Allen's playing career and although England lost a marvellous rubber 3-2 after winning the first two Tests, he returned with reputation enhanced.

During the War, Allen served as a spy exposing the siting of Germany's ground-to-air defences, but one of the more colourful incidents of his military career was more hilarious than heroic. When he heard his brother had been wounded in Dunkirk, he flew to break the news to his mother and landed in an Eton playing field near her home. The plane — the first one he could find — had Belgian markings and when Allen returned to it, he found it surrounded by the Eton Home Guard who promptly arrested him as a German spy.

After the War, Allen's cricket future lay in administration but he was to make an astonishing playing return, leading England to the West Indies in 1947-48, aged 45, having played in only one match for Middlesex the previous summer. Tom Pearce of Essex had been invited by Warner to lead the side, made arrangements to be away from work for the winter, then read in the newspapers that Allen had been made captain for the tour, from which many of England's leading players had opted out. Allen pulled a muscle skipping on the voyage to the Caribbean and missed the first Test in the four-match series which England lost 2-0. Selectorial foibles are nothing new.

Off the field, Allen served as MCC president and treasurer, and as a successful chairman of selectors from 1955 to '61. His influence spread throughout the game and in 1952 he co-wrote the *MCC Coaching Book* which has sold more than 100,000 copies and is still regarded as something of a cricket 'bible'. It is said that the book, and Allen's dogmatic belief in its creed, condemned a number of potentially fine Test bowlers, who were overlooked because they did not conform to his idea of a classic action. Allen completed a family hat-trick in 1986 when, like his grandfather and father, he was knighted.

G.O.B. ALLEN born 31.7.02 (Sydney, Australia). Died 29.11.89. Tests 25 runs 750 average 24.19 100s 1 wickets 81 average 29.37

Gubby Allen (left) greets Australian captain Don Bradman when the 1938 tourists arrive from Southampton at Waterloo.

DENNIS AMISS

Warwickshire 50 Tests 1966-77

THE sight of Dennis Amiss chugging benignly into a cricket ground behind his pipe was one of the most misleading images in cricket. The gentle Brummie nature that served him well in his later career as an undertaker, disguised one of the most hardened and often unappreciated batsmen to play for England in the post-War period. He had to fight battles with himself and with others before he emerged at the end of a splendid career with 102 first-class centuries, an England record over 50 Tests that ranked with the best and an MBE for his services to the game.

But it was never easy. Amiss probably realised fate had strewn a few trip-wires in his path when at 17 he suffered a bad back injury playing soccer, which meant for the rest of his sporting life he had to start each day with a stretching routine to loosen up. He made his Warwickshire debut in 1960 and his England debut in 1966 but it was not until the following year that he scored his first championship century.

For someone who topped 100 hundreds, he was a remarkably late starter. Amiss' batting was watchful and intense. He had powerful forearms and loved to get on the front foot to drive — yet there lurked the suspicion that he did not have the stomach for the big occasion, a suspicion fed by a return of only one half-century in his first 12 Tests. He appeared to be an instinctive flincher when faced with short-pitched bowling and had struggled against

spin, but he conquered both through his own determination and strength of character.

Amiss lost his Test place at the start of 1973 in India yet in that year he fought back to score 1,356 runs — a record for a calendar year by an England player — at an average of 79.76. His voracious appetite for runs was demonstrated by the fact that meagre centuries did not satisfy him; of the 11 he scored for England, only three fell short of the 150 mark.

'Dennis was always tinkering with his game, he was a bigger perfectionist than Colin Cowdrey,' says his former Edgbaston colleague Jack Bannister. To overcome his trouble with spin, Amiss managed to persuade two of India's finest — Bishen Bedi and Chandrasekhar — to bowl at him for hours on end in the nets on England's 1972-73 tour of the sub-continent; to overcome his trouble with bouncers he ignored the scorn of many observers to become the pioneer of the batting helmet.

Yet perhaps his biggest battle was to come not against the world's finest bowlers but against the attitudes of his fellow professionals at Edgbaston where a great servant of the county found himself despised and shunned. The cause was his decision to turn his back on England and take the money on offer in Australia to join Kerry Packer's cricket circus.

The initial revolt in county cricket against the Packer players was beginning to subside in 1978, everywhere but at Edgbaston where

Bob Willis, who had himself considered an offer from Packer, partly orchestrated the anti-Amiss feelings. Amiss would often go through a whole day's play without exchanging a word with his team-mates; in the dressing room he changed in his own silent corner. Yet instead of forcing him out, the situation made the phlegmatic Amiss even more determined to stay on when his contract expired at the end of the summer. Amiss became a *cause celebre* for a group of supporters trying to oust the Warwickshire committee, Lord's saw the impasse as an obstacle to resolving the Packer affair — and eventually when Warwickshire offered him a new contract for 1979 and everyone breathed a sigh of relief, Amiss said typically: 'I'll think about it.'

Sign he did, however, and play on magnificently for another nine seasons, but he never had another chance for England and in 1982 threw in his lot with the next group of privately paid cricketers to leave these shores, Graham Gooch's rebel side bound for South Africa. After his playing days, Amiss' strength of character proved an important part in the resurgence of Warwickshire, where he became cricket chairman, and in 1992 he was made an England selector.

D.L. AMISS born 7.4.43 (Birmingham). Tests 50 runs 3612 average 46.3 100s 11

Dennis Amiss — the man behind the mask.

Paul Allott

PAUL ALLOTT
Lancashire 13 Tests 1981-85

APOWERFULLY built, skilful swing bowler, Paul Allott just lacked that extra zip to enjoy anything more than a respectable Test career. He was a consistent and cagey county performer who was at his best in English conditions, and he played only two Tests abroad. Back trouble, which forced him home from the 1984-85 Indian tour after the first Test, did not help his progress.

P.J.W. ALLOTT born 14.10.56 (Altrincham, Cheshire). Tests 13 runs 213 average 14.20 wickets 26 average 41.69

BOB APPLEYARD
Yorkshire 9 Tests 1954-67

BOB Appleyard had the most extraordinary career. In his limited Test life he had a remarkable strike rate of a wicket every 51 balls — Trueman's ratio was one every 49 — and in first-class cricket his 708 wickets cost a miserly 15 runs apiece. When health gave him a chance, Appleyard was one of England's finest bowlers.

An engineer in the Navy during the War, the strong, forthright Appleyard played Bradford League cricket until Yorkshire gave him two games in 1950 at 26. The next year, he had a full season and took 200 wickets at an average of 14. He was taken ill during the first match of 1952, then spent 11 months in hospital recovering from tuberculosis after losing part of a lung, and missed the next year recuperating.

He returned in 1954, took 154 wickets at 14 apiece and was selected for England, starting with 5 for 51 in his first innings. His bowling was a canny mixture. He would often open for Yorkshire, with Trueman, bowling fast-medium seamers. Then he would switch to self-taught off-cutters. His reasoning for being a multi-purpose bowler was 'You can't take wickets with your sweater on.'

The TB left him weaker and made

Bob Appleyard

him change to a more orthodox off-spin which was still good enough to see him picked ahead of Jim Laker for the 1954-55 tour of Australasia. Yet by 1958, at the age of 34, it was all over for Appleyard as abruptly as it had started, a shoulder injury influencing Yorkshire's decision to release him.

He enjoyed another rare achievement, winning an out-of-court settlement for unfair dismissal from printing magnate Robert Maxwell, whom he had threatened to sue. Appleyard now puts much of his energy into developing Yorkshire's youth trust scheme at Bradford.

R. APPLEYARD born 27.6.24 (Wibsey, Yorkshire). Tests 9 runs 51 average 17 wickets 31 average 17.87

KEITH ANDREW
Northamptonshire 2 Tests 1954-63

KEITH Andrew was a high-quality wicketkeeper but was unfortunate that the early part of his career coincided with the reign of Godfrey Evans, who allowed him only one brief look-in on the 1954-55 Ashes tour when he was suffering from sunstroke. In 1963, England recalled Andrew for the first Test against the West Indies but then decided they needed a wicketkeeper-batsman to bolster the side and called up Jim Parks. A former Northamptonshire captain, Andrew plays a vital role in youth cricket as chief executive of the National Cricket Association.

K.V. ANDREW born 15.12.29 (Oldham, Lancashire). Tests 2 runs 29 average 9.66 dismissals 1 caught 1

Keith Andrew

Geoff Arnold

GEOFF ARNOLD
Surrey and Sussex 34 Tests 1967-75

WHEN Geoff Arnold emerged at the Oval as a swing and seam bowler of genuine class, England thought they had at last found a regular new-ball partner for the hostile John Snow. It was not to be. They played only eight Tests together; it seemed that when Arnold was in favour, Snow was not.

Arnold, with his powerful shoulders and good action, could be devastating when conditions suited and he was an intelligent, aggressive bowler. Unfortunately, knee trouble took the edge off his pace, which probably stopped him developing into a world-class performer. For three years, however, he was an England regular, uncomplaining when he had to shoulder a heavy workload.

He bowled tirelessly on the gruelling 1972-73 tour of India and Pakistan, which he started with match figures of 9 for 91 — his best — in the victory in Delhi. The next summer he bowled his heart out against both New Zealand and the West Indies, delivering 310 overs and taking 31 wickets. He and Snow routed the Kiwis, but that was to be the last summer their paths crossed.

In 1978 Arnold quit Surrey and moved south to Sussex, in effect replacing Snow who had finished the previous year. 'Horse' (his initials are GG) had five seasons at Hove before returning to the Oval as coach, and in recent years his expertise has been harnessed by England, who use him as adviser for the pace bowlers.

G.G. ARNOLD born 3.9.44 (Earlsfield, Surrey). Tests 34 runs 421 average 12.02 wickets 115 average 28.29

MICHAEL ATHERTON
Lancashire 23 Tests 1989-

EVEN before he had played a Test match, Michael Atherton was being touted as a 'future England captain'. The epithet was added to his name so often by the media that his Lancashire team-mates nicknamed him 'Fec'. It was unfair on one so young but he had the temperament and talent to handle it, and indeed, everything was going according to plan until fate hurled a nasty spanner into the works in 1991.

Atherton, with his sound technique and composed nature, was always destined to open for England. He captained England Under-19s at the age of 16, then captained Cambridge University; by 21 he was in the Test team and in his third Test in 1990 he scored 151 off the New Zealand bowling. His partnership with Graham Gooch developed into the most successful opening pairing England had seen for years. A refreshingly independent voice in the England camp, Atherton was installed as Gooch's vice-captain in 1991 for the visit of the West Indies and at 23 was clearly being groomed as his successor.

He had a disastrous series, averaging 8 in five Tests, which was later explained partially by a back problem which forced him to give up his leg-break bowling. The injury, sustained through too much cricket when he was at school, demanded an operation and he missed the 1991-92 World Cup winter, Alec Stewart taking over as opener and vice-captain to great effect. Atherton won his place back in 1992 but curious selectorial decisions left him still struggling to re-establish himself after an unhappy tour of India in '93.

M.A. ATHERTON born 23.3.68 (Manchester). Tests 23 runs 1374 average 32.71 100s 3 wickets 1 average 282

Michael Atherton

Bill Athey

BILL ATHEY
Yorkshire, Gloucestershire and Sussex 23 Tests 1980-88

WITH the Union Jack tattooed on his arm, no-one could doubt the bulldog spirit of Bill Athey, an early-order batsman who enjoyed a long run in the England side once he had escaped the internecine politics of his native Yorkshire in 1983. He missed only one in 20 Tests between 1986 and '88 but never quite graduated with honours at international level, passing 50 only five times in 41 attempts. Joined the 1990 rebel tour to South Africa.

C.W.J. ATHEY born 27.9.57 (Middlesbrough, Yorkshire). Tests 23 runs 919 average 22.97 100s 1

ROB BAILEY
Northamptonshire 4 Tests 1988-90

A POWERFUL, imposing middle-order batsman, Rob Bailey rejected offers to lure him on to the 1990 rebel tour of South Africa because of his desire to play for England. His reward was a place on that winter's trip to the West Indies, the opponents he had faced in his sole Test appearance two years previously. Bailey, like many before him, was found wanting against the Caribbean pace machine, failing to reach a half-century in six innings.

Rob Bailey

Since then his loyalty to English cricket has not been recognised and his destructive batting not seen against more genteel attacks.

R.J. BAILEY born 28.10.63 (Biddulph, Staffordshire). Tests 4 runs 119 average 14.87

DAVID BAIRSTOW
Yorkshire 4 Tests 1979-81

FLAME-HAIRED and passionate about his cricket, 'Bluey' Bairstow served Yorkshire with distinction as wicketkeeper and defiant batsman for

David Bairstow

21 seasons, three as skipper. He took an A-level at 6 am in order to make his debut as a schoolboy in 1970 and turned down a contract with Bradford City FC, such were his ambitions in the summer sport. His ebullient style was seen in the Test arena only fleetingly but he never let anyone down.

D.L. BAIRSTOW born 1.9.51 (Horton, Yorkshire). Tests 4 runs 125 average 20.83 dismissals 13 caught 12 stumped 1

CHRIS BALDERSTONE
Yorkshire and Leicestershire 2 Tests 1976

BUT for his love of soccer, Chris Balderstone might have achieved much more as a Test cricketer. His football career with Huddersfield, Carlisle, Doncaster and Queen of the South often curtailed his summer job as a middle-order batsman and left-arm spinner in August, although he once played both sports on the same day, turning out for Doncaster in the evening after a day's championship play. His cricket flourished as the soccer subsided and his two Test caps came against the West Indies when he was 35. Now a first-class umpire.

J.C. BALDERSTONE born 16.11.40 (Longwood, Yorkshire). Tests 2 runs 39 average 9.75 wickets 1 average 80.00

Chris Balderstone

GRAHAM BARLOW
Middlesex 3 Tests 1976-77

GRAHAM Barlow was a confident batsman — possibly over-confident when it came to his fleeting Test opportunity. In five innings, this attacking left-hander, who was a brilliant taker of the quick single, never reached double figures, and flaws in his defence persuaded the selectors to look elsewhere. A former England under-23 rugby union cap, Barlow was plagued by back and hip trouble in his latter career and emigrated to South Africa.

G.D. BARLOW born 26.3.50 (Folkestone, Kent). Tests 3 runs 17 average 4.25

CHARLIE BARNETT
Gloucestershire 20 Tests 1933-48

WHEN the War started, Charlie Barnett was 29 and was in all probability reaching his prime years as a strong, thrilling opening batsman. In 1938 he had cracked an undefeated 98 before lunch on the first day of the Ashes series, the closest an Englishman has come to scoring a century before lunch on the first day of a Test against Australia. After the conflict, he slipped down the order and played in four more Tests but was never the same force, producing a top score of 33. He became a school coach until his retirement.

For illustration see also Tony Greig

C.J. BARNETT born 3.7.10 (Cheltenham, Gloucestershire). Died 28.5.93. Tests 20 runs 1098 average 35.41 100s 2

BOB BARBER
Lancashire and Warwickshire
28 Tests 1960-68

ONE-DAY cricket is so often blamed for ruining young cricketers, but in the case of Bob Barber, it was the making of him. An inveterate pusher and nudger for nine summers at Lancashire, he appeared to have ended his England days when he moved to Warwickshire for the 1963 season. He had played nine Tests, eight of them in India and Pakistan, and had passed 50 only twice.

The summer of his move to Edgbaston coincided with the start of one-day county cricket in the Gillette Cup. Barber, with his style, did not think he should be in the side but he was picked anyway, decided to slog and saw the light. He became a born-again batsman, transformed from the doughty blocker into an enterprising, dangerous left-handed opener who always gave the bowlers a chance and was a joy to watch.

He won his England place back at the end of the 1964 summer and that winter set off for a highly successful tour of South Africa, where he averaged 72. Barber was inevitably happier on faster foreign wickets and his greatest achievement was a magnificent 185 off 255 deliveries against Australia in the third Test of the 1965-66 tour. It remains the highest score by an England player on the opening day of an Ashes Test and was the best score of Barber's first-class career.

Something of a law unto himself, Barber was a good leg-spinner but did not rate himself and was often reluctant to bowl. An intelligent man whose family ran a building business, he quit cricket in 1969 at 33 to go into business himself, and now lives in Switzerland.

R.W. BARBER born 26.9.35 (Withington, Lancashire). Tests 28 runs 1495 average 35.59 100s 1 wickets 42 average 43.00

Graham Barlow

Charlie Barnett

TREVOR BAILEY
Essex 61 Tests 1949-59

The patented Bailey Block

TREVOR Bailey, England's premier all-rounder throughout the 1950s, is convinced that a few careless words, if not costing lives, cost him the chance to captain his country. For a decade Bailey was virtually an automatic choice in the England side. He batted in every position from 1 to 9, often shoring up the innings with his renowned forward-defensive and love of a crisis; he provided valuable support for Bedser, Statham and Tyson with his reliable fast-medium swing and seam bowling and was an excellent close fielder.

In short, he was an integral member of the teams led by Len Hutton and Peter May. Yet somewhere in between the reigns of these two giant cricketers, Bailey, a highly-regarded, astute skipper of Essex (where he was also county secretary), could rightly have expected the opportunity to gain the highest honour in the English game.

He was tipped to be Hutton's successor when a ghost-written book under his name returned to haunt him in 1954. The book was not seen and approved by the game's lords and masters at the MCC and, worse still, was serialised and sensationalised in a Sunday newspaper. On the Saturday morning before publication, the sports editor was on the telephone asking Bailey if he would like to see a proof of what was going to appear the next day. Bailey pointed out that he was, in fact, fairly tied up at that time playing for Essex and so, in the days when the nearest thing to a fax machine was a carrier pigeon, the article was printed without him seeing it.

Bailey says: 'There was nothing vaguely controversial in the book but the newspaper changed the words entirely and Lord's were upset with some comments under my name about West Indian cricket. I have little doubt it cost me a shot at the captaincy.'

If Bailey's tactical acumen was not utilised to the full, his cricket skills certainly were and the 'Bailey Block' became a treasured national event in the summer calendar. He stuck around so much that soon he became known as 'The Barnacle', a name he delighted in although it was at odds with the fluent stroke-play he regularly demonstrated with Essex. Bailey says: 'Just as Frankie Vaughan was expected to sing *Give Me The Moonlight* every time he went on stage, the broad bat was expected of me every time I went out to play. It so happened that England at that time were an attacking side and they often needed someone to play that role.'

There have been few more epic efforts in Test cricket than Bailey's 257-minute match-saving 71 on the last day of the 1953 Lord's Test against the Australians. Four wickets down before lunch and staring defeat in the eyes, Bailey and Willie Watson (who scored 109) pulled up the drawbridge until 40 minutes before close to save the Test in a series England won 1-0. Five years later Bailey was to go one better in the first Test in Brisbane. Viewers of the first televised match in Australia were treated to an epic 50 scored in three minutes under six hours, still the slowest recorded half-century in cricket. In all Bailey scored 68 in seven hours 38 minutes with 40 scoring shots from the 425 deliveries he faced. It still remains arguably the most exciting programme put out by Australian television.

Bailey, while he lives with being type-cast as a blocker, was much more than that. He became only the third England player — after Wilf Rhodes and Maurice Tate — to do the double of 1,000 runs and 100 wickets, a feat he achieved eight times in a championship season with Essex. In his youthful days Bailey was also a fine footballer, winning an FA Amateur Cup winner's medal with Walthamstow, and after his sporting career, his clipped, incisive comments made him a respected and regular member of the Test Match Special radio team.

T.E. BAILEY born 3.12.23 (Westcliff-on-Sea, Essex). Tests 61 runs 2290 average 29.74 100s 1 wickets 132 average 29.12

All-round effort... Trevor Bailey

For illustration see also Brian Close

KIM BARNETT
Derbyshire 4 Tests 1988-89

KIM Barnett sensed that his face did not fit and took the money on offer on the 1990 rebel tour to South Africa, aborting his England career in its embryonic stage and ignoring suggestions that he might be captain one day. An attacking, resourceful player and a popular skipper of Derbyshire, Barnett should have been picked before his Test debut in 1988. He was selected for that winter's cancelled tour of India and played part of the next summer against Australia before joining the rebels and suffering a three-year ban.

K.J. BARNETT born 17.7.60 (Stoke-on-Trent, Staffordshire). Tests 4 runs 207 average 29.57

Kim Barnett

Mark Benson

MARK BENSON
Kent 1 Test 1986

A FINE player of fast bowling, Mark Benson has been woefully unlucky to have played just once for England. Called up against India in 1986 as a replacement for Wayne Larkins, the modest left-handed Kent opener made a handy debut, batting for four hours. He was dropped to give Martyn Moxon his debut and, despite scoring consistently in county cricket, has never had any other international recognition, a fact which puzzles most fellow professionals. Became Kent captain in 1991.

M.R. BENSON born 6.7.58 (Shoreham, Sussex). Tests 1 runs 51 average 25.50

BOB BERRY
Lancashire, Worcestershire and Derbyshire 2 Tests 1950

THE first player to be capped by three counties, Bob Berry won only two caps for his country. The first he wore with pride, taking 9 for 118 on a crumbling Old Trafford wicket on which another debutant spinner, Alf Valentine, took 11 for 204. In his second Test, Berry's gentle left-arm spin met with no success and after a fruitless tour of Australia, he disappeared from the international scene. His travels took him to Mansfield where he became a publican.

R. BERRY born 29.1.26 (Manchester). Tests 2 runs 6 average 3 wickets 9 average 25.33

Bob Berry

Jack Birkinshaw

JACK BIRKENSHAW
Yorkshire, Leicestershire and Worcestershire 5 Tests 1973-74

JACK Birkenshaw was the epitome of a good all-round county cricketer: a probing off-spinner who used flight and guile, a handy batsman who could grind it out or go for the slog, a dependable fielder and great competitor. At Test level, though, his chances were limited to tours, and his appearances were all overseas in India, Pakistan and the West Indies. After becoming a Test match umpire he turned to coaching, first at Somerset and then back at Leicester.

J. BIRKENSHAW born 13.11.40 (Rothwell, Yorkshire). Tests 5 runs 148 average 21.14 wickets 13 average 36.07

JIMMY BINKS
Yorkshire 2 Tests 1964

ON HIS second tour of India, Jimmy Binks made his Test debut when England were reduced to 11 fit men. First-choice wicketkeeper Jim Parks played as a specialist batsman while Binks took the gloves for two matches, but oddly he failed to reproduce the elegant assurance he brought to his work with Yorkshire. It may have had something to do with the fact that he was also asked to act as emergency opener. Incredibly, he missed only one of the 492 championship matches played during his 15-year career with Yorkshire.

J.G. BINKS born 5.10.35 (Hull, Yorkshire). Tests 2 runs 91 average 22.75 dismissals 8 caught 8

Jimmy Binks

KEN BARRINGTON
Surrey 82 Tests 1955-68

WHEN Ken Barrington died suddenly at the age of 50 in a Barbados hotel on the 1981 tour of the West Indies, a wave of deep sadness swamped English cricket. For 30 years he had lived for his cricket and his country as a player, selector, manager and finally coach. And, quite seriously, he died for it too, succumbing to a heart attack he always knew might happen.

There have been few more popular cricketers than Ken Barrington. A craggy yeoman of a man, he turned himself into one of the most dependable and courageous batsmen England have produced. His

run scoring was monumental rather than majestic, he was as solid and pretty as a battering ram and no-one in the post-War period — not Hutton, Compton, Cowdrey or May — could touch his Test average of 58.67.

He was intense about his cricket, he fretted continuously, yet he was also a wonderful mimic and comic, a loyal colleague and good-natured man. It was said of him that when he marched out to bat you could almost sense the Union Jack fluttering behind him and hear him whistling *Colonel Bogey*. The military metaphors are not unapt. Barrington was the son of a professional soldier, brought up

in spartan barracks in Reading where luxury was enough hot water to fill the tin tub used by him, his two brothers and sister.

He joined Surrey principally as a leg-spinner but, after his National Service, returned and shone as an attractive stroke-maker. He won his first cap in 1955 but scores of 0, 34 and 18 in two Tests saw him discarded as being patently not good enough. That experience changed Barrington, who opened his stance, moved on to the back foot and became essentially a defensive player.

Four years later his run-making caught the selectors' attention again

AN ENGLISHMAN ABROAD... Barrington (centre) watches Indian cricket official Dr. Radha Kishan greet Peter Richardson for the third Test in 1961 in New Delhi. Tony Lock is on Barrington's left, Ted Dexter is doing the introductions.

and he was back for keeps. At home his efforts often went unsung, overshadowed by the flashing blades of Cowdrey, Graveney and Dexter, but his colleagues knew his worth and from 1959 to '68 he never missed a senior tour, averaging 69 on foreign soil and scoring nine overseas centuries before reaching the landmark at home — with 256 against the 1964 Australians.

The following summer he scored his second home century against New Zealand — and it cost him his place. The weather was so cold on the first day of the first Test in Birmingham that the umpires wore pyjamas under their trousers and hot drinks were served on the field — and Barrington's unbeaten 61 in more than three hours did little to warm the heart. The next day, not heeding instructions from captain Mike Smith, Barrington plodded on; he went through an hour on 85 without scoring, and in all spent more than seven hours scoring 137. Although England won the Test, Barrington was dropped but he returned for the third Test and, typical of Ken's 'I'll bloody show 'em' approach, he drilled 26 fours in an innings of 163.

While the slow-scoring saga depressed Barrington he was more upset by the 'Griffith Affair' which led to him refusing to face the fearsome West Indian paceman because he was convinced Charlie was a chucker. Griffith's action had been the subject of constant suspicion since his early days in Barbados but when the 1963 West Indians arrived in England it was believed the home umpires had been warned not to call him because of racial problems already brewing in the country.

During the series, Barrington was convinced Griffith had 'thrown him out' and the next summer, when the West Indies returned for some exhibition matches, he refused to face the big Bajan. Barrington hated the hostility this stirred up between himself and the West Indians on the field and on their 1966 tour the stress led to a nervous breakdown which forced him to pull out of the side after two Tests.

Two years later Barrington faced Griffith again in the more relaxed

Another day's work... Barrington accepts the acclaim after scoring a century at Sydney in 1963

atmosphere of a double-wicket championship in Australia but after winning the first encounter, he collapsed in the dressing room. He had suffered a heart attack. After that Barrington gave up cricket — but didn't. Although he stopped playing he continued to devote his life to the game and sadly, 13 years later, the game consumed him.

K.F. BARRINGTON born 24.11.30 (Reading, Berkshire). Died 14.3.81. Tests 82 runs 6806 average 58.67 100s 20 wickets 29 average 44.82

ALEC BEDSER

Surrey 51 Tests 1946-55

THEY don't make them like Alec Bedser any more. When Bedser's England career ended in 1955 he had set a world Test record of 236 wickets, every one paid for with buckets of sweat and hours of endeavour. And when 'Big Al' was chairman of England's selectors for 13 years from 1969, woe betide any young pace bowler who suggested to him that he was being over-bowled and feeling a touch jaded. The withering look from one of English cricket's great yeomen was legendary. 'I dunno,' he used to say, shaking his head. 'These kids nowadays, 20 overs a day and they're moaning. I blame all these bloomin' sponsored cars and bloomin' winter contracts...they don't know they're born, they don't.' Alec, you see, was from a different era. An era when you did not speak to your amateur captain unless spoken to, an era when you would bowl all day, uphill and into the teeth of a Force 10 if required — and be grateful.

But for all his gruff determination to stay faithful to his generation, he was a kind-hearted man and knew class when he saw it — and there should be no doubting that he was a bowler of the highest calibre himself. From little more than half-a-dozen paces, he produced an unerring in-swinger, developed wet and dry wicket leg-cutters in the days when pitches were left uncovered and conditions varied, and his powerful

6ft 3in frame extracted bounce from the most supine of wickets. For much of his career he was England's strike bowler as well as stock bowler — out of choice as well as necessity. He was also a doughty lower-order batsman and loved to be asked to be nightwatchman.

But above all, Alec loved to bowl. Rhythm and stamina were what he was all about. He shared the new ball with a host of pace bowlers including Bill Edrich, Trevor Bailey, Derek Shackleton, and later on with Brian Statham and a youthful Fred Trueman, but for much of the time he was expected to carry the attack.

His career started in spectacular style with 11 wickets at Lord's in 1946 against India and he followed that with another 11-wicket haul in his second Test. His favourite battles, however, were against the Australians. In 1950-51 Bedser took 30 wickets in the series while the other bowlers claimed 49 between them, in 1953 he took 39 out of 91 including 14 for 99 at Trent Bridge, which remains a Test record for Nottingham.

No profile of Alec Bedser would be complete, however, without mention of his mirror-image Eric, his twin brother. The pair were unfathomably similar and still are, wearing identical clothes down to their socks. They still live together, sound the same and are seen regularly at the Oval, side by side,

causing many a spectator to rub his eyes in disbelief. Eric never made it as a Test player but was a good county performer who bowled similarly to his younger brother until he realised it would be wise to switch to off-spin if he wanted to get in the side. To help the scorers, Alec would wear his MCC sweater so they could tell the pair apart. Sometimes, when one was out, the brothers would mischievously swap sweaters and cause consternation to protesting opponents, who thought the same man was batting twice, and distraught umpires, left to sort out the confusion. The story is even told that once Alec, rather busy at the time, realised their passports had run out and sent Eric off to the photo-booth to have four pictures taken for the pair of them. If it is not true, it should be.

For several years, Alec was vice-captain to Peter May at the Oval but the thought of taking over would not have entered his head. He was 'only' a professional from working-class stock who lived to serve. He loved the game and he loved his country, and few men have given more to English cricket than Alec Bedser, whose services were recognised with a CBE.

A.V. BEDSER born 4.7.18 (Reading, Berkshire). Tests 51 runs 714 average 12.75 wickets 236 average 24.89

The Bedser Boys... Alec is the one with the filling in his top molar, right side

For further illustrations see Godfrey Evans and John Warr.

IAN BOTHAM
Somerset, Worcestershire and Durham 102 Tests 1977-92

IAN Botham has not swum the Channel, been an MP (yet) or mud-wrestled with Esther Rantzen — other than that, there are not many gaps in the Botham CV. He has, quite simply, been English cricket's most recognisable figure since WG Grace. He is the best all-round player England has produced, worth his place as either batsman or bowler alone for most of his 15 years at the top. He became the first player in the world to top 3,000 runs and 300 wickets, his 383 wickets is an English record, his 65 consecutive Test appearances equals Alan Knott's record, and his 120 catches — mostly spectacular affairs in the slips — equals Colin Cowdrey's England record. In one summer with Somerset he hit a record 80 sixes and his 200 off 220 balls against India at the Oval in 1982 remains the fastest double-century in Test cricket.

The statistics roll on yet don't tell an iota of the man's story. He is a powerful, courageous yet technically correct batsman and a swing bowler who was bounding with aggression in his early days, brimming with cunning and audacity in his latter days after a back operation reduced his pace. All of this was fuelled by intense self-belief and bravado.

But what he did on the field is only half the story. Being busted for drugs, suspended by the authorities and accused of all sorts of mayhem from bed-busting to nose-breaking only added to the hell-raising image that was some way from the truth but did his career as a showman no harm at all. Botham became a television personality, a pantomime star, and a one-man stage act.

For a brief spell he was a shin-crunching professional footballer in Scunthorpe's defence and he was constantly a champion of charities, particularly Leukaemia Research, walking the length and breadth of Britain and over the Alps with a string of elephants to raise literally millions of pounds. He raced cars, flew planes, knocked Australian skippers from bar-stools, upset the whole of the Pakistan nation by refusing to send his mother-in-law there for a holiday and kept his solicitor a busy and happy man.

Botham came a long way from the insecure, mop-haired Yeovil boy who joined Somerset in 1974 to be taken under the wing of bowling mentor Tom Cartwright and Brian Close, the man he still admires most. His career is littered with marvellous moments but no summer encapsulated Botham's talent like that of 1981 when against Australia, he transformed the series and became a hero for grannies, children and MCC cricket buffs alike.

The year started in despair because the one thing Botham was not was ready for the England captaincy at 24, despite Mike Brearley's recommendation. After leading England through two torrid

Scunthorpe's Mr Fixit

series against the West Indies without a victory, Botham lost the first Test of the '81 summer against Australia, suffered a pair at Lord's in the second and jumped before he was pushed by the selectors.

Brearley was recalled and the country witnessed the most astonishing Test of the modern era. England followed on at Leeds and Botham came in at 105 for 5 with the team still 122 behind. Soon it was 92 behind with three wickets remaining. Graham Dilley came in and he and Botham decided the only thing to do was attack. The result was an innings full of anarchic hitting, Botham scoring 149 not out and Australia, shell-shocked, needed 130 to win. Botham's efforts inspired Bob Willis to his greatest Test performance, 8 for 43, and England won amazingly by 18 runs, only the second time in history a team following on had won a Test.

In the fourth Test at Edgbaston Australia needed only 151 to win but this time Botham blitzed them with the ball, taking their last five wickets for one run in 28 balls to put England 2-1 ahead in the series. In the fifth Test at Old Trafford he devastated Australia — including Dennis Lillee — with a great show of controlled hitting, scoring a century off 86 balls to set up another victory to clinch the series. Was it little wonder Australian skipper Kim Hughes wept?

Botham's county career was no less colourful. After helping homely Somerset to one-day successes he quit in acrimony in 1986 when his pals Viv Richards and Joel Garner were sacked. More success in five years at Worcester was followed by a swansong move to Durham in 1992 for their first season in the championship and the opportunity to prove the doubters wrong once again by becoming the first player to represent England while playing for three different counties.

I.T. BOTHAM born 24.11.55 (Heswall, Cheshire). Tests 102 runs 5200 average 33.54 100s 14 wickets 383 average 28.40

There's only one Ian Botham...

GEOFF BOYCOTT
Yorkshire 108 Tests 1964-82

NO NAME sparks more extreme feelings in bar-room debates on cricket's greats than Geoffrey Boycott. He was to some 'a bloody marvel' while to others he is 'that selfish bugger.' This is what John Arlott said of him: 'He is the most single-minded cricketer one can imagine; some people would say the most self-centred; others, the most perfectionist.'

Boycott lived for making runs and, it often appeared, making them for himself rather than for the good of the team although he would always argue that if he did well, the team usually prospered. When his Test career ended with him signing for the first group of England rebels to go to South Africa in 1982, he was the most prolific run-maker in Test history with 8,114, a total since passed by Sunil Gavaskar, Allan Border, Viv Richards, Javed Miandad and David Gower. If he had not imposed three years of Test exile on himself between 1974 and '77 (30 matches) or incurred a three-year suspension for going to South Africa, he could well be in an impregnable position as the greatest run-maker of all time.

Yet while 'Boyks' set out to achieve most of his ambitions, a few — probably the most treasured few — remained out of reach. His burning desire to captain his country successfully flickered only dimly for four Tests as a stand-in after Mike Brearley broke an arm, and during his reign as Yorkshire captain from 1971 to '78 he failed to recapture the White Rose county's past glories. In the end his single-minded pursuit of runs hampered his leadership ambitions; many lesser players found him blunt, dogmatic and unsympathetic.

The environment the young Boycott found himself growing up in was pretty blunt and unsympathetic too. His father suffered terrible injuries in a pit accident and sport offered the main distraction from the hardships of the mining community. As an under-18 trialist with Leeds United alongside a young Scot named Billy Bremner, Boycott was not good enough to make the grade at soccer, but the young bespectacled clerk from the Ministry of Pensions in Barnsley soon found his way on to the staff at Headingley in 1962. Two years later he was opening for England.

Boycott had great virtuosity as a stroke-player but he began to eliminate chance and develop the capacity to score off almost any delivery — particularly if it was the last ball of the over and he wanted to keep the strike. His patience was rock solid but that of the selectors was not, and after spending the best part of 10 hours accumulating what was his best Test score, 246 against India at Leeds in 1967, he was dropped for slow scoring.

His biggest disappointment, however, was his failure to be given the chance to captain England after Ray Illingworth in 1973. Instead the job went to Mike Denness whom Boycott resented intensely. He almost refused to tour that winter in the West Indies because of the appointment of Denness whom he described as 'the worst England captain I have played under.' He admits: 'I had little respect for the man as a captain... and he was not good enough as a player to command a place. It was a mess from start to finish, an absolute joke.' Denness, and increasing problems as captain of a county riddled with schisms, were what drove Boycott away from international cricket although it was easy to suggest at the time that he had lost the stomach for the coming battles with the Australian pace attack of Lillee and Thomson or the West Indian quicks.

He returned in 1977 to become the first player to score his 100th first-class hundred in a Test, and he did it at Headingley, but for all his efforts for England he was never a player to whom the public warmed. In his first-class career he scored 151 hundreds — only four men have scored more — and he is the only player to have averaged more than 100 twice over a whole English season. During his final Test in Calcutta he was unable to field because of stomach trouble but was later discovered playing golf on a nearby course, which earned him an early plane home — and out of Test cricket. Although he failed to break through into the Lord's hierarchy, he remains a much-respected coach and a pungent, entertaining writer and broadcaster on the game.

G. BOYCOTT born 21.10.40 (Fitzwilliam, Yorkshire). Tests 108 runs 8114 average 47.72 100s 22 wickets 7 average 54.57

MASTER CLASS... eyes on the ball, perfectly poised, Boycott shows the net admirers at Lord's how it's done

For further illustration see Geoff Miller

RICHARD BLAKEY
Yorkshire 2 Tests 1993-

ENGLAND'S controversial strategy of playing a wicketkeeping batsman ahead of a specialist 'keeper gave Richard Blakey an unexpected taste of Test action on the disappointing 1993 tour of India. A capable and popular county player, Blakey was chosen as No. 2 to Alec Stewart, but illness to front-line batsmen saw him pushed into action. While his 'keeping was clean, Blakey was out of his depth against the Indian spinners and suffered a torrid baptism.

R.J. BLAKEY born 15.1.67 (Huddersfield, Yorkshire). Tests 2 runs 7 average 1.75 dismissals 2 caught 2

BRIAN BOLUS
Yorkshire, Nottinghamshire and Derbyshire 7 Tests 1963-64

BRIAN Bolus opens his hilarious after-dinner act with: 'For those of you who saw me bat... let me apologise.' Bolus was essentially an accumulator, dependably totting up 25,000 runs over 20 summers. Typically, when his England chance came as an opener he never let anyone down, first against the West Indies, then on the 1963-64 tour of India. A loss of form in 1964 gave a young Geoff Boycott a chance — and once in, he took some shifting. A committee man at Trent Bridge, Bolus has become an aspiring Test selector.

J.B. BOLUS born 31.1.34 (Whitkirk, Yorkshire). Tests 7 runs 496 average 41.33

Brian Bolus

BILL BOWES
Yorkshire 15 Tests 1932-46

A CLUMSY 6ft 4in tall with thick horn-rimmed glasses, Bill Bowes looked anything but one of the finest medium-paced bowlers English cricket has seen. In the field he was expected to try to stop the ball but if he missed it, one of his Yorkshire colleagues would do the chasing; with the bat he scored fewer runs in his career (1,528) than the number of wickets he took (1,639). But with the ball in his hand off a measured 10 paces, he was the master, making it swing both ways and bounce sharply, when he was in the mood.

A modest, gentle man, Bowes worked tirelessly at his game with the great Yorkshire side that won seven championships in the 1930s. He would

Bill Bowes

have played far more often for England had the selectors not hankered after bowlers with a yard more pace but less ability.

He received the call-up for the 'Bodyline' tour only three days before the boat sailed and played in only one Test during the series — but in that match he was sharp enough to bowl Don Bradman first ball. The 1930s were prosperous times for batsmen but Bowes plugged away intrepidly and even Bradman, when he went on the rampage in 1938, could not get the better of him.

During the War, three years in an Italian PoW camp cost Bowes four stone, weight his sparse frame could not afford to lose, and when peace was restored he bowled at a much reduced pace for only two more seasons. He made his final England appearance in the first Test after the conflict, against India. Bowes' Test bowling average of 22 runs per wicket is outstanding for his era, his career average of 16 is quite astonishing. After his playing days he became a respected cricket writer.

W.E. BOWES born 25.7.08 (Elland, Yorkshire). Died 5.9.87. Tests 15 runs 28 average 4.66 wickets 68 average 22.33

DON BRENNAN
Yorkshire 2 Tests 1951

DON Brennan, with his distinctive white gloves, was a good enough wicketkeeper to evict Godfrey Evans from the England side in 1951. There can be few higher tributes to his 'keeping skills than that. Brennan toured India that winter but lost out to Dick Spooner, a fine batsman in his own right, and his representative days were numbered. He continued

Chris Broad

keeping impeccably for Yorkshire, pulling off many spectacular leg-side stumpings until the demands of the family textile business forced him to quit in 1953.

D.V. BRENNAN born 10.2.20 (Eccleshill, Yorkshire). Died 9.1.85. Tests 2 runs 16 average 16 dismissals 1 stumped 1

CHRIS BROAD
Gloucestershire and Nottinghamshire 23 Tests 1984-89

CHRIS Broad pressed the self-destruct button on a career that promised so much. His lack of self-control at the crease brought a sad end to his reign as England opener at the age of 30 when he should have been enjoying his prime years.

An imposing straight-hitting left-hander, Broad left Gloucestershire looking to better his England chances and within three months of moving to Trent Bridge in 1984 he was making his Test debut. He faced up to the West Indies' pace onslaught better than most and was unlucky to be dropped at the end of that summer, but he made a sensational return on the 1986-87 tour of Australia, becoming only the fourth

English batsman to score centuries in three successive Tests.

The next winter he scored another three centuries in four Tests and England looked at last to have found a long-term partner for Graham Gooch. But Broad, never one to hide his opinions under a bushel, could not contain his emotions either. In Lahore he refused to leave the crease when given out. A month later, with England's players under the microscope because of dissent shown in Pakistan, he smashed his stumps down in the Bicentenary Test at Sydney when he played on after scoring 139. The next summer, at Lord's of all places, Broad mouthed his anger for all to see on television when out leg-before for a duck, and he was dropped.

Disillusioned, he soon joined Gatting's rebel team to South Africa and wrote off the best years of his playing life. Amiable but often outspoken, he was disappointed not to be made Nottinghamshire captain, and an uneasy relationship with the incumbent Tim Robinson ended at the end of 1992 when he rejoined Gloucestershire.

B.C. BROAD born 29.9.57 (Knowle, Bristol). Tests 23 runs 1661 average 39.54 100s 6

IT WAS a chance move by two Middlesex committee men, Mike Murray and Charles Robins, in 1970 which was to change the course of English cricket history. The county, despite a strong squad, had been under-achievers; Fred Titmus and Peter Parfitt, two leading Test players of their time, had failed to get the best out of a dressing room with more than its share of strong personalities. Someone with a fresh approach was being sought — and Murray and Robins turned their attention to California and a university lecturer: Mike Brearley.

Brearley, an academically brilliant philosopher, had dabbled in the professional game with moderate success and taken himself off for a life of teaching. At Cambridge University this wicketkeeper-batsman had scored more runs than anyone before him and had toured South Africa with England in 1964-65 without playing a Test. Two years later he captained an MCC under-25 team in Pakistan, scoring 312 not out in a day against the North Zone in Peshawar, but his sporting ambitions petered out.

For a few seasons he was available for Middlesex only when he was not teaching at Newcastle University, and then he moved across the Atlantic with seemingly just the odd mention in Wisden to mark a modest career. Little could he have dreamed that he would go down as one of the most successful captains England has seen.

Murray and Robins saw in Brearley a man who still possessed the ethos of an amateur captain; a great talker, listener, negotiator and motivator of men. In short, a philosopher. Brearley was fascinated by the challenge presented at Lord's, despite the dressing-room pockets of resentment directed towards him at first, and he returned to bring success to his county and his country.

He wrote: 'I like to be bossy. I hate to get bored. I want to be doing something all the time, and the tactics of the game fascinated me. I liked the idea of the inter-relation with people, and, above all, I like trying to get the best out of people.' He did that to great effect, with no better example than the youthful, headstrong Ian Botham. The pair were opposites: Brearley, the thoughtful, tentative cricketer; Botham the boisterous, belligerent cricketer brimming with bravado. It was perfect chemistry.

Brearley captained England 31 times between 1977 and '81, winning 18 Tests and losing four. He became the first skipper to lead England to five victories in an Ashes series (1978-79) and presided over a record run of 19 home Tests without defeat. In 1980 he announced his retirement from Test cricket, handing over to the sorcerer's apprentice, Botham, but it was an ill-conceived transfer of power. The 24-year-old all-rounder had a miserable 12 months, failing to win a Test, before Brearley was tempted back for one final encore to win an astonishing 1981 series against the Aussies, with Botham in full cry again.

Brearley, of course, has his detractors and they point out that his reign coincided with the arrival of a crop of exceptionally gifted young players such as Botham, David Gower, Mike Gatting, Graham Gooch and Bob Willis. It also came at a time when Australia were well below strength because of the defection of their top players to the Kerry Packer circus; when England under Brearley did play a full-strength Australian team they lost 3-0. But, as all sportsmen will point out, you can do no better than beat the opposition presented to you, and Brearley's England did that.

He took over because Tony Greig defected to Packer but then insisted cleverly that Greig and the other Packer players should retain their places. He also fought hard for increased pay for his players and held a unique position of strength and respect within the England dressing room — a position made all the more remarkable because of his own shortcomings as a batsman. Despite his prolific scores as a student, Brearley's efforts in the professional game disappointed and frustrated him although it is often forgotten that he was originally selected by England as a batsman.

One winter he was so worried about his batting that he took himself off to Tom Cartwright for private tuition and for the second half of his international career he regularly slipped down the order from his familiar opener's position, but still the big scores remained elusive. In 66 Test innings his top score was 91 and his average of 22 frustrated him to the end. He once said on the problems of being a captain who could not deliver the goods himself: 'It is easier for a football manager to 'play God', to read the riot act to players, because he does not have to perform himself. Sales managers don't sell, foremen don't hump bricks but all cricket captains bat and field and some bowl. We receive repeated intimations of our own fallibility.'

When Brearley stopped playing in 1982, Middlesex and England failed to tempt him into using his charm and skill in man-management off the field. Instead he turned to running a psycho-therapy practice in London and stayed in touch with cricket only through journalism.

J.M. BREARLEY born 28.4.42 (Harrow, Middlesex). Tests 39 runs 1442 average 22.88 100s 0

Mike Brearley... practice never quite made perfect

DENNIS BROOKES
Northamptonshire 1 Test 1948

A CULTURED and prolific opener, Dennis Brookes, having played in Test trials and been England's 12th man twice, finally had his chance in Gubby Allen's experimental party bound for the Caribbean late in 1947. He was one of five new caps in the first Test but a fractured finger suffered in a friendly game forced him home early and, despite consistently scoring heavily for Northamptonshire, he was never on the Test team sheet again. The first professional skipper at Northampton, he became county president and a JP.

D. BROOKES born 29.10.15 (Kippax, Yorkshire). Tests 1 runs 17 average 8.50

ALAN BROWN
Kent 2 Tests 1961

A LAN Brown was one of seven new caps on a long, arduous but happy tour of India, Pakistan and Sri Lanka (neé Ceylon) under Ted Dexter, which was given a wide berth

Alan Brown

by the more established fast bowlers such as Trueman and Statham. Powerful and popular, Brown did his opening bowler's job with honest endeavour, as he did over 14 seasons with Kent, but he was never to get close to a full-strength England side for a home Test.

A. BROWN born 17.10.35 (Rainworth, Nottinghamshire). Tests 2 runs 3 average — wickets 3 average 50

David Brown

DAVID BROWN
Warwickshire 26 Tests 1965-69

D AVID Brown was enjoying his most successful summer as an England fast bowler when the selectors decided to answer the public clamour for an exciting young Derbyshire tearaway named Alan Ward. In the first half of 1969, Brown had taken 14 wickets in three Tests at 20 apiece as England beat the West Indies 2-0 in a three-match series. New Zealand were the next visitors and an injury to John Snow let Alan Ward in for the first Test. Snow was fit to return for the second but, instead of relegating Ward, Brown was axed, not for under-achievement, simply because the selectors wanted to look at Ward in a series they expected to win comfortably. Ward's career sadly spluttered like a faulty firework, while Brown never returned to the international stage.

The Warwickshire man had to overcome major surgery on a frightening stomach-muscle tear after slipping in a wet foot-hole at Bristol at the start of his county career, and it was his gutsy determination and uncomplaining effort that was to be

the hallmark of an England career interrupted by the usual collection of fast bowlers' injuries.

The rangy, popular paceman played musical chairs with Snow, Jeff Jones and Ken Higgs for much of his England career. His most rewarding tour was the successful trip to the Caribbean in 1967-68 when his unstinting effort on the hard West Indian wickets earned 14 wickets in four Tests. He continued to enjoy himself against the West Indians two summers later but the selectors had other ideas. Brown finished playing in 1979 to become cricket manager at Edgbaston for eight years, before leaving the game to concentrate on his racehorse stud farm in the Midlands.

D.J. BROWN born 30.1.42 (Walsall, Staffordshire). Tests 26 runs 342 average 11.79 wickets 79 average 28.31

FREDDIE BROWN
Surrey and Northamptonshire
22 Tests 1931-53

T HE story of Freddie Brown could happen only in cricket. His 22 Tests spanned as many years, he rarely played the game regularly, yet he transformed Northamptonshire and became something of a folk hero in Australia at the age of 40 for his bravura leadership of England into calamitous defeat.

Right from the start, Brown was unique. He was born in Lima where his father, who was a trader, forced him to switch from being a natural left-hander to doing everything right-handed. Brown had a brilliant Cambridge career as a bold batsman and a nippy leg-break or off-cutter bowler. His silk kerchief knotted around his neck, he became a robust trier for Surrey, enlivening county games. He went on the 'Bodyline' tour without making Jardine's controversial side and played a scattering of six Tests before the War with little distinction.

Hostilities saw him captured in Italy where, as a PoW with Bill Bowes for three years, his powerful 14-stone frame wasted to 10 stone. After the War, cricket appeared virtually forgotten when a business move took

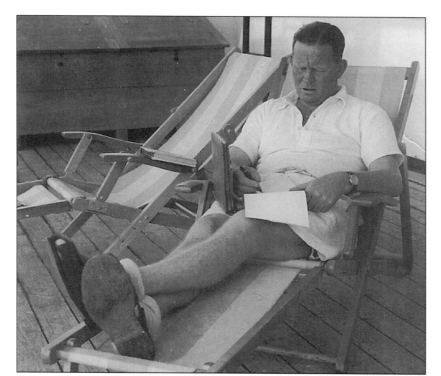
Freddie Brown

ALAN BUTCHER
Surrey and Glamorgan 1 Test 1979

A POPULAR and accomplished left-handed opener, Alan Butcher was unlucky to be consigned to membership of the 'One Cap Club'. He replaced an injured Wayne Larkins for the last Test of 1979 and, although he did not fail, he did not get enough runs to win a tour place. Despite consistent county performances and an ability to tackle quick bowlers, Butcher was passed over. Brothers Ian and Martin played county cricket and in 1991 as Glamorgan skipper, he had the pleasure of playing against his son Mark on his Surrey debut. Became Essex coach in 1993.

A.R. BUTCHER born 7.1.54 (Croydon, Surrey). Tests 1 runs 34 average 17

him to Northampton and he assumed the county captaincy. The fleeting Test appearances continued, but now as captain when Norman Yardley and George Mann had business commitments. Both were unavailable for the 1950-51 tour to Australia; the selectors were at their wits' end — and then saw Brown score a spectacular 122 in a Gentlemen v Players match, and their minds were made up.

Brown, an occasional county cricketer who had never looked good enough as a Test player and was approaching his 40th birthday, was put in charge. England suffered a 4-1 Ashes defeat but Brown's leadership won friends. He was not universally popular among his own players, he could be intolerant and brusque, yet no-one doubted his wholeheartedness at the head of a poorly balanced side.

He enjoyed success the next summer, beating the South Africans, and in 1953, now chairman of selectors, he was persuaded back for a final Test. He became an energetic administrator, managed two MCC tours and was a member of the BBC radio commentary team.

F.R. BROWN born 16.12.10 (Lima, Peru). Died 7.24.91. Tests 22 runs 734 average 25.31 wickets 45 average 31.06

Alan Butcher

ROLAND BUTCHER
Middlesex 3 Tests 1981

IN THE autumn of 1980 Roland Butcher's selection became the focus of attention. He was set to become the first black West Indian-born player to represent England — and on a tour of the Caribbean. There was enormous interest in this pleasant Barbadian — a cousin of West Indian batting star Basil Butcher — who had come to England when he was 13 but whose intuitive batting had never lost its calypso flair. In the event, in the wake of the death of Ken Barrington and the 'Jackman Affair', Butcher's debut in his native Barbados passed virtually unnoticed and his impact on Test cricket was forgotten after the tour.

R.O. BUTCHER born 14.10.53 (St Philip, Barbados). Tests 3 runs 71 average 14.20

Harold Butler

HAROLD BUTLER
Nottinghamshire 2 Tests 1947-48

A BURLY swing bowler, Harold Butler had every reason to feel let down by England. He succeeded Harold Larwood at Nottinghamshire and lost his prime years to the War but when the Test call came at 34 he was an instant success with match figures of 7 for 66 against the 1947 South Africans. He went to the West Indies that winter as main strike bowler but a calf injury and then malaria restricted him to just one Test. He was then discarded, injury and weight problems counting against him.

H.J. BUTLER born 12.3.13 (Clifton, Nottinghamshire). Died 17.7.91. Tests 2 runs 15 average 15 wickets 12 average 17.91

DAVID CAPEL
Northamptonshire 15 Tests 1987-90

DAVID Capel was one of those unfortunate cricketers who became tagged as being the next all-rounder to fill Ian Botham's boots. He couldn't, of course. An irrepressible enthusiast, Capel was principally a batsman who bowled but because he did both jobs, his run-making abilities were pushed down the order. He found it difficult to convince England captains of his ability in either department and injuries also disrupted his progress, but he found himself back in the reckoning when he was picked for the 1993 'A' team tour of Australia.

D.J. CAPEL born 6.2.63 (Northampton). Tests 15 runs 374 average 15.58 wickets 21 average 50.66

TOM CARTWRIGHT
Warwickshire, Somerset and Glamorgan 5 Tests 1964-65

TOM Cartwright was an exceptional bowler whose talents could not find a regular niche in the England side, much to the discredit of the selectors. His high, flowing action off a few steady paces produced unerring accuracy and nip for his rich assortment of seam and swing deliveries, but England looked

David Capel

usually for a first-change bowler with extra pace. He played two Tests in 1964, one in South Africa that winter on his only tour and was then dropped in 1965 after taking 6 for 94 against South Africa. His lasting legacy to cricket, however, was as the man who taught Ian Botham to bowl.

T.W. CARTWRIGHT born 22.7.35 (Coventry, Warwickshire). Tests 5 runs 26 average 5.20 wickets 15 average 36.26

Tom Cartwright

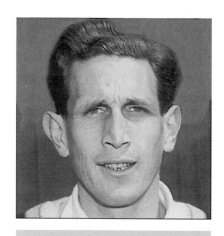

DONALD CARR
Derbyshire 2 Tests 1951-52

DONALD Carr's impact on Test cricket as a player was minimal but as an administrator he played a leading role in the post-War game, healing wounds and building bridges as revolution followed bloody revolution.

Carr, a thinking man's all-rounder, was something of a schoolboy prodigy and as the 18-year-old captain of Repton School made his first-class debut in 1945 in the third 'Victory Test' (an unofficial one) against Australia at Lord's. No sooner had he left Oxford University than he was made vice-captain to Nigel Howard for a marathon tour of India lasting seven months and taking in Pakistan and Ceylon (Sri Lanka). A makeweight MCC party saw five English players make their debuts in the first Test, including Carr and Howard. Carr did not play again in the series until Howard went down with pleurisy and he became captain for the final Test, having the misfortune to become the first English skipper to lose to India.

That was the extent of Carr's Test experience, although as an enterprising batsman and slow left-arm bowler, he made a successful Derbyshire captain. After 12 years as assistant secretary of the MCC, he took over as secretary of the fledgling organisation running the English game, the Test and County Cricket Board, in 1973. It was in this role as the most influential figure in English cricket that Carr mixed diplomacy with a sense of justice as first the

Packer Affair, and then the first rebel tour to South Africa, threatened to split the world game. He was also in charge during an era when commercialism changed the face of cricket and England staged the first three World Cups in 1975, '79 and '83. He retired in 1986 but continues to work in committee and is a Test match referee. His son John plays for Middlesex.

D.B. CARR born 28.12.26 (Wiesbaden, Germany). Tests 2 runs 135 average 33.75 wickets 2 average 70.00

JOHN CHILDS
Gloucestershire and Essex 2 Tests 1988

A CHANGE of county at the age of 33 proved an inspired move for John Childs. Coaching at Essex, particularly from Fred Titmus, extended his run-up and brought success for Childs' left-arm spin, and at the age of 36 years 320 days, he became the oldest player since Dick Howorth in 1947 to make his England debut. It was a tough baptism against the rampant 1988

John Childs

West Indies but his continued success for Essex kept him in the selectors' minds. Come 1992 he was back in the squad, though he did not play.

J.H. CHILDS born 15.8.51 (Plymouth, Devon). Tests 2 runs 2 average — wickets 3 average 61.00

Len Coldwell

LEN COLDWELL
Worcestershire 7 Tests 1962-64

A DEVONIAN built to last, Len Coldwell was a great Worcestershire servant whose new-ball pairing with Jack Flavell was respected and feared throughout the county circuit. While his partner relied on sheer pace, Coldwell's weapons were accuracy and swing, backed up by a big heart which often saw him ignore the pain of injured knees. His Test career started with match figures of 9 for 110 at Lord's against Pakistan in 1962 and he toured Australasia that winter, but he could never make a place his own in the Trueman-Statham era.

L.J. COLDWELL born 10.1.33 (Newton Abbot, Devon). Tests 7 runs 9 average 4.5 wickets 22 average 27.72

BRIAN CLOSE
Yorkshire and Somerset 22 Tests 1949-76

IT IS no surprise that the man Ian Botham cites as the greatest influence on his career is Brian Close. They were both marvellous maverick cricketers, and while Close never fulfilled the great potential of his youth as Botham did, their stories ran a similar course and finally converged in Somerset as one career was coming to an end and one was just blossoming.

Close, like Botham, was brimming with audacity and talent as a young man. He should have set standards and records as an England all-rounder that even Botham would have struggled to emulate; he was a better, more inspirational captain than Botham but both were allowed only a brief flirtation with the England job by selectors forever suspicious of their style.

Close was a games player of extraordinary talent. He played soccer for Arsenal, Leeds and Bradford City, he was an outstanding right-handed golfer who decided to switch to playing left-handed so he could drive further and, at 18 years 149 days, he became the youngest Test player in English history. It was a tag which he came to loathe, describing it as 'an albatross around my neck.'

In those early days he was an aggressive left-handed batsman and bowled as fast as the other young talent on the Headingley staff in 1949, Fred Trueman. That year Close won his Yorkshire and England caps and in 1950 set sail for Australia with Freddie Brown's MCC team as a 19-year-old. It became a tour of misery for the young Close who found himself overawed in the

Pain Barrier... Close takes another blow from Andy Roberts, Old Trafford 1976

company of his schoolday heroes Hutton, Compton and Washbrook. When he returned home from a disappointing trip, many say the sparkle of youth had been dimmed, and he was never the same player again. The fast bowling made way for off-spin and occasional seamers, injuries dogged him and his temperament was questioned.

His England career never got going. He played just 22 Tests over an astonishing span of 27 years, finally being recalled at 45 to take a battering from the fearsome West Indian attack of 1976. By then Close had become known as the iron man of cricket, a character of immense courage epitomised by his bravery in fielding close to the wicket, collecting 813 catches and twice as many bruises.

His career was restored to some extent by the challenge of the Yorkshire captaincy from 1963 to '70, his most successful period as a Test player — and eventually most bitter. He was installed as captain for the last Test of 1966 and led England to a rare victory against the West Indies. He became a national hero, a somewhat eccentric but honest figure, and the next summer he led England to three victories over India and two against Pakistan. England, under his leadership, had been unbeaten, winning six Tests out of seven and he was the natural choice for the tough winter tour to the Caribbean.

However, the Establishment were still uneasy about his presence and, it is suggested, looking for the first opportunity to dump him. They got it when Close was accused of time-wasting and criticised for a confrontation with a spectator during a Championship match at Edgbaston. He was on the carpet, bluntly refused to apologise and, within minutes of winning the series against Pakistan, was informed that he was being sacked as skipper. The job went to Colin Cowdrey. Close's own words summed up the feelings of most England fans: 'It was all so bloody, horribly unfair.'

Three years later things turned sour at Yorkshire and Close left to breathe fire into Somerset for seven seasons. He became an England

The great competitor... even when Brian Close is playing quoits against Trevor Bailey on the voyage to Australia in 1950

selector for three years, was still playing first-class cricket at the age of 55 at the Scarborough Festival and rebuilt bridges at Headingley where he became manager and then club chairman.

D.B. CLOSE born 24.2.31 (Leeds, Yorkshire). Tests 22 runs 887 average 25.34 wickets 18 average 29.55

DENIS COMPTON
Middlesex 78 Tests 1937-57

DENIS Compton captured the spirit of an age. After the War, the public wanted new heroes with a sense of flair and fun; they wanted optimism and charm. 'Compo' personified all that. He was their egalitarian hero. It is difficult to transmit quality across the generations, perspectives and demands change, but there is no doubt that Compton was something very special. He was handsome, friendly and, to the public's delight, prone to mistakes that would embarrass any village cricketer. His running between the wickets was a hazard to fellow batsmen while stories about his time-keeping are legendary. It is true that he would sometimes turn up for play still in full evening dress, having come straight to the ground from the night before. His face was known to the nation long before the age of television coverage

as he beamed down from posters as 'The Brylcreem Boy.' With his great mucker Bill Edrich, he packed the grounds like they had never been packed before — or since — as cricket enjoyed a golden era.

His skill as a games player came naturally. At 14 he was on the staff at Lord's by summer, at Highbury by winter. He won a League Championship medal with Arsenal and played for England in 14 wartime internationals. This soccer career, however, was to cost him dearly in his latter days as a cricketer. An old knee injury flared up frequently, restricting his mobility and finally leading to the removal of his right kneecap. His batting was full of improvisation and he would often take a pre-determined stroll down the wicket and invent a shot. His left-arm bowling was an experimental concoction of chinamen and googlies. His fielding

was superb — anywhere. His captaincy? 'A disaster... but always fun,' says a contemporary who adds: 'He was the most unselfish cricketer I knew, and he would have been a wonderful player in today's one-day cricket. He made it up as he went along.'

Compton scored 1,000 runs in his first season with Middlesex and by the age of 19 was in the Test team. In 1938 at 20 years 19 days he became the youngest player to score a Test century for England — the record still stands — and it can only be imagined what might have happened if hostilities had not stopped cricket until 1946. When Germany were all out, Compton came out to bat again and in 1947 he made 3,816 runs (average 90.86) including 18 centuries, world records for a single season. He posted the fastest 300 (181 minutes) on record playing for the

BOY'S OWN HERO... Denis Compton was certainly that with bat or ball — for further illustration see Godfrey Evans

MCC in South Africa and he reached his 100 centuries in fewer innings (552) than anyone but Sir Don Bradman.

Compton's standing as a national hero was firmly established in 1948 against the Australians at Old Trafford. England were being overwhelmed that summer by the Australian pace attack of Lindwall and Miller and were in trouble again when Compton hooked a no-ball on to his forehead and left the field, his shirt stained crimson. Wickets fell while Compton was stitched up, and he returned to the crease, still bleeding, head in bandages, to score an unbeaten 145, an innings of

brilliance and courage. One of his adversaries that day was Keith Miller, a joyful man who became great friends with Compton. They still speak to each other every week from their different hemispheres by telephone.

Like any genius, Compton was not consistent. He had unsuccessful times, notably the 1950-51 trip to Australia. On that tour, as vice-captain to Freddie Brown, he became the first professional to lead England this century but captaincy was not his forte, although he shared the job for a few years at Middlesex with Edrich. The 'Compton Knee' became an increasing national concern and finally, in 1956, he had

to have an operation. He played one more series in South Africa that winter before leaving the international stage. He became president of Middlesex and until recently wrote regularly on the game. He is still regarded as a national treasure and, as Arlott once wrote: 'The very mention of Denis Compton's name in all the cricketing countries where he played is sufficient, even nowadays, to produce sentimental smiles on the faces of elderly ladies who were maidens when he was a young man.'

D.C.S. COMPTON born 23.5.18 (Hendon, London). Tests 78 runs 5807 average 50.06 wickets 25 average 56.40

CECIL 'SAM' COOK
Gloucestershire 1 Test 1947

A COUNTRY lad just starting off in cricket, Sam Cook was a surprise choice in the experimental years after the War. An accurate left-arm spinner, he was only 25 with little first-class experience when he played in the first Test of 1947 against South Africa. Almost 1,500 runs were scored on a shirt-front Trent Bridge wicket and Cook finished his 30 overs wicketless. Having been tried too early, he was callously discarded too early, but Sam continued to enjoy his cricket and his pint for 19 years at Bristol before putting in 16 seasons as an umpire.

C. COOK born 23.8.21 (Tetbury, Gloucestershire). Tests 1 runs 4 average 2

GEOFF COOK
Northamptonshire 7 Tests 1982-83

A PLAYER held in great respect by his fellow professionals, Geoff Cook got his big chance when the first rebel team went to South Africa in 1982, but he was unable to convert his consistent county form into Test success. In 13 Test innings as a diligent opener he passed 50 only twice. A commanding captain of Northamptonshire for eight summers, he has been a leading figure in the game as chairman and secretary of the Cricketers' Association and is currently director of cricket at Durham.

G. COOK born 9.10.51 (Middlesbrough, Yorkshire). Tests 7 runs 203 average 15.61

Nick Cook

NICK COOK
Leicestershire and Northamptonshire 15 Tests 1983-89

N O BOWLER has enjoyed such a sensational start to his England career as left-arm spinner Nick Cook, who claimed 32 wickets in his first four Tests, including a return of 11 for 83 against Pakistan in Karachi. The next summer, however, the confidence of youth was undermined by the West Indian batsmen and success, even in county cricket, became elusive. A move to

Geoff Cook — See also Allan Lamb

Northampton helped and Cook toured Pakistan again but a third return in 1989, into an England team in turmoil during the Ashes series, proved an unhappy last act to his Test career.

N.G.B. COOK born 17.6.56 (Leicester). Tests 15 runs 179 average 8.52 wickets 52 average 32.48

GEOFF COPE
Yorkshire 3 Tests 1977-78

G EOFF Cope's career was blighted by suspicions that his off-spinner's action was illegal and twice — in 1972 and 1978— he was suspended by Lord's. The second suspension came after he had broken through into the Test side the previous winter in Pakistan, where he came tantalisingly close to a debut hat-trick. Having dismissed Qadir and Sarfraz, he had Iqbal Qasim given out caught first ball only for the catcher, Mike Brearley, to withdraw the appeal, uncertain the ball had carried. Cope went through agonies to sort out his action and succeeded with the help of Johnny Wardle.

G.A. COPE born 23.2.47 (Leeds, Yorkshire). Tests 3 runs 40 average 13.33 wickets 8 average 34.62

Geoff Cope

BILL COPSON
Derbyshire 3 Tests 1939-47

BILL Copson, a flame-haired pace bowler with a temper to match, became a cricketer by accident. A miner, he first played at 17 to kill time during the General Strike, and discovered that off six paces with a slingy action, he could generate surprising pace and movement. After much success with Derbyshire, Copson, never an Establishment favourite, was belatedly called into the Test team in 1939, taking nine wickets on his debut. The War intervened but he played one Test when peace returned in his 40th year. Umpired between 1958 and '67.

W.H. COPSON born 27.4.08 (Stonebroom, Derbyshire). Died 14.9.71. Tests 3 runs 6 average 6 wickets 15 average 19.80

BOB COTTAM
Hampshire and Northamptonshire 4 Tests 1969-73

BOB Cottam's ability to bowl sharp seamers or cutters at a reduced pace on turning wickets made him a useful tourist, and his four England caps came on two tours of the Indian sub-continent. Also selected for the aborted 1968-69 South Africa trip, he never figured at home, yet always provided sterling service for his county employers, taking 1,010 first-class wickets at 20 apiece. After a spell as Warwickshire manager, he took over at Somerset, where son Andrew plays, in 1992.

R.M.H. COTTAM born 16.10.44 (Cleethorpes, Lincolnshire). Tests 4 runs 27 average 6.75 wickets 14 average 23.35

NORMAN COWANS
Middlesex 19 Tests 1982-85

NORMAN Cowans did not receive a glowing report about his application on the 'B' tour of Sri Lanka in 1986 and he has not played for England since. Before that winter, this easy-going fast bowler had been on the England scene for three years without ever taking the quantity of wickets expected of him. On song — as he was in Melbourne in 1983 when he took a match-winning 6 for 77 — he had everything going for him but too often 'Flash' was not tuned in. Injuries have added to his frustration in recent summers.

N.G. COWANS born 17.4.61 (St Mary, Jamaica). Tests 19 runs 175 average 7.95 wickets 51 average 39.27

CHRIS COWDREY
Kent and Glamorgan 6 Tests 1984-88

CHRIS Cowdrey was fortunate to play Test cricket at all but he did not deserve the shabby treatment which ended his brief England career. Faced with the daunting task of following his famous father at Kent, he was a very different type of player. A bustling enthusiast, Cowdrey was invited to fill the all-rounder's spot on the 1984-85 tour of India, led by his good friend David Gower. He had modest success on a happy tour and returned to county cricket.

In 1988, chairman of selectors Peter May sprang a surprise by opting for Cowdrey, his godson, to be the captain to bring a fresh image to an England side in turmoil and being

Bob Cottam

Norman Cowans

crushed by the West Indies after Mike Gatting and John Emburey had both been jettisoned as skippers. It was a bold appointment which had a whiff of a return to the days of the amateur skipper, which would hardly have aligned itself to the thinking of team manager Micky Stewart.

Cowdrey was appointed for two Tests but could not stop the rot at Leeds, scoring five runs and failing to take a wicket. He damaged his foot before the last Test but instead of being given until the morning of the match to check his fitness, he was summarily replaced by Graham Gooch. A bitter newspaper article which followed landed him in trouble with Lord's and in 1990 he joined a rebel tour to South Africa.

C.S. COWDREY born 20.10.57 (Farnborough, Kent). Tests 6 runs 101 average 14.42 wickets 4 average 77.25

Chris Cowdrey

SIR COLIN COWDREY
Kent 114 Tests 1954-75

THE mention of Colin Cowdrey's name in any gathering of former players will cause an astonishingly diverse reaction. Some will pay dreamy tribute to his silken batting skills, explaining he did not so much hit the ball to the boundary as charm it there. Other contemporaries will shuffle uneasily and look down at their feet, not willing to besmirch the public image of one of the game's greats.

Cowdrey was not universally liked inside cricket. The benign exterior hid a calculating, complex character. He was a player of moods who one day could make the world's finest look like village green bowlers and the next would become bored and bogged down by county trundlers. He fell out with colleagues including Kent team-mate Mike Denness and his own son Chris, who was to follow the family trail to become Kent and England captain. A man reputed to be driven by Corinthian ideals, Cowdrey so infuriated Garfield Sobers with England's go-slow tactics in Trinidad in 1968 that the West Indian skipper declared with a meagre lead, allowing England to win the decisive Test of the series. Cowdrey, the captain, dithered over the chase for 215 until Ken Barrington confronted him in the dressing room toilets at the tea interval and convinced him England could win. 'Kipper' captained England 27 times in all but his indecision and introspection led to the England selectors overlooking him more than once.

But if not a born leader, a beautifully natural run-maker he certainly was — probably from the moment his cricket-loving father, a tea-planter in India, gave him the initials MCC. Large but well-balanced, Cowdrey was an outstanding schools player and was introduced to Tonbridge School's first XI at the age of 13 as a leg-spinner and No. 3 bat. He played for Kent while still at school and at 18 became the youngest player to be capped by the county. By the age of 22, as an Oxford undergraduate, he was on the boat to Australia with Len Hutton's team. His father died while he was on the voyage but he steeled himself for instant success, playing in all five Tests, scoring a century in his third. It was an innings that marked him out as something special, scoring as he did 102 out of a total of 191 on a Melbourne green-top. England won the Test and Cowdrey won his spurs.

The records followed although some still believe he never did himself full justice. He converted only three of his 107 centuries into double-hundreds, which perhaps shows a lack of a killer instinct, yet when it came to bravery he was not found wanting. He will always be remembered for appearing in the 1963 Lord's Test against the West Indies with a broken left wrist in plaster ready to face the fearsome Wes Hall if necessary. Cowdrey had had his wrist broken earlier by Hall and came out for the final two deliveries with England needing six to win and the West Indies needing one wicket for victory. Without him, England would have had to concede defeat but they survived, No. 10 David Allen playing out the last two deliveries.

Along the way he shared a 411-run partnership with Peter May in the West Indies, an English record, and became the first man to score centuries against all the Test-playing nations of the time. He was 42 when England recalled him for a final time to fly out to Australia in an injury crisis to face Lillee and Thomson, and he was happy to step into a Test within four days of arriving, after three years absence from the international game.

When Cowdrey left international cricket, his 114 Tests and 7,624 runs were records and his 22 centuries were an all-time best he shared with Hammond and Boycott. A superb slip fielder, he had also held 120 catches, a record he was to share with Botham. He was awarded the CBE, made MCC president for the club's bicentenary in 1987 and went on to become chairman of the International Cricket Council. The position made him potentially the most powerful single figure in the world game. Cowdrey introduced an international code of conduct and match referees to clean up cricket's tarnished image but his lack of decisiveness, or possibly a desire to be all things to all men, led to a disappointing term in office.

M.C. COWDREY born 24.12.32 (Putumala, India). Tests 114 runs 7624 average 44.06 100s 22

Another kind of National Service for AC2 Cowdrey at RAF Cardington

ALEC COXON
Yorkshire 1 Test 1948

ALEC Coxon's Test career was abrupt — much like the man himself. An ever-willing seam bowler, he was one of several tried in the search for a partner for Alec Bedser, but he did himself no favours with a brusqueness which could upset. After six successful seasons with Yorkshire, Coxon quit unexpectedly to play league cricket in the north-east. As he was only 34 and had taken 131 wickets the previous summer, his departure sparked the same speculation as his brief Test career: that he had upset someone. Even 40 years on, Alec refuses to talk about it.

A. COXON born 18.1.16 (Huddersfield, Yorkshire). Tests 1 runs 19 average 9.50 wickets 3 average 57.33

KEN CRANSTON
Lancashire 8 Tests 1947-48

A LIVERPOOL dentist and fine all-round cricketer, Ken Cranston allowed himself just two seasons of first-class cricket as skipper of Lancashire in

1947 and 1948. He also forced his way into the England side and was a member of a weak touring party sent to the West Indies in '48. Skipper Gubby Allen pulled a muscle skipping on the banana boat taking the team out, and Cranston was made captain for the drawn first Test. Cranston played one Test the following summer before returning to his surgery.

K. CRANSTON born 20.10.17 (Liverpool). Tests 8 runs 209 average 14.92 wickets 18 average 25.61

JACK CRAPP
Gloucestershire 7 Tests 1948-49

BUT for an interruption for the more serious business of World War Two, Jack Crapp lived for cricket. He was a sound rather than spectacular left-handed batsman who scored 1,000 runs in all but one of his 15 seasons — that was 1954, when he struggled with the Gloucestershire captaincy. After the War and at 35, he became the first Cornishman to play Test cricket when he appeared in three Tests at home and four in South Africa with conservative success. After his playing days, he dedicated 22 summers to umpiring and stood in four Tests.

J.F. CRAPP born 14.10.12 (St Columb Major, Cornwall). Died 13.2.81. Tests 7 runs 319 average 29.00

TIM CURTIS
Worcestershire 5 Tests 1988-89

A DILIGENT, determined opener, Tim Curtis was brought in to stop the rot against the 1988 West Indians with about as much success as those who had gone

Tim Curtis

before him. The next summer during the Ashes series he was asked to do a similar job in a disintegrating England team, but he was never able to reproduce his consistent county form at the highest level. An English teacher by winter, Curtis took over the Worcestershire captaincy in 1992 and is a thoughtful and articulate chairman of the Cricketers' Association, the players' 'union'.

T.S. CURTIS born 15.1.60 (Chislehurst, Kent). Tests 5 runs 140 average 15.55

PHILLIP DeFREITAS
Leicestershire and Lancashire
32 Tests 1986-

FINDING himself left out of the 1990-91 Ashes tour was the best thing that could have happened to Phillip DeFreitas. Four years earlier, DeFreitas had gone to Australia as a 20-year-old with a handful of first-class games behind him and played an exciting part in victory for Mike Gatting's team. Adopted by Ian Botham and likened to Ian Botham, it was all too much, too soon, for the impressionable 'Daffy'.

The comparisons were inescapable. DeFreitas was an explosive hitter when the mood took him, an aggressive pace bowler, inclined to pitch everything short and a spectacular fielder. But like the others who have tried to fill the

Phillip DeFreitas

to withdraw.

If there was any complacency left in DeFreitas it was knocked out of him when he missed out on the 1990-91 Ashes trip. Then injuries saw him flown out as a replacement and he showed his consistency to make him a regular Test choice at last. Sadly a persistent groin injury hindered that progress in 1992 and on the 1993 India tour.

P.A.J. DeFREITAS born 18.2.66 (Scotts Head, Dominica, West Indies). Tests 32 runs 550 average 12.50 wickets 93 average 33.24

MIKE DENNESS
Kent and Essex 28 Tests 1969-75

THE first Scotsman to captain England, Mike Denness found himself penned in by controversy through most of his 19-match reign. A positive, attractive stroke-maker, Denness impressed with his unselfish leadership of Kent and had played only one Test when he was made number two to Tony Lewis in India in 1972-73. Although he did not command a place the next summer, he was appointed to succeed Illingworth for that winter's trip to the West Indies — much to the disgust of Geoff Boycott, whose antipathy towards him was never disguised.

After only two days of Test cricket, Denness found himself having to resolve a potentially explosive situation in Trinidad when Tony Greig ran out Alvin Kallicharran at the close of play. A three-hour meeting that evening ended with Denness diplomatically withdrawing the appeal. Somehow, England scraped a draw out of that series, and the next summer against India, England and Denness flourished.

Against anything but the most hostile of bowling, he looked in control at the crease. Unfortunately that winter, 1974-75, Australia had in Lillee and Thomson the most fearsome of attacks. The decision to retain Denness had been criticised by Illingworth, John Snow was scandalously left out, Boycott refused to tour and Tony Greig began imposing himself by being critical of selections — all before they had boarded the plane. Denness failed to inspire his troops in the face of the onslaught and, after six single-figure scores, he bravely dropped himself for

Mike Denness

the fourth Test. He returned and, with great character, scored 188 to inspire victory in the final Test but by then the Ashes were unobtainable. After a massive defeat in the first Test against Australia the next summer, Denness was replaced by Greig and his England career closed.

At Kent the next year he left after a dispute but finished his days in happy circumstances, helping Essex to their first championship. He is still heavily involved in the game with his own public relations company.

M.H. DENNESS born 1.12.40 (Bellshill, Lanarkshire). Tests 28 runs 1667 average 39.69 100s 4

all-rounder's position — Pringle, Capel, Cowdrey, Lewis — DeFreitas suffered when measured against the great man.

A lack of maturity led to problems at Grace Road. Team-mate Jon Agnew hurled his kit off the dressing room balcony in one famous confrontation, the committee dropped him because of his attitude and in 1989 he left to join Lancashire. The move worked, for DeFreitas became a much more relaxed character and while his batting rarely blossomed, his bowling began to develop. He made a rash decision to join the 1990 South Africa rebel tour but the angry reaction of the black community in England persuaded him

TED DEXTER
Sussex 62 Tests 1958-68

LONG before David Gower buzzed an up-country cricket ground in Australia aboard a Tiger Moth, Ted Dexter was performing many an airborne trick. He once flew his family to Australia in a light aircraft and, so it is said, popped over to France on the rest day of a Test in which he was playing to watch a horse race. The trouble with life was that there was too much going on for the restless Dexter to cram it all in. His interest in cricket was only one piece in the jigsaw. One former Test player says: 'Talk to him during a Test about the game and you'd get a blank look, talk to him about golf or horse racing and you were away.' Dexter owned horses and greyhounds, he loved powerful cars and motorbikes, he stood for Parliament (against Jim Callaghan) shortly before a tour, he collaborated on two novels, he became a journalist and broadcaster and set up his own public relations company. Currently he is the first paid chairman of selectors and throughout it all, he has found time for golf. He seriously considered a career in golf; one year he failed to qualify for the Open by one shot after missing a short putt on the 18th. But he opted for cricket, and for a decade illuminated the game before his all-too-early retirement.

Dexter was — still is — known as 'Lord Ted' because of his rather aristocratic air. He was dashing, charming and good at games. He first emerged as a frenetic pace bowler but it soon became apparent his batting was something special. He could hit imperiously, and the faster the bowling the more he seemed to relish it. He was at his best when adversity concentrated his mind and he always wanted to carry the fight to the bowlers. Few have hit a ball harder and his record bears testimony to his courage as well as technique.

After an indifferent Test initiation, he came of age in the West Indies in 1960 with two centuries and an average of 65, and 18 months later, when Peter May retired, the 26-year-old Dexter took charge. Dexter, the Corinthian, bridged the gap at the end of the amateur-professional days. He had been the last player to lead the Gentlemen against the Players at Lord's in 1962. He was to captain England 30 times but players found his methods eccentric and at times inflexible. He would come up with a game plan and stick to it dogmatically.

The selectors were never quite sure, just as they were never convinced about Colin Cowdrey's leadership qualities. In 1962 they came up with the novel idea of putting them both on trial. Dexter captained the first two against Pakistan and won handsomely, Cowdrey took charge for the third and won equally comfortably. Dexter was to get the job but he opted out of a tour to India and the next winter toured under Mike Smith because the selectors were unsure whether he would be playing cricket that winter or making his maiden speech in Parliament. The next summer he broke his leg in an accident which had a touch of black farce about it, and decided to retire. Driving back from an advertising assignment with a Champagne house, his Jaguar ran out of petrol on the A4 and, when Dexter tried to push it off the road, the car rolled back, crushing his leg against the gates of the Martini factory and setting off the alarms. In a way, the injury gave Dexter an excuse, perhaps a drastic one, to give up playing at 29. He was in his prime but other challenges called.

As if to make a point, three years later he returned to the Sussex side and scored 203, the second 100 coming at quicker than a run a minute. The selectors could not resist bringing him back for two Tests against the Australians but Dexter, although he acquitted himself well, decided not to try to revive former glories. He became an entertaining writer and broadcaster on the game but in 1989 gave up journalism to become chairman of selectors, forming a successful axis with manager Micky Stewart and captain Graham Gooch.

E.R. DEXTER born 15.5.35 (Milan, Italy).
Tests 62 runs 4502 average 47.89
100s 9 wickets 66 average 34.93

A man of many parts and many runs...
Ted Dexter after scoring 180 against
Australia, Edgbaston 1961

For further illustration see Ken Barrington

GRAHAM DILLEY

Kent and Worcestershire 39 Tests 1979-88

GRAHAM Dilley was an enigma. He had the makings of a world-class fast bowler yet, depressingly, failed to quite grasp the moment. He was tall — 6ft 3in — and powerfully built with an aggressive streak. Genuinely fast, he was born into an era of opportunity when England were crying out for someone to help take the strain off Willis' creaking knees. The selectors showed belief in him, plucking him from obscurity at the age of 20 for Mike Brearley's team in Australia in 1979-80. In all, Dilley went on seven official tours, played in 14 series at home and abroad yet completed only two of them — and neither of these were five-match affairs.

Injury was partly to blame but so too, it seems, was the Dilley temperament. His massive, thumping delivery stride put much pressure on his body and he suffered serious problems with his neck, back and knees. He showed considerable courage overcoming those problems yet had a reputation for succumbing to the first twinge. Possibly he always feared the worst. His desire was questioned, too. He could appear uninterested, even sullen, when the dice were not rolling for him, yet that mood is at odds with the explosion of frustration he showed in New Zealand in 1988. At Christchurch he pulled out everything and in the first innings he took 6 for 38, his best return in Test cricket. In the second innings, as the home side battled for safety on the last day, he removed both openers but then had a series of appeals turned down and finally snapped, screaming expletives which could be heard all over Lancaster Park. It earned him a £250 fine, but no-one doubted his desire that day.

On other days, however, he could appear so diffident. One former colleague says: 'A fine bowler but he could be idle with it. I think his greatest problem was the lack of competition.' Dilley could also be an effective late-order hitter and it was his enterprising 56 at Leeds in 1981 which inspired Ian Botham's famous century, setting up England's victory after following on against Australia.

Dilley had barely given up his job as a diamond-setter in Hatton Garden and completed his first full season at Kent when England decided to gamble on his raw talent. He took only seven first-class wickets on that tour — '£7,000 for seven wickets,' as tour manager Alec Bedser put it — and the potential was slow to be realised. In 1984, back surgery kept him out of cricket for a year but he fought back finally to take his first five-wicket return in his 23rd Test in Australia in 1986-87. He reached his peak on that happy tour under Mike Gatting and also made a major career move by deciding to quit Kent and join Worcestershire. His disenchantment with his home county had dragged on for a few years, first because of a dispute over money during his year of convalescence and then because of the sacking of Chris Tavare as skipper in favour of Chris Cowdrey.

The constant threat of injury and his decision to give up the chance of a benefit at Kent made Dilley more conscious of his lack of financial security and he always regretted his decision to pull out of the first rebel tour to go to South Africa in 1982. So when the chance to join Gatting's rebel squad came along in 1989 he did not need persuading. The decision marked the end of his England career at a time when he was enjoying his most consistent run, having played in nine consecutive Tests. Dilley's destructive ability still played a vital part in Worcestershire's success in the late 1980s but he was forced to retire in 1992 because of recurring injury problems.

G.R. DILLEY born 18.5.59 (Dartford, Kent). Tests 39 runs 479 average 12.94 wickets 133 average 28.48

GRAHAM DILLEY... when it all worked, it worked beautifully

BASIL D'OLIVEIRA
Worcestershire 44 Tests 1966-72

WHEN South Africa were accepted back into the fold of world cricket in 1991, Basil D'Oliveira kept a typically low profile. Who but the man who had been the catalyst of South Africa's 21 years of isolation because of their apartheid policy could offer a more pertinent comment about their return? But D'Oliveira, then coach at Worcester, declined to cash in, just as he has never wanted to glory in the 'D'Oliveira Affair' which will forever make his name part of cricket history.

What many tend to overlook is that D'Oliveira was an exceptionally good batsman as well as a useful medium-pacer, whose whole career was a remarkable story of determination to overcome the odds fate had stacked against him. Categorised in South Africa as a 'Cape-Coloured', he learned his cricket on rough pitches and playing in the streets, dodging the police patrols which would have dragged him off to the local jail for such a heinous offence. The future for a non-white cricketer was bleak and so he wrote, initially to John Arlott, whom he had heard and read, asking how he could get coaching instruction so he could then teach cricket to his fellow 'Cape-Coloureds.'

Reports of his ability filtered back and in 1960, with donations to pay his air fare, 'Dolly' came to England at 29 to start a career in the Lancashire League with Middleton. He had never played on grass before — and never experienced such a climate — and his first few weeks were miserable, but soon he adapted and by the end of the season he had finished ahead of even Garfield Sobers in the League averages.

A few years later his ability caught Tom Graveney's eye and he was invited to join Worcestershire in 1964. Two years on, even his wildest dreams were exceeded when he walked out at Lord's wearing an England cap. His early grounding on untrustworthy wickets taught him to employ a remarkably short backlift yet still hit the ball with great power.

His strong presence became an important factor in England's middle order until, it seemed, 1968. Behind the scenes the MCC had been made aware of the political ramifications of picking D'Oliveira for that winter's tour to South Africa, who had let it be known they would not allow him to play there. Unexpectedly, D'Oliveira was dropped after the first Test against Australia that summer, despite scoring 87 not out. Conveniently he was left out for the rest of the series but an uncanny catalogue of injuries to Tom Cartwright, Barry Knight and then Roger Prideaux gave the selectors no option but to pick D'Oliveira for the final Test.

A believer in fate, he rang his wife Naomi before play on the second morning and told her to make sure she did not miss a ball on television. He felt it was going to be his day. He was dropped on 31 but his conviction never wavered and the result was a magnificent 158 that set up England to win the Test and level the series. He even made the breakthrough with his bowling in the last hour of a match Derek Underwood won famously on a 'sticky dog' with five minutes to spare.

That evening the selectors — Insole, Bedser, Kenyon, May, Cowdrey, Gilligan and Gubby Allen — picked their squad for South Africa and omitted the Worcestershire man. The dignified D'Oliveira appeared to have been betrayed. There was public outrage. The next morning Arlott wrote: 'There is no case for leaving out D'Oliveira on cricketing grounds... the MCC have never made a sadder, more dramatic or potentially damaging decision.'

But fate was not done yet. Cartwright withdrew, reporting a sore shoulder, and the selectors had to pick D'Oliveira. The South African government claimed the Anti-Apartheid Movement had picked the side and cancelled the tour.

D'Oliveira relished the rest of his career, making friends all along the way. In 1969 he received the OBE and in 1980 he became Worcestershire coach, a position he held until his retirement in 1991.

B.L. D'OLIVEIRA born 4.10.31 (Signal Hill, Cape Town). Tests 44 runs 2484 average 40.06 100s 5 wickets 47 average 39.55

BASIL D'OLIVEIRA... under the spotlight

TOM Dollery was the mainstay of Warwickshire's batting for two decades. Powerful, with a full array of strokes, he amassed 24,414 first-class runs (average 37), a considerable achievement as his prime years between 25 and 32 were lost to the War. Tom was chosen for the aborted India tour of 1939 and his Test chance finally arrived after the conflict, but he failed to make an immediate impression and made way for younger talent. The first professional county captain this century, he was coach at Edgbaston for 14 years and an England selector for two.

H.E. DOLLERY born 14.10.14 (Reading, Berkshire). Died 20.1.87. Tests 4 runs 72 average 10.20

PAUL DOWNTON
Kent and Middlesex 30 Tests 1981-88

PAUL Downton was unfortunate to have to pick up the gauntlets thrown down by Alan Knott and Bob Taylor. They had both worn the wicketkeeping gloves with artistry in their hands and any successor was liable to suffer by comparison. And so it was for Downton, although he was a much better 'keeper than many gave him credit for.

His father was Godfrey Evans' deputy for a couple of summers at Kent and Downton followed him to Canterbury. With a law degree, a coaching certificate and a taste of international recognition in both cricket and rugby union at youth level, Downton was naturally ambitious. He toured New Zealand and Pakistan as Taylor's deputy in 1977-78 with only seven first-class matches behind him, but was frustrated by the lack of opportunity at Kent, filling in only when Knott was on Test duty.

In 1980 he moved to Middlesex and that winter broke through into Test cricket in the Caribbean, but opportunities remained rare until the West Indies came along again in 1984. England, sensing a need to bolster the batting, summoned

JOHN DEWES
Middlesex 5 Tests 1948-50

AN OUTSTANDING batsman at Cambridge University, John Dewes played most of his Test cricket while still a student. For the Light Blues he was an aggressively entertaining left-hander, sharing a second-wicket partnership of 429 — then an English record — with David Sheppard. But with Middlesex, caution infiltrated his game while his duties as a schoolmaster restricted his appearances. He ended his Test days on a disappointing Ashes tour in 1950-51.

J.G. DEWES born 11.10.26 (North Latchford, Cheshire). Tests 5 runs 121 average 12.10

HUBERT DOGGART
Sussex 2 Tests 1950

AN UNBEATEN 215 against Lancashire on his Cambridge University debut — a record debut score in English cricket — marked out Hubert Doggart as a batsman of great potential. In his last year as a student in 1950 he captained Cambridge and was introduced to Test cricket in the first two matches against the touring West Indians. But it turned out to be a modest start — and end — to Doggart's Test career, his teaching commitments restricting him to just one full summer of county cricket after that. He is a former president and treasurer of the MCC.

G.H.G. DOGGART born 18.7.25 (Earl's Court, London). Tests 2 runs 76 average 19.00

Hubert Doggart

Downton and that was to be the start of a 23-match run in the team. His 'keeping was safe and acrobatic, his batting resourceful, particularly when others were ducking below the parapet. Captains trusted 'Nobby', perhaps that is why 16 of his Tests, more than half, were against the West Indies when they were at their most fearsome.

A trusted, affable team member, he played a major role in Middlesex's success through the 1980s but was forced to quit cricket for a life in the City in 1990 after a flying bail caught him in the eye and blurred his vision.

P.R. DOWNTON born 4.4.57 (Farnborough, Kent). Tests 30 runs 785 average 19.62 dismissals 75 caught 70 stumped 5

Paul Downton

Tom Dollery (seated 3rd from left) with his 1951 Warwickshire Championship-winning side. Back (l to r) D. Taylor, R.T. Weeks, T.L. Pritchard, A. Townsend, R.G. Thompson, F.C. Gardner, R.E. Hitchcock. Front (l to r) A.V. Wolton, W.E. Hollies, Dollery, J.S. Ord, C.W. Grove, R.T. Spooner

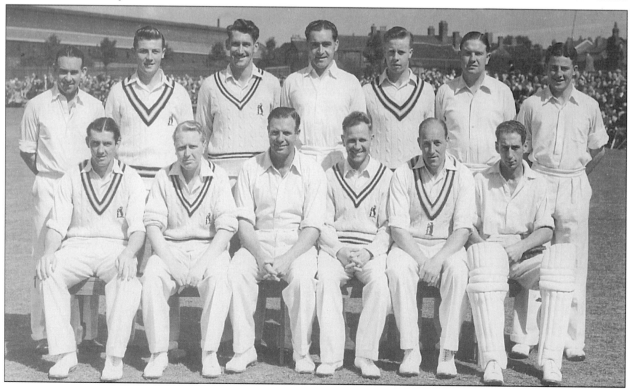

PHIL EDMONDS
Middlesex 51 Tests 1975-87

THERE was at least one person who thought Phil Edmonds should have been captain of England: Phil Edmonds. But it was never really on. He was always too much of a *Singular Man*, the perfect title of a recent Edmonds' biography. Cricket should be thankful for people like Phillippe Henri Edmonds who could illuminate even the dullest of contests. At Calcutta in 1984-85, India refused to up the tempo of a Test doomed for a draw so Edmonds, fielding at square leg, produced a *Daily Telegraph* and started to read.

His bowling was orthodox left-arm, delivered with powerful shoulders from a high, easy action. He took risks and he spun the ball. He also had the aggression of a fast bowler and more than once let rip with a bouncer off his usual six paces if the batsman irritated him enough. He was so strong, although back problems forced him to wear a support in latter days, that when the bowling 'yips' struck in India and he lost his run-up completely, he was just as effective bowling off one pace.

He was — still is — an argumentative soul. He could be cussedly abrasive or engagingly charming but he could never bring himself to conform to the fist-clenching, grim-faced trait of most professional sportsmen. It was this independent spirit that saw him clash so frequently with Mike Brearley at Middlesex. While the equally opinionated John Emburey would agree to differ with Brearley, there was no common ground between Edmonds and his captain, and their disagreements were loud and famous. Edmonds had been skipper at Cambridge but committee men and England captains were often wary of him, the reason why he never achieved the two jobs he fancied most: leader of Middlesex and England.

Edmonds developed much of his competitive nature in southern Africa, where he was born to an English father and Belgian mother in Lusaka. He was schooled in Tunbridge Wells and went to Cambridge in 1971, the same year he joined Middlesex. At Lord's he had the knowledge of Fred Titmus to call upon and was to develop a fruitful partnership with another young slow bowler, John Emburey. He celebrated his Test debut against the 1975 Australians at Leeds with 5 for 17 inside his first 12 overs for England, but appearances were to be sporadic. He was unfortunate that his youthful promise coincided with the expertise of Derek Underwood.

His career hit a two-year hiatus between 1980 and '82 when he did not play a Test and it was not until the advent of David Gower as captain that Edmonds produced his best. The relaxed, youthful Gower was not worried about tales of Edmonds being hard to handle. He was the best left-arm spinner in the country and Gower wanted him in India in partnership with another lively character, Pat Pocock. The combination worked well and England enjoyed their best time under Gower, beating the Indians and Australia at home, Edmonds taking 29 wickets in the two series. Although now established as a regular Test performer, Edmonds found that various business interests became increasingly demanding and in 1987 he suggested to Middlesex he continue to play for them but as an amateur. They refused, so Edmonds left the game, his only link being his often provocative thoughts in a weekly newspaper column... until 1992, and an injury crisis at Lord's. Middlesex called him up and he threw his kit in the boot of his Rolls-Royce, motored up to Trent Bridge and showed that the years had not dulled the spirit.

P.H. EDMONDS born 8.3.51 (Lusaka, Northern Rhodesia). Tests 51 runs 975 average 17.50 wickets 125 average 34.18

A man with a vision... Phil Edmonds always had a few of those

BILL EDRICH
Middlesex 39 Tests 1938-55

Walking out to play... Bill Edrich

IF **BILL** Edrich had his career again in the current era, he would be like an agent's dream. Bill made Ian Botham's lifestyle look like that of a Trappist monk. One of four cricket-playing brothers, Bill married five times, was a war hero, a flying winger with Norwich and Tottenham and on the cricket field he could bat and bowl a bit, too. He will always be mentioned in the same breath as Denis Compton; they were the 'Terrible Twins' of Middlesex in cricket's halcyon days after the War. Two great mates who did not waste a minute of life getting bored, they are commemorated today in a concrete stand — the Compton and Edrich Stand — at the Nursery End at Lord's. It is a dull, practical structure which does little justice to their mercurial talents and indomitable spirits.

Edrich's story started before the War but only really took off after it when he returned a hero, decorated with the DFC for his daring exploits as a daylight bomber pilot. Only 5ft 6in, he was a fearless fellow, an aggressive, jaunty batsman who the more he was struck by a fast bowler, the harder he would try to hook him out of the ground. He could also answer like with like, being a wild-card fast bowler, although later he converted to off-spin!

His introduction to Test cricket was something of a disaster. In his first eight Tests he failed to pass 28 but in his ninth, with the ship anchored and steaming impatiently in the Indian Ocean off the South African coast waiting to take the MCC party home, he scored 219 in the second innings of the timeless Test in Durban.

And then the War interrupted rudely. He finished his RAF career an officer, enjoyed the lifestyle and, supported by his wife who was a squadron officer in the WRAF, thought it befitting his rank that he should give up his professional status and play as an amateur. He had seen Wally Hammond turn amateur and be given the England captaincy and he hoped the same honour would come his way. Compton says: 'That, I'm sure, was Bill's great ambition. More's the pity he never achieved it because no bigger-hearted cricketer ever drew breath and few men ever dared more for King and country. Certainly he merited the honour more than some who received it. I am certain it was a bitter disappointment but he never moped or whined, he just lived life to the full.'

Edrich was never Compton's equal as a batsman but together they made the summer of 1947 their own. Between them they scored 7,355 first-class runs including 30 centuries, and on their own ground at Lord's they gave a virtuoso performance in the second Test against South Africa. Edrich scored 189, Compton 208, as they shared a third wicket partnership of 370, an English record. In the next Test Compton scored his third successive hundred and Edrich cracked 191, as well as taking eight wickets opening the bowling.

Those heights were never touched again and, as the big scores became infrequent, he had a three-year break from Test cricket before returning in 1953 to help England regain the Ashes. A year later he returned to Australia to make sure the Ashes were retained but, at 38, that was his final shot for his country. After that his energies were channelled into Middlesex. For two summers, Bill and Denis had shared the captaincy, but in 1953, Edrich took sole charge and led the side for five years before leaving the first-class game — with 36,965 runs, 86 centuries and 479 wickets to his name — to captain his native Norfolk in the Minor Counties League.

W.J. EDRICH born 26.3.16 (Lingwood, Norfolk). Died 24.4.86. Tests 39 runs 2440 average 40.00 100s 6 wickets 41 average 41.29

An officer and a gentleman

JOHN EDRICH
Surrey 77 Tests 1963-76

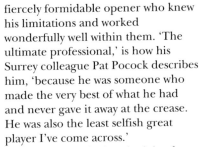

ASK someone to pick one of John Edrich's great innings or even one of his classical strokes and it will be head-scratching time. Yet ask the professionals to name their 20 leading batsmen since the War and the Surrey left-hander will be on most lists. The Edrich family in Norfolk produced such a talented line of cricket-playing males that they

formed their own team. Five, four of them brothers, went on to play county cricket but it was John, on the Oval staff for 20 years and captain for six, who stood out even above his dashing older cousin Bill, whom he followed into the England team.

Unflinching, unselfish, and often unsmiling while going about his business in the middle, he was a

fiercely formidable opener who knew his limitations and worked wonderfully well within them. 'The ultimate professional,' is how his Surrey colleague Pat Pocock describes him, 'because he was someone who made the very best of what he had and never gave it away at the crease. He was also the least selfish great player I've come across.'

Edrich was 21 when he joined Surrey and in his second match — against Nottinghamshire at Trent Bridge — he scored a century in each innings and averaged 52 in his first season. In the early days his bushy-browed concentration failed to convince the selectors, who shuttled him in and out of the Test team, but in 1965 he returned against New Zealand at Leeds and, on a seaming wicket, scored an unbeaten 310. His Herculean effort contained 57 boundaries, a record for a Test innings. It was the first triple-century for an Englishman since 1938 and kept him on the field for the whole match — but it kept him in the team for only one more Test before he was dropped again.

That winter, however, he went to Australia, scored two centuries in successive Tests batting at No. 3 and that laid the foundations for a regular place in the top three for the next decade, much of it in reliable partnership with Geoff Boycott. Despite his triple-century, Edrich will always be associated with his many innings of courage in the face of hostile fast bowling from Australian pair Lillee and Thomson, in the Caribbean against Hall and Griffith and, at the age of 39 in his last series, the West Indians Holding, Holder and Daniel.

In that last heroic stand in 1976, with fellow hardened pros Brian Close and David Steele for company in the firing line, Edrich would often let the ball thud into his body rather than surrender his wicket. At the end of the day his right side would be covered with violent violet bruises, a hazard of the trade he would dismiss with a friendly grin and a shrug.

In 1974-75, when England were being battered by Lillee and Thomson, skipper Mike Denness dropped himself for the fourth Test and Edrich took over for his first and only taste of the English captaincy. As England batted to save the match and the Ashes, Edrich was hit first ball by Lillee and had to leave the field. He returned from hospital with two ribs broken and, at 156 for 6, went out again to try to save a match which England finally lost in the last hour with Edrich still undefeated on 33.

Despite his enormous application when he had a bat in his hand, his captaincy at Surrey between 1973 and '78 strangely lacked conviction and success. He had an alert mind and various business interests, and would often, say colleagues, give the impression he had better things to do than play cricket seven days a week, slipping away from nets to make a string of phone calls. He was an England selector for a year in 1981 after Ken Barrington died, but he gave that up too. Probably he had better things to do.

J.E. EDRICH born 21.6.37 (Blofield, Norfolk). Tests 77 runs 5138 average 43.54 100s 12

John Edrich... thou shalt not pass

JOHN EMBUREY
Middlesex 62 Tests 1978-

JOHN Emburey's career, successful as it has been, must be consigned to the what-might-have-been tray when it is over. When the critics come to write the tributes to his lasting and worthy contributions for England and Middlesex, question marks will be scattered liberally, but they will all revolve around one central theme — what if he had not been the one player to join both rebel tours to South Africa at the start of the 1980s and '90s? Those money-chasing excursions cost him six lost years as far as Test cricket was concerned: potentially around 50 matches and more than 100 wickets — and, more significantly, probably an extended run as England captain, a job for which he was better suited than some who held the position post-Mike Brearley.

Emburey served his apprenticeship as an off-spinner under Fred Titmus at Lord's and with his Middlesex left-arm colleague, Phil Edmonds, formed the outstanding spin combination of their day. It was a difficult era for slow bowlers as the game moved into the age of bland covered batting wickets, one-day cricket and bats as heavy as railway sleepers that sent even an edged shot flying away to the boundary. It was an age many traditionalist spinners shuddered at and shied away from, but Emburey adapted.

His weapon has been his masterful control and patience; a relentless talker off the field,

'Embers' nags away on it with his probing spin, like a neglected wife, until the batsman's willpower snaps. The opponent who confronts Emburey with a lunging pad and a broad bat presents a challenge he knows he can win; it has been only the boldest batsmen who have succeeded against him. At 6ft 2in and powerfully built with a smooth action, Emburey can plug away all day and he has a textbook 'arm ball' which he drifts away from the right-hander. Much of his prime time was spent trying to curb the West Indian stroke-makers during Viv Richards' reign while England's pace bowlers rested, a task about as thankless as painting the Forth Road Bridge.

Possibly 'Embers' has never taken as many wickets as he should have at the top level and when presented occasionally with a spinners' track, he has rarely terrorised the opposition's batsmen, as his record of only six returns of five wickets or more in his first 60 Tests suggests. His ability, however, has always been appreciated by his fellow professionals and Edmonds had no qualms about including him in his book *100 Greatest Bowlers* which covers practitioners from all eras and all nations. Emburey, he writes, 'accomplished for hours on end the hardest job in modern bowling — imposing some measure of control over the West Indian stroke-makers while in the ascendancy on their own grounds, equipped as they are with short

boundaries.'

Throughout his career Emburey has been a pragmatist. Realising his batting technique was limited he adapted his game and while he makes batting coaches weep, his mow to leg and carve through the off side make him a highly effective and always entertaining late middle-order batsman. His fielding is also of the highest class and his thinking on the game astute and decisive, which makes his decisions to go to South Africa (another pragmatic choice in a limited career of limited rewards) even more of a loss to English cricket. His first ban from Test cricket probably cost him the captaincy at Middlesex — where Mike Gatting took over from Brearley — and restricted him to no more than a caretaker role as England skipper for two Tests late in his career in the troubled summer of 1988 when four captains were used against the West Indies.

It was a mark of Emburey's durability and continued effectiveness as a one-day performer that even at the age of 40, when the second rebel ban was lifted, he was instantly recalled for the 1993 tour of India to shepherd his new left-arm spin twin from Middlesex, Phil Tufnell.

J. EMBUREY born 20.8.52 (Peckham, London). Tests 62 runs 1613 average 21.79 wickets 144 average 37.59

GODFREY EVANS
Kent 91 Tests 1946-59

IT IS said that wicketkeepers are noticed only when they make a mistake. Not true. If you failed to notice Godfrey Evans on a cricket field it was time to whistle up your guide dog. Evans was one of the game's great showmen; an extrovert and crowd-pleaser but also a great gloveman. For more than a decade he was the best 'keeper, standing up or back, in the world and he set the standards for modern stumpers to follow. Over 13 years Evans was an automatic choice for England. With hands as deft as a magician's and the enthusiasm of a schoolboy, he played a major part in England's resurgence towards the end of the 1950s. In the last hour of a long hard day in the field it was usually Evans cheerfully chiding Trueman or Statham that they were not turning it much at his end. Very little hit his pads, so much so that he often said he would have liked to have kept without pads on, but feared spectators would have thought he was showing off. His 'keeping was an integral part of the Laker-Lock spin strategy but he would also stand up to bowlers of the sharp pace of Bedser and Shackleton.

England seems to be good at producing men who can catch a ball with gloves on. Just as the soccer team has been blessed with a string of world-class goalkeepers, so the Test team has never had any worries about the quality of 'keeper available. Before the War Les Ames was an outstanding all-round performer and after it, Evans took over the mantle.

Born in Middlesex, Evans spent his childhood in Kent — in a house near Faversham, aptly named 'Lord's' — and Ames soon became his idol. Evans' dream came true when he joined Kent just before the War and started to learn from Ames. Later he was to continue this great Kent tradition by helping to school Alan Knott, the next great England 'keeper. Evans, strong and stocky, soon impressed with his agility and swiftly usurped Paul Gibb as England's post-War 'keeper.

The Showman... Evans

His batting, usually performed from No. 7 or 8, was also useful enough to score two Test centuries. He loved to give the ball a whack and at Lord's in 1952 plundered 98 runs before lunch off India's attack on his way to 104. He could also defend if the situation demanded and his performance in Adelaide in 1947 has earned him an unusual slot in the record books: he took 97 minutes to get off the mark, a first-class record. He finished unbeaten on 10 that day after a 133-minute partnership with Denis Compton that saved the Test.

While he was always willing to stand up and risk surrendering the odd bye for the chance of taking a wicket, his ability to take the ball on even the most unreliable of surfaces was like a sixth sense. He did not concede a bye in his first Ashes match in Sydney in 1946 from 1,384 balls delivered. Australia's first innings 659 in that match is still the highest Test total scored without a bye. Runs from the Evans bat became more scarce in his latter years and when he gave way in 1959 to Roy Swetman and Jim Parks, it was in no way a reflection on his 'keeping ability. He became the first 'keeper to achieve the double of 200 dismissals and 2,000 runs, and his 91 Test appearances and 219 dismissals were wicketkeeping world records until Knott topped them both 20 years later.

He retired soon after his last Test but in 1967 celebrated his 47th birthday back behind the stumps for Kent when the county asked him to stand in while Knott was making his Test debut. His jolly countenance and bushy mutton-chop whiskers remain a delight on the Test scene, which he kept in touch with as a representative for Ladbrokes, offering odds on anything that moved on a cricket field.

T.G. EVANS born 18.8.20 (Finchley, Middlesex). Tests 91 runs 2439 average 20.49 100s 2 wickets 219 average 173 stumped 46

TEST SHOOT... Godfrey Evans during the filming of 'The Final Test' at Elstree Studios with actor Jack Warner (batting) and team-mates (from left) Denis Compton, Len Hutton, Jim Laker and Alec Bedser, 1952

George Emmett

Laurie Fishlock

RICHARD ELLISON
Kent 11 Tests 1984-86

IN THE right conditions, Richard Ellison could be a lethal swing bowler, and in 1985 he returned for the last two Tests with the Ashes series all-square and inspired England to innings victories in both matches, taking 17 wickets. A qualified teacher, Ellison could never, however, be sure of his place when conditions were not suitable. His chances were curtailed when a serious back injury kept him out of the whole of the 1987 season and in 1990 he signed up for the South African rebel trip, ending his Test ambitions.

R.M. ELLISON born 21.9.59 (Ashford, Kent). Tests 11 runs 202 average 13.46 wickets 35 average 29.94

GEORGE EMMETT
Gloucestershire 1 Test 1948

GEORGE Emmett's solitary Test appearance caused something approaching national outrage. It was not so much the choice of Emmett, a highly-rated attacking opening batsman, that caused the stir as the absence of the man he replaced: Len Hutton. In a show of strength by the selectors, Hutton was dropped after two Tests for being too negative against the Australian attack. The point made, Hutton was restored and Emmett slipped back into county cricket where he played with distinction, captaining Gloucestershire for four seasons.

G.M. EMMETT born 2.12.12 (Agra, India). Died 18.12.76. Tests 1 runs 10 average 5

NEIL FAIRBROTHER
Lancashire 10 Tests 1987-

SENT out on his Test debut to face the Pakistan pace attack in dire circumstances, Neil Fairbrother was out without touching the ball. England's management was castigated for not using a nightwatchman and Fairbrother was dropped. An inventive, intelligent left-hander, Neil Harvey Fairbrother — he was named after the famous Australian batsman — reappeared on the troubled Pakistan-New Zealand tour but never reached double figures. He was condemned as being a one-day dasher but when given another chance on the difficult 1993 India tour he at last began to look the part as a Test batsman. Lancashire skipper since 1992.

N.H. FAIRBROTHER born 9.9.63 (Warrington, Lancashire). Tests 10 runs 219 average 15.64

LAURIE FISHLOCK
Surrey 4 Tests 1936-47

LAURIE Fishlock, a good county performer, was astonishingly unlucky when his Test chance did come along. A forcing left-hander, he went on two Ashes tours (1936-37 and 1946-47) and suffered hand injuries both times, restricting him to one Test overseas. He won two caps at home before the War and returned after the conflict to win back his Test place at 39, going on to collect a championship medal at 45. An England amateur soccer cap, he played professionally for Aldershot, Crystal Palace, Gillingham, Millwall and Southampton.

L.B. FISHLOCK born 2.1.07 (Battersea, London). Died 26.6.86. Tests 4 runs 47 average 11.75

Neil Fairbrother

JACK FLAVELL
Worcestershire 4 Tests 1961-64

A RED-HAIRED, fiery competitor, Jack Flavell was a wicket-to-wicket fast bowler, running in close to the stumps and bowling straight; if the batsman missed he was in trouble. In harness with Len Coldwell, who was a gear slower but swung the ball, he formed the best new-ball partnership in the country for a few years, helping Worcestershire to the championship in 1964 and '65. Jack's ventures into Test cricket were unspectacular, however, even in the one Test in which he shared the bowling with Coldwell, against Australia in 1964.

J.A. FLAVELL born 15.5.29 (Wall Heath, Staffordshire). Tests 4 runs 31 average 7.75 wickets 7 average 52.42

NEIL FOSTER
Essex 28 Tests 1983-

IT IS difficult to know whether Neil Foster has suffered more at the hands of the England selectors or his surgeon. A tall, slim fast bowler, Foster has frequently found his body in rebellion over the demands put on it. As a teenager who flirted with the idea of a professional football career with Ipswich and Colchester, he had a plate inserted in his back, and at the last count both knees had been given

running repairs at least three times.

The injuries held him back, but so too did the selectors, who took some convincing that this articulate and often outspoken Essex country boy was Test material. At a time when England were searching for support for Ian Botham and a successor for Bob Willis, Foster was one of more than a dozen fast bowlers used over three years.

Between 1983 and 1986 he played five home Tests, four of them at Lord's on an unforgiving batting wicket. On tour in India in 1984-85 he took a memorable 11-wicket haul in the sweltering heat of Madras but still had to wait until 1987 to establish

himself. The Foster-Dilley partnership had promised better things for England but breakdowns shared on almost a rota basis restricted the pair to just seven appearances together.

In 1988 further surgery interrupted Foster's career and in 1989 he opted to join Mike Gatting's rebel team in South Africa, suspecting it might be his last big pay-day. Without the burden of Test cricket, however, he continued to flourish in a successful Essex side and still harbours international ambitions.

N.A. FOSTER born 6.5.62 (Colchester, Essex). Tests 28 runs 410 average 11.38 wickets 88 average 31.78

Neil Foster

KEITH FLETCHER

Essex 59 Tests 1968-82

THE sacking of Keith Fletcher as England captain remains one of English cricket's shabbiest sagas. It taught the man currently in charge of the England team as manager all he needed to know about showing loyalty to his players. As a skipper, Fletcher did not have the flamboyance of Tony Greig or the cerebral eloquence of Mike Brearley. He was what the players call a cricketer's cricketer. When he was belatedly made England skipper for the 1981-82 tour of India, the dressing room reaction around the country was: 'about time too.'

Fletcher was a tough cookie, a shrewd man who could bluff opponents like the most disarming of poker players. He evoked loyalty in his team-mates and admiration from opponents, even when they were beaten by the sucker punch. For some in authority, however, he did not look or sound right. Fletcher appeared a diffident character. Shuffling out to bat, he gave the impression he would be just as happy traipsing the Essex countryside following his other loves, shooting and fishing. He was a bit of a country boy and sounded it, but he was not to be underrated. At 17 he was playing for Essex and soon quietly offering advice to the county's ebullient leader, 'Tonker' Taylor. In a team of extroverts, 'Fletch' soon became 'The Gnome', so christened by Ray East because his well-worn winklepickers began to curl up at the toes, pixie-style. Anyway 'Gnome' suited him perfectly.

Fletcher was obviously captaincy material and he turned a county of cheerful losers into an even happier bunch as the most successful side in the country through the 1980s. He groomed Graham Gooch for the England captaincy and was pulling the strings at Chelmsford until England made him manager in 1992. He had always been an exciting middle-order batsman, full of resourcefulness and with quick feet that made him an excellent player of spin.

His England debut arrived in 1968 at Leeds against the Australians but it turned into a sombre experience for the young Fletcher. The Headingley crowd thought their own Phil Sharpe should have been given another chance in the Test, and Fletcher's selection reawakened mutterings of southern bias. On top of everything, Sharpe was a brilliant slip fielder and when Fletcher, himself usually very safe, spilled a few chances, the crowd turned against him. A duck in his first innings did not help and the experience appeared to make Fletcher of England a far more introverted batsman than Fletcher of Essex. He did not score his first England century until his 20th Test but went on to add six more at a rate of one every four appearances. His resilience made him a popular choice with captains if not always the public. Tony Lewis, who fielded away from the bat, was grateful for Fletcher's know-how, posting him at first slip so he could pass on advice; Greig often relied upon Fletcher's acumen to back up his battle cries, and the pair became close friends. Fletcher, never pushy or conceited, did not pose a threat to his captains and when the job passed on to Brearley in 1977, Fletcher's England days looked numbered.

After Brearley's retirement and the chastening experience of trying Ian Botham in the captaincy, however, Fletcher was recalled after a four-year gap to take the side to India. It should have been a golden autumn for Fletcher's career but the contest became depressingly negative as he and Gavaskar locked tactical horns. Complaints from England about the umpiring in the first Test, which was lost, caused offence, and in the second Fletcher's disgust at being given out resulted in him flicking the bails off with his bat as he left the crease. He apologised but the die was cast.

There was increasing trouble with Geoff Boycott — eventually sent home early — and at the end of the

tour half the team, under Fletcher's Essex colleague Gooch, disappeared to South Africa for a rebel tour. Fletcher knew nothing about it in India — for which he was also blamed — and a few weeks later turned down the chance to join the rebels himself because of loyalty to England. His reward was the sack from the new chairman of selectors Peter May, whose appointment of Bob Willis brought modest results. Fletcher was hurt by his treatment, an experience he should not forget as England manager.

K.W.R. FLETCHER born 20.5.44 (Worcester). Tests 59 runs 3272 average 39.90 100s 7 wickets 2 average 96.50

Keith Fletcher... an underrated batsman

ANGUS FRASER
Middlesex 11 Tests 1989-

JUST how Angus Fraser suffered a distressing injury which has blighted a highly promising Test career will probably remain a mystery. When he went to Australia in 1990-91, the young Middlesex fast-medium bowler with an old head on his shoulders looked the answer to a Lord's prayer. While others strove for pace and control, 'Big Gus' was always there, a reliable, intelligent and hard-working bowler.

At 6ft 5in and a trundling 15½ stone, he reminded observers of a young Alec Bedser with all his good, old-fashioned English virtues. He could bang the ball into any pitch and make quality batsmen grope and flinch. He had done well in the West Indies on his maiden tour early in 1990 and also that summer after shaking off a rib injury. In Australia he was to be the heart of the attack and when England found themselves one down after the first Test, it was Fraser to whom they turned.

There was a glimmer of hope in the second Test and Fraser was in metronome mood. He bowled his heart out for Gooch at Melbourne for a career best 6 for 82 — but at what cost? After banging down 39 overs on an unforgiving wicket, he complained of a painful hip, tried to compete in the fourth Test and has been absent from the England scene since. He played in only two county matches the following summer and while he was a regular performer for Middlesex in 1992, he was in pain and distressingly ineffective.

Various diagnoses and treatments, including operations, had not cured his hip and he went back for more surgery after the season. Was he over-bowled in Melbourne that day, was he given the right treatment or was the weakness always there? Fraser still strives to find the answers.

A.R.C. FRASER born 8.8.68 (Billinge, Lancashire). Tests 11 runs 88 average 6.76 wickets 47 average 26.70

GRAEME FOWLER
Lancashire and Durham
21 Tests 1982-85

GRAEME Fowler never had any pretensions about his Test career. His chance came when England lost 16 players, including their two established openers Graham Gooch and Geoff Boycott, to the first rebel tour of South Africa. It went when the rebels' three-year ban was over and they were welcomed back into the Test team. Fowler filled a void for those three years and made the most of it. Whether England were grateful, they never said. They should have been.

A risk-taking left-hander, Fowler rarely bored anyone with his batting. He played cricket with a smile and was not reticent about enjoying himself afterwards. He was 12 when he first picked up a cricket bat and at 15 he became the youngest opener in the Lancashire League. He did not have time to worry about the coaching manuals, his eye and nimble feet saw him through.

In July 1982 'Foxy' pulled off the unique feat of scoring two centuries in a championship match, both with the aid of a runner, and it was enough to make the selectors take notice. A month later he was in the Test side but he could never curb his style. His scores fluctuated wildly: 105 and 1 against New Zealand, 106 and 11 against the West Indies, 201 and 2 against India.

A double-hundred in the sapping heat of Madras was Fowler's greatest moment, yet after just one more Test he found himself discarded to make way for the returning Gooch. His fall from grace was dramatic, the summer of 1985 going nightmarishly wrong for him when he slipped during fielding practice before a county match, tearing his neck muscles and suffering partial paralysis for several weeks. Fowler's 20-year association with Lancashire was ended by the 1992 clear-out at Old Trafford.

G. FOWLER born 20.4.57 (Accrington, Lancashire). Tests 21 runs 1307 average 35.32 100s 3

Angus Fraser

BRUCE FRENCH
Nottinghamshire 16 Tests 1986-88

A **WICKETKEEPER** of the highest calibre, Bruce French spent two tours as uncomplaining understudy to Paul Downton, the better batsman, before his Test debut in 1986. He made the job his own until a finger injury kept him out and Jack Russell took his chance. For a mountaineer, French is alarmingly prone to accidents on tour, such as being bitten by a dog, hit by a ball thrown by a spectator at practice and then knocked over by a car when he arrived at hospital for treatment. Joined the 1990 rebel tour to South Africa.

B.N. FRENCH born 13.8.59 (Warsop, Nottinghamshire). Tests 16 runs 308 average 18.11 dismissals 39 caught 38 stumped 1

PAUL GIBB
Yorkshire and Essex 8 Tests 1938-46

A **SLIGHT**, bespectacled man, Paul Gibb was a solitary teetotaller yet his value was always appreciated by his team-mates. He was a resolute run-maker and broke through as a specialist batsman in South Africa in 1938-39, scoring 93 and 106 on his debut. After the War he played three more Tests as wicketkeeper-batsman, although his glovework was no more than competent. He left the game after the 1946-47 Ashes tour but reappeared for Essex four years later as a professional, causing the MCC to suspend his membership. After five years at Chelmsford he spent 10 years as an umpire, travelling the circuit by caravan, before becoming a bus driver.

P.A. GIBB born 11.7.13 (Brandsby, Yorkshire). Died 7.12.77. Tests 8 runs 581 average 44.69 100s 2 dismissals 4 caught 3 stumped 1

Bruce French

Paul Gibb

moved on to Edgbaston aged 43 and took 100 wickets in his first season. After three decades as a player, 14 as captain, 'Giff' continued to be a major influence as manager on England senior and A tours and is currently pumping his enthusiasm into his job as coach at Sussex.

N. GIFFORD born 30.3.40 (Ulverston, Lancashire). Tests 15 runs 179 average 16.27 wickets 33 average 31.09

CLIFF GLADWIN
Derbyshire 8 Tests 1947-49

CLIFF Gladwin was so proud of his miserly bowling that he would correct the scorers at the close of play if there was an error in their figures. Powerfully built, he could bowl his inswingers all day, and for a decade after the War, he formed with Les Jackson the most feared opening attack on the county scene. Taking 100 wickets a season was routine for Gladwin but at Test level he found success scarce, his most famous achievement being his scampered leg-bye in Durban in 1948 to achieve the only last-ball victory in Test history.

C. GLADWIN born 3.4.16 (Doe Lea, Derbyshire). Died 10.4.88. Tests 8 runs 170 average 28.33 wickets 15 average 38.06

NORMAN GIFFORD
Worcestershire and Warwickshire
15 Tests 1964-73

A SPINNER who pushed Derek Underwood out of the England side has to be something special, and Norman Gifford was just that. A great competitor with a deep knowledge of the game, 'Giff' could find turn from most surfaces despite firing in his left-arm deliveries. He played two Tests prematurely in 1964 but after a seven-year gap made himself a regular on the England scene for two years. He would have played many more Tests but for Underwood's unique ability although when a bigger spinner of the ball was needed, he was the slow bowler captains turned to. His doughty batting often produced valuable runs in a crisis and as a close fielder he missed little. He led Worcestershire to the Championship in 1974 and then after 23 seasons at New Road

Cliff Gladwin

Alf Gover, master coach

ALF GOVER
Surrey 4 Tests 1936-46

IT **IS** impossible to quantify Alf Gover's impact on cricket. As a tall fast bowler with adroit control he took 1,555 first-class wickets, including 200 in a season twice, and played three Tests before the War and one after. But it was as a coach that Alf inspired so many. At his homely South London indoor school he was patiently passing on his expertise to the great — Viv Richards was one pupil — and not so great, the young and not so young alike into his eighties. Good cricket was a crusade for one of the game's kindest men.

A.R. GOVER born 29.2.08 (Epsom, Surrey). Tests 4 runs 2 average — wickets 8 average 44.87

TOMMY GREENHOUGH
Lancashire 4 Tests 1959-60

IT **WAS** amazing that Tommy Greenhough played Test cricket at all. As a young player with Lancashire, he took a job in a cotton mill during the winter and fell from a gantry. Both ankles were badly broken and his feet ended up different sizes. He overcame his handicap to become one of the most inventive leg-break bowlers in the country, performing well when called up in 1959. He could, however, lose confidence, as happened on the 1960 tour of the West Indies where he did not play a Test.

T. GREENHOUGH born 9.11.31 (Rochdale, Lancashire). Tests 4 runs 4 average 1.33 wickets 16 average 22.31

STEWART 'BILLY' GRIFFITH
Surrey and Sussex 3 Tests 1948-49

ONE of cricket's leading administrators since the War with the TCCB, MCC and Sussex, Billy Griffith had a remarkable playing career. After wartime service as an Airborne Division glider pilot, during which he rose to Lieutenant Colonel and won the DFC, he went on the 1948 Caribbean tour as reserve wicketkeeper. However, he played as an emergency opener and scored 140, making him the only England player to have made his maiden century on his Test debut. The following winter in South Africa he returned to his more orthodox role and ousted Godfrey Evans for two Tests but never played a home international. His son Mike also captained Sussex.

S.C. GRIFFITH born 16.6.14 (Wandsworth, London). Died 7.4.93 Tests 3 runs 157 average 31.40 100s 1 dismissals 5 caught 5

Tommy Greenhough

MIKE GATTING

Middlesex 72 Tests 1977-

IT **IS** said Mike Gatting never sat on the fence in his life... if he had done, he would have broken it. Whichever way you take the joke, it is true. People have views on Gatting: he is liked or disliked, admired or abused but never ignored. For someone who just set out to enjoy his sport, Gatting has found himself wandering a pothole-ridden path that has led him into some glorious battles and murky skirmishes.

At times his career seemed to be buried under an avalanche of controversy but he has always emerged the same approachable, straightforward, likeable 'Gatt'. Most high-profile sportsmen change their telephone number every year but

Gatting's has remained the same throughout a career including the unhappy time when he decided to lead a rebel team of England players to South Africa and was the target of hate mail and even death threats.

Talk of Gatting the batsman always evokes adjectives such as pugnacious, bold, brave and belligerent. He was an outstanding young footballer but as a 14-year-old goalkeeper on trial at Queen's Park Rangers he was told he was too short and fat, so Gatting decided to concentrate on cricket while QPR were left to sign the other teenage trialist that day, Phil Parkes. Gatting is, in fact, 5ft 10in tall but his stocky frame makes him look much shorter.

He marches to the wicket with the bulldog determination of one of his mentors, Ken Barrington; he refuses to be intimidated by the most hostile fast bowling and generally takes the attitude that spinners should not be on the same field as him.

From the moment he started clubbing runs for Middlesex in 1975 as an 18-year-old he was destined for Test cricket and he arrived on the international scene only two years later. He took an inexplicably long time — 54 innings — to score his first Test century, but when it did arrive in India in 1985 it opened the floodgates and was followed a few weeks later by a double-century. Gatting by this stage was England

The Defiant Bulldog... Gatting in action

vice-captain, an honour given him by David Gower, the man he was soon to succeed with dramatic and shocking consequences.

Between heroic deeds, Gatting was prone to some very public pitfalls which eventually led to him being dubbed by the press 'Captain Cock-up', an insult he laughed off like other jibes — but it hurt, nonetheless. He had a penchant for getting himself out playing no shot or attempting the reverse sweep — the most agonising example of which cost England the World Cup Final against Australia in Calcutta in 1987.

Earlier that year at Edgbaston his team had been watching the television in the dressing room during a break for bad light oblivious of the umpires back out in the middle waiting to restart the game, while more seriously he found himself losing a match-winning opportunity in Faisalabad when he was sucked into an infamous slanging contest with umpire Shakoor Rana which cost a day's play. Many observers thought Gatting should have been stripped of the leadership — something he had never sought — then and there, but he survived until the next summer, and a chance meeting with a barmaid in Leicestershire during the series against the West Indians. Allegations of a nocturnal net practice were met with denials which were, publicly at least, accepted by Lord's, but Gatting was sacked all the same, a decision which reeked of revenge for the Shakoor Rana affair. Still, though, he was considered by many — including his leading advocate, England manager Micky Stewart — to be the best man to captain his country and the following year was the choice of both Stewart and the new chairman of selectors, Ted Dexter, to lead England against the Australians. Their decision was, however, vetoed by higher powers and Gower was reinstated with miserable consequences.

Gatting, having been fined £5,000 for his account of the Shakoor Rana row in a book, was by now totally disillusioned with cricket's hierarchy and in the middle of 1989 agreed to lead a team to South Africa, for which he collected a reported £200,000 and

a statutory five-year ban from Test cricket. That ban was lifted in 1992 and Gatting was immediately selected for the winter tour to India. Thus he was afforded a belated chance to fulfil his promise of being one of England's great post-War batsmen, instead of just a good one.

M. GATTING born 6.6.57 (Kingsbury, Middlesex). Tests 72 runs 4136 average 37.26 100s 9 wickets 4 average 79.25

The Defiant Bulldog... Mike Gatting sweats it out in Faisalabad 1987 with Graham Dilley and Chris Broad (right) seated

GRAHAM GOOCH
Essex 101 Tests 1975-

WHEN Graham Gooch was made England captain in 1988 it was a stop-gap move — and he has stopped in the gap ever since, with the occasional intermission caused by injury or selectorial lameness. By very good luck, England stumbled across a reticent leader who transformed his own career and England's fortunes at the same time. When Gooch took over, England had been through three captains in four Tests against the West Indies — Gatting, Emburey and Chris Cowdrey — and had suffered a sequence of 17 Tests without a victory. What the pragmatic, dedicated Gooch did was to transform England into a world force again, leading by example on and off the field, demanding everyone show the same commitment and pride as he and bringing continuity to selection.

He goes into the autumn of his career very firmly established in the top drawer of English post-War players yet the ride along the way has, like that famous stubbled chin, been anything but smooth. A powerful, straight middle-order hitter and useful support swing bowler, he was in the England side at 21 and started against the Australians with a pair. He had to wait another five years through a total of 36 innings before he recorded his first Test century, which may explain the patience Gooch the captain has often shown to young batsmen.

His career had taken off as an opener when, in 1982, he signed up for the first rebel tour to South Africa and found himself pushed into the captaincy. Their team was forever to be known as 'Gooch's Rebels'. Whether Gooch refused to understand or simply did not understand the condemnation of the rest of the world of the rebels' mercenary undertaking is difficult to say, but a three-year ban from international cricket was resented by many of the squad.

Gooch returned to England's side in 1985 but still opposition to his presence lingered, culminating in his request to come home from the 1986 tour of the Caribbean because of anti-apartheid protests. Captain David Gower pleaded with him to stay and Lord's flew out Alan (A.C.) Smith to talk him round, and finally, grudgingly, Gooch completed the tour. Touring was to become something of a chore, his demeanour to the outside world became increasingly bleak and he fretted about minor alterations in his technique. All of this belied a quiet, often self-mocking humour which occasionally surfaced when he would run through his hilarious routine of bowling impersonations from Bob Willis to Dilip Doshi.

While his England career surged on, he gave up the captaincy at Essex temporarily because his batting slumped, and the possibility of leading England appeared to have passed him by. Yet in 1988 the chance arose when Cowdrey, having been given the captaincy for two Tests, was summarily levered out after one because of injury doubts, and Gooch, who had a strong supporter in manager Micky Stewart, was installed. Gooch had already decided he did not want to play for England in India that winter and had agreed to return to South Africa to play for Western Province, but the carrot of the captaincy made him change his mind. He was named as skipper for the tour, which was then promptly cancelled when the Indian government refused visas for him and seven other blacklisted players because of their South African connections. The next spring, Gooch was overlooked, Gatting was vetoed and Gower was reinstated for what turned out to be a disastrous Ashes series. By the end of the year Gooch, despite having had his inspirational qualities once likened by the new England chairman of selectors Ted Dexter to being slapped in the face with a wet fish, was back in charge.

He led England to the West Indies, almost pulling off a sensational result, and very quickly he became the most powerful England leader since Brearley. Gooch grew in stature and his batting, which had always left suspicions of under-achievement, flourished astonishingly. Before the captaincy he had scored eight centuries in 63 Tests, as captain between 1990 and 1992 he scored nine in 36 Tests including 333 against India at Lord's, the second highest Test score by an Englishman behind Sir Len Hutton's 364. He won every county honour as Essex captain and, but for his own fumbled catch in the final against Pakistan, would have almost certainly crowned his international career by becoming the first England skipper to lift the World Cup in Melbourne in March 1992.

G.A. GOOCH born 23.7.53 (Leytonstone, East London). Tests 101 runs 7620 average 42.56 100s 17 wickets 22 average 40.63

REBELLIOUS DAYS... Gooch in 'Test' action against South Africa in 1982. The wicketkeeper is Ray Jennings

DAVID GOWER
Leicestershire and Hampshire 117 Tests 1978-

DAVID Gower became not so much a great cricketer as a national treasure. If he was abused or misused by those in authority a wave of public indignation would sweep the land. Those feelings of protectiveness and admiration were never greater than in the autumn of 1992 when, a few weeks after becoming his country's greatest run-maker and most capped player, Gower was jettisoned again for another tour for reasons other than ability.

That ability and his appeal was obvious even to his detractors. His talent for hitting a cricket ball was a gift from the gods and to that he added a grace and charm that went with his blond curls and blue-eyed good looks. He was a cricket cavalier in the age of the roundhead. Articulate and easy-natured, he rarely pounded the ground with his fists or the ears of his opponents with

obscenities, which led to a misconception that he was too laid back to care. Nothing infuriated Gower more than that accusation because underneath the genteel exterior lurked a steely calculating determination. It must be remembered that Gower never flinched in the face of the fearsome West Indian attack that dominated world cricket in the 1980s, nor did he take the easy well-paid option of joining rebel tours to South Africa.

He came from a well-heeled family of diplomats and servicemen, was educated at all the right schools and thought about a career in law before realising cricket was the easier and more natural option. At 21 he pulled his first ball in Test cricket nonchalantly for four and never looked back — except, possibly, to ensure the Champagne was on ice.

His strokes were full of grace and lazy timing, he put a patent on the leg-side swivel off his hips and refused to let caution cloud his tactics, sometimes to the hair-tearing frustration of his colleagues when he chased the ball into the slip cordon. He didn't score as many Test centuries as he should simply because he refused to play safe in the eighties and nineties.

Gower's style on the field matched his love of life off it. Showbiz friends and Champagne were never far away, he revelled in the Cresta Run, once consigned a car to the bottom of a Swiss lake attempting a midnight spin on the ice, chased big game through Africa and India with his camera, and tried to relieve the tension of a fraught 1990-91 Ashes tour with a Tiger Moth swoop over the ground during an up-country

game, a prank which brought the wrath of the Establishment down on his head again.

That same Establishment had twice made the mistake of assuming that a great player must make a great captain. Gower brought his own style to the captaincy by picking individuals, giving them latitude and expecting them to do the rest, and for two renaissance series against India and Australia it worked like a charm. But the five victories in that period were Gower's only triumphs in 26 matches in charge, which included two 5-0 'black-washes' by the West Indies.

When things went wrong they slipped alarmingly and probably Gower's darkest hour was the summer of 1989 when he was recalled to lead England against Australia. England were now into the era of the full-time manager and Gower could never see eye-to-eye with the work ethic of the man in charge, Micky Stewart. The results were disastrous: England losing abysmally, 4-0, and Gower looking close to breaking point. He stormed out of one press conference at Lord's, announcing he was off to the theatre, banged his head on the table in frustration during another at Edgbaston, and at Old Trafford was forced to issue an apology for an obscene gesture to the supporters. That was the start of an unrelenting battle to convince Stewart and the next captain, Gooch, that he was more than a dilettante, a battle he finally won to regain his place and top Geoff Boycott's run-scoring record.

One of Gower's most eminent ancestors was Admiral Sir Erasmus Gower, Governor and Commander-in-Chief of Newfoundland in the early 19th century. His motto was: 'You can break but not bend us.' At times, David Gower's grip on a Test place was broken, but none could bend his devotion to fun, style and excellence.

D.I. GOWER born 1.4.57 (Tunbridge Wells, Kent). Tests 117 runs 8231 average 44.25 100s 18 wickets 1 average 20.0

THE POWER... Gower in full flow

AND THE GLORY... Ashes and splashes in 1985 at the Oval

TOM GRAVENEY
Gloucestershire and Worcestershire 79 Tests 1951-69

IN HIS retirement Tom Graveney chuckles over the miscarriages of justice and misconceptions of attitude that blighted his Test career. 'For an inoffensive sort of chap,' says Graveney, 'I did have my fair share of controversy.' Everyone's cheery favourite-uncle, he now regards his sporting setbacks simply as another few jigsaw pieces that made up the picture of a rich and varied career.

Certainly any England side including Graveney during his 18 years on the international scene was the better for his rich and varied batting skills. His strokes oozed class, the pick of which was a cover drive brought up in a charm school, but while he played 79 Tests, few of his peers have any doubts that he should be one of that select band to have represented their country 100 times. Like another player blessed with effortless talent 30 years later, David Gower, Graveney in his day had trouble convincing those in authority he really meant business. Indeed, two of his England captains, Len Hutton and Peter May, lacked complete faith in a player to whom cricket had not been a compulsion. Graveney came out of the Army an officer and had the talent to follow a career as a professional golfer and the openings to train as an accountant. Instead he chose cricket at Gloucestershire, where elder brother Ken was already on the staff. His talent soon carried him into the Test team and his second innings for England brought him 175 runs in Bombay.

Results in those early years, however, were not spectacular, partly, believes Graveney, because he was overawed by the likes of Hutton and Compton. In later years when his talent was in full bloom, England's selectors often turned up their noses. Graveney says: 'I had two breaks of three years away from the Test scene and during one of them, around 1964-65 when Worcestershire were winning the championship, I reckon I was the best batsman in England.' His first break from international cricket coincided with a dispute at

Gloucester which led him to quit and move to New Road, missing the whole of the 1961 championship season. He batted his way back into the England side in 1962 but a year later was isolated for another three years until 1966 when he returned to enjoy some of his most sumptuous batting in the international arena until his career ended in more controversy in 1969.

That summer coincided with his benefit at Worcester and he had been offered a £1,000 contribution if he

turned out in an exhibition match in Luton on the Sunday of the first Test — a rest day — against the West Indies. As £1,000 was likely to amount to almost a fifth of what Graveney could expect to pick up during his whole benefit year, he was not inclined to turn it down. Before the England team was selected Graveney told chairman of selectors Alec Bedser about the benefit match and added that if they were not happy with him playing, they should not select him.

Tom Graveney... the cap fits perfectly

When, much to Graveney's surprise, he was named for the Test at Old Trafford, he took that to mean his Sunday excursion had been approved and, after scoring 75 in England's first innings, he played his benefit game. The next day, however, on his 42nd birthday, he found himself reported to the disciplinary committee and suspended for the next three Tests which, in effect, finished an England career that had illuminated two decades. Throughout it all, Graveney remained philosophical and his relaxed, friendly nature made him a popular television and radio commentator on the game in later years.

T.W. GRAVENEY born 16.6.27 (Riding Mill, Northumberland). Tests 79 runs 4882 average 44.38 100s 11 wickets 1 average 167.0

TONY GREIG
Sussex 58 Tests 1972-77

TONY Greig was larger than life — and standing at 6ft 7in, that took some doing. Cricket was never the same post-Greig. Vilified by some, admired by others, he will always be linked with Kerry Packer, the bull-necked Australian entrepreneur who bought up the world's best for his own television station and forced the game's Establishment to come to terms with commercialism and bring the pay of international cricketers into the 20th century.

Greig, the tallest player to represent England, was the country's leading all-rounder through the mid-1970s, playing in an uninterrupted run of 58 Tests. He became captain, enjoyed reasonable success and then recruited from within for the Packer circus, an act which Lord's saw as treachery — particularly coming from a South African who had been allowed to play for his adopted country. He was not, as is the tradition with England captains, made an honorary member of the MCC and his name still causes mutterings in some committee rooms — if few dressing rooms.

His father was a Scottish RAF bomber pilot, his mother hailed from South Africa, where he was born and learned a brash, combative style of cricket which was still alien to the English game. Blond and demonstrative, you could not miss Greig even in a crowd, and when he launched his Sussex career with 156 in his first championship match, the selectors quickly checked out his qualification credentials. He was an aggressive stroke-player by trade but was willing to show enormous courage for the cause, whether it be defying the hostility of Lillee and Thomson or coping with a debilitating stomach bug during his match-winning 103 at Calcutta in 1977, probably the greatest innings of his life.

He was also a bounding, unpredictable pace bowler who could deliver off-breaks if the situation

ADVERSARIES... Tony Greig punishing his favourite opponents, Australia, in 1977. Rick McCosker (slip) and Rod Marsh are powerless

demanded, and was a fine slip fielder. He was flashy in the middle and boisterous in the dressing room, totally intolerant of team-mates he thought were not giving everything. He became the first England player to score 3,000 runs and take 100 wickets but, through it all, many on the sidelines remained suspicious of this ruthless cricketer who was smart enough to use the media, which lapped up his gregarious approach. His infamous remark about making the West Indies 'grovel' on their tour of 1976 when he was skipper was taken out of context but did not sound good however it was dressed up, being delivered in a Springbok accent at a time when anti-apartheid feelings were at their most sensitive. It was not too clever either, as England vice-captain in 1974, to run out Alvin Kallicharran in Jamaica as the West Indian batsman headed back to the pavilion at the close of play. The appeal was later withdrawn and the batsman reinstated but Greig was widely criticised and lost the vice-captaincy for the next tour.

However, in 1975 he was finally installed as captain, replacing Denness, to lift flagging English spirit and the remaining three Tests that summer were drawn. The next summer brought a 3-0 defeat against the 'non-grovelling' West Indies but he led England to a magnificent 3-1 success in India and then into the Centenary Test in Melbourne. The next summer, 1977, Australia were the visitors and Greig was the obvious choice to lead the battle for the Ashes. Early in the tour he threw a typically extravagant party in a marquee on the lawns of his Brighton home for the Sussex and Australian players, and word leaked out about Packer's plans for later that year. Greig, it was revealed, was heavily involved with the planning as well as recruitment.

The Test and County Cricket Board was in turmoil and Greig was pilloried. He lost the captaincy but his successor Mike Brearley insisted the Packer men stay in the side that series. Mid-way through the next summer, Greig quit the Sussex captaincy and left the English game, aged 31. He emigrated to Australia

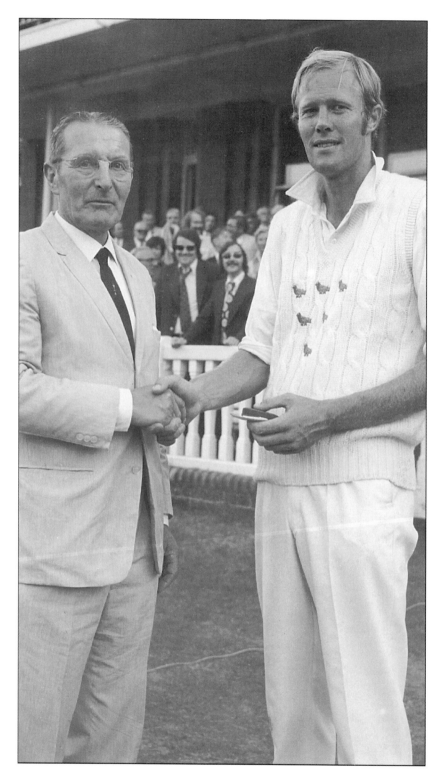

England men young and old... Charlie Barnett makes a presentation to Tony Greig

where he worked for Packer and became the anchorman of Channel Nine's cricket coverage. He also revealed after his playing days that he suffered from epilepsy.

A.W. GREIG born 6.10.46 (Queenstown, South Africa). Tests 58 runs 3599 average 40.43 100s 8 wickets 141 average 32.20

IAN GREIG
Sussex and Surrey 2 Tests 1982

IAN Greig was in every sense a scaled-down version of his more famous brother Tony: not as big, not as demonstrative, not as good. He was, nonetheless, a determined county all-rounder, and the selectors decided to see what he could do against Pakistan in 1982 when Derek Pringle was injured. He did not progress beyond the standard two-Test trial. When Sussex released him as a cost-cutting exercise in 1985, Greig emigrated to Australia, but Surrey astutely brought him back as skipper between 1987 and '91.

I.A. GREIG born 8.12.55 (Queenstown, South Africa). Tests 2 runs 26 average 6.50 wickets 4 average 28.50

John Hampshire (right) celebrates with Ray Illingworth

JOHN HAMPSHIRE
Yorkshire and Derbyshire
8 Tests 1969-75

JOHN Hampshire thrilled English cricket supporters when he scored a century at Lord's on his Test debut — a unique achievement for an England player. An attractive middle-order stroke-player, Hampshire looked one for the future but he was dropped after one more match. It was an erratic decision but only mirrored Hampshire's own enigmatic form. Despite possessing great natural talent, he failed to apply it consistently. He was given a four-Test run on the 1970-71 Australasia tour but, frustratingly, again failed to convince. John captained Yorkshire briefly, moving to Derbyshire and then becoming an umpire, joining the Test list in 1989.

J.H. HAMPSHIRE born 10.2.41 (Thurnscoe, Yorkshire). Tests 8 runs 403 average 26.86 100s 1

Ian Greig

84

Joe Hardstaff

JOE HARDSTAFF
Nottinghamshire 23 Tests 1935-48

JOE Hardstaff was one of the most artistic batsmen ever to set foot on a cricket field but he paid the high price of falling out with Gubby Allen. The son of Joe Hardstaff, who played four Tests before the first War, Joe junior followed his father into the Nottinghamshire team and established himself in England's middle order with 16 Tests before the second War.

Tall and handsome, an impeccable stroke-maker, he was denied the chance to play cricket when his powers were at their peak because of the conflict, but when play resumed in 1946, he marked the return of Test cricket to England with an unbeaten 205 at Lord's against India. He was dropped two innings later and that winter played in a solitary Test in Australia.

The following winter he toured again under Allen in the West Indies but the autocratic Allen and the volatile Hardstaff never saw eye-to-eye. On their return from the Caribbean, Gubby assured the Nottinghamshire man he would never play another Test. Hardstaff asked him to name his odds, Allen gave him 100-1 and Joe junior backed himself with a fiver. Hardstaff played the first Test that summer against Australia and received a cheque for £500 from Allen, which he tore up and posted back.

Hardstaff, at 36 and with a Test average of 46, was never to play for England again. The Press campaign for his return was ignored, even during the summer of 1949 when he headed the national averages with 2,251 runs at 72. He almost found himself banned from county cricket in 1950 when Allen raised questions in the MCC committee suggesting that his winter appearances for Auckland in New Zealand infringed his Nottinghamshire registration.

Hardstaff's son — now Middlesex secretary — became confusingly the third Joe Hardstaff to play first-class cricket when he turned out for Free Foresters.

J. HARDSTAFF born 3.7.11 (Nuncargate, Nottinghamshire). Died 1.1.90. Tests 23 runs 1636 average 46.74 100s 4

FRANK HAYES
Lancashire 9 Tests 1973-76

FRANK Hayes was heralded as the 'new Compton' when his free-flowing stroke-play brought him a century on his Test debut — the 13th and most recent time the feat has been achieved by an Englishman. The euphoria did not last. Nerves and an impulsive hook made Hayes vulnerable, and it did not help that he was asked to play all his Test cricket against the West Indian pace attack. After his century, he failed to reach 30 in his remaining 15 innings, suffering six ducks along the way. A science graduate, he now teaches.

F.C. HAYES born 6.12.46 (Preston, Lancashire). Tests 9 runs 244 average 15.25 100s 1

Frank Hayes

WALLY HAMMOND
Gloucestershire 85 Tests 1927-47

THE cricket folk of Gloucester, Bristol and Cheltenham are proud of their contribution to the English game. The West Country county hardly has a monopoly on producing Test players but when it does, they tend to be in the Mayfair class rather than the Old Kent Road. They will tell you that they provided the greatest cricketer of the last century — Dr. W.G. Grace — and the greatest player of this century — Wally Hammond. There is no doubt that Hammond was one of the very finest to have played in any age. His Test average (58.45) is bettered by only two Englishmen, Sutcliffe and Barrington, but unlike those two, he was also a front-line pace bowler, and as a fielder, standing erect in the slips, he had the hands of an apple-picker.

Hammond played only eight of his 85 Tests after the War but his imprint on cricket is indelible, taking up the England captaincy where he had left off in 1939. His final Test innings before the hostilities was a masterful 138 against the West Indies. Without the six-year hiatus and another summer he had lost early in his career fighting an illness that threatened his life, his final aggregate score could have been staggering. As it was his 7,249 runs remained a world record until Colin Cowdrey passed it in 1970 and his total of 22 Test centuries has never been bettered by an English player, despite the amount of international cricket now played.

Yet, alongside the glorious achievements, Hammond's story is coloured by sadness. Born in Kent, his father's postings as a soldier meant he spent much of his childhood in China and then Malta, where he played his cricket against a gun shed. His family finally settled in Gloucestershire but soon he lost his father, killed in the Great War. He was keen to play for Gloucestershire but Lord Harris at Canterbury, in mean mood, had him banned for two years while he qualified, a break

which gave Hammond the chance to enjoy his soccer with Bristol Rovers.

Superbly athletic, Hammond was tall and powerfully built, a vivid stroke-maker mainly off the back foot with a penchant for very big scores — he hit 36 double-centuries and four triple-centuries. His bowling was controlled and menacing and his fielding magnetic — his 78 catches in 1928, including 10 in one match, is a record for out-fielders. Quite simply, he had no equal in the world as a cricketer until Don Bradman emerged to claim the batting crown at least. Off the field he was a composed, withdrawn figure, yet on it his being appeared to find true expression. He hated boring cricket and once, when Lancashire's batsmen put up the shutters, he bowled an over of grubbers — underarm all along the ground — in protest. He was an important member of the 'Bodyline' tour of 1932-33 and was impressed and influenced by Douglas Jardine's no-mercy approach.

Hammond's game started to become more circumspect with maturity and nothing demonstrates that better than a run of Test scores on that Australasia tour of 101, 75 not out, 227 and 336 not out, the highest score in Test cricket at the time. His 240 in adversity against Australia at Lord's in 1938 was his most famous moment and after the War the great man's life had a sad final chapter. He captained in Australia in 1946-47 under the strain of problems in his personal life and, it is said, spent much of the tour alone, frequently travelling separately. It was an unsuccessful tour and his England career ended.

He also suffered from lumbago and when he finished playing for Gloucestershire in 1951, he settled in South Africa, where he invested — and lost — his savings in the motor trade. One of cricket's legends ended up thankful to be offered a job as groundsman-coach at Natal University. He died, aged 62, in Durban in 1962 from an illness

caused in part by severe injuries he had suffered in a road accident a few years earlier.

W.R. HAMMOND born 19.6.03 (Dover, Kent). Died 1.7.65. Tests 85 runs 7249 average 58.45 100s 22 wickets 83 average 37.80

The epitome of style... Wally Hammond

86

EDDIE HEMMINGS
Warwickshire, Nottinghamshire and Sussex 16 Tests 1982-91

ORIGINALLY a seam bowler, Eddie Hemmings saw his career transformed by a change of county. His dependable off-spin bowling developed so well at Trent Bridge that at 33 he became a Test newcomer. He was on the England scene for the next decade, touring regularly but never cementing his place. For the Tests, bigger spinners of the ball were often preferred but 'Steady Eddie', also a doughty batsman, remained a combative performer, particularly in the one-day side.

E.E. HEMMINGS born 20.2.49 (Leamington Spa, Warwickshire). Tests 16 runs 383 average 22.52 wickets 43 average 42.44

MIKE HENDRICK
Derbyshire and Nottinghamshire 30 Tests 1974-81

IN 30 Test appearances, Mike Hendrick never claimed a five-wicket return, the traditional benchmark of a good bowling performance. Team-mates and coaches — including England manager Ken Barrington — told him that bowling too short was holding him back, but Hendrick never achieved security. Over seven years he was more out of the side than in it, being recalled no fewer than 13 times.

At 6ft 3in, Hendrick was a lively fast-medium seam bowler who could produce plenty of bounce to trouble county batsmen. His 770 first-class wickets came at the impressive cost of just 20 apiece. He loved to pin batsmen down with his accuracy and force errors, and to do so he bowled negatively and slightly short — too short to take wickets consistently at the top level. Also Hendrick did not have the best of luck with injuries: a torn hamstring ended his first tour of Australia (1974-75) after one full Test and in 1980-81 he returned home with shoulder trouble suffered during his first bowl of the trip. When he did see out a tour Down Under he enjoyed his most successful time, taking 19 wickets in five Tests in 1978-79.

In 1981 he made two career moves, leaving Derbyshire to join neighbours Nottinghamshire to see out his playing days before injuries forced him to retire in 1984. He also signed up for the first rebel tour of South Africa, incurring a three-year ban which confirmed the end of his England career. When he stopped playing, Hendrick's laconic wit helped him on the after-dinner speaking circuit, in the commentary box and, no doubt, in a brief interlude as an umpire. In 1992 he made a welcome return to the first-class game as coach at Trent Bridge.

M. HENDRICK born 22.10.48 (Darley Dale, Derbyshire). Tests 30 runs 126 average 6.40 wickets 87 average 25.83

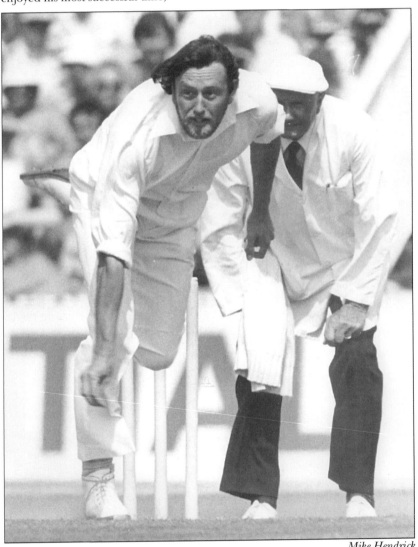

Mike Hendrick

GRAEME HICK
Worcestershire 15 Tests 1991-

RARELY has so much been expected of a player on his Test debut than of Graeme Hick when he walked out at Headingley on June 6 1991 to face the West Indies. Here was the Great White Hope: the batsman to lead England into the next century. Sport — happy to relate — is not that predictable.

Hick, the son of a Zimbabwe tobacco farmer, had been scoring centuries since he was six. He was a member of the 1983 Zimbabwe World Cup squad but, with no sign of his country's admittance to Test cricket, he came to England to serve a seven-year qualification period and proceeded to demolish county batting records. In 1986 he became the youngest player to score 2,000 runs in a summer; two years later he scored 405 not out against Somerset, the highest score in England this century; in 1990, shortly after his 24th birthday, he became the youngest player to record 50 first-class centuries.

Never had a player come into Test cricket with so many achievements behind him, and England waited for him to put the world's bowlers to flight. The awakening was a rude one. Out for 6 and 6 in that first Test, Hick was dropped after four appearances, tormented by the West Indian pacemen who ruthlessly exposed failings in his technique against short-pitched bowling.

The following winter in New Zealand, Hick was expected to rehabilitate himself against the friendlier Kiwi attack but he fell below expectations again, each failure planting more doubts in the mind of this shy Zimbabwean prone to introspection. Pakistan's rampant attack did not let him recover in 1992 but he found the Indian spinners more to his liking on the '93 winter tour, and England hope a superb 178 in the final Test in Bombay will be a portent of things to come.

Hick's steady off-spin bowling and brilliant slip fielding also make him a potent force in the limited-overs game.

G.A. HICK born 23.5.66 (Salisbury, Rhodesia). Tests 15 runs 716 average 28.64 100s 1 wickets 14 average 39.0

Ken Higgs

KEN HIGGS
Lancashire and Leicestershire 15 Tests 1965-68

BUILT like the proverbial brick out-house, Ken Higgs was a fine medium-fast bowler with an impressive pedigree who suddenly went out of fashion with the selectors after one Test of the 1968 Ashes series. At 31, Higgs was discarded with a Test record to be proud of, and a new-ball partnership with John Snow was halted when it looked to have several series ahead of it.

Higgs forced his way into the England side in 1965 and soon established himself with his no-nonsense expertise. In 1966 he was England's only ever-present as the West Indies went on the rampage, but Higgs still finished with 24 wickets in the series as well as sharing a 128-run 10th wicket partnership with Snow, a record for England at home. The next summer, Higgs took 17 Pakistan wickets at 14 apiece but did not get into the team that winter in the Caribbean and played only one more Test.

Big-hearted and broad of beam, Ken did not suffer officialdom gladly and walked out of the game prematurely in 1969 to play league cricket. After several offers, he was tempted back in 1972 by Leicestershire, where he became captain and then coach, turning out and showing the young 'uns a thing or two by taking 5 for 22 against Yorkshire when he was 49. As a bone-shuddering centre half, he also played soccer for Port Vale. Ken went on to work in the car trade.

K. HIGGS born 14.1.37 (Sandyford, Staffordshire). Tests 15 runs 185 average 11.56 wickets 71 average 20.74

MALCOLM HILTON
Lancashire 4 Tests 1950-52

AS A 19-year-old, Malcolm Hilton won national acclaim when he accounted for Don Bradman twice in a match with his beguiling left-arm spin. He was the best slow left-arm bowler Lancashire had seen this century and, at 22, was in the Test side, seemingly set for life. Hilton, however, suffered the spinners' nightmare, the jitters, and lost his way at times. He also, say colleagues, enjoyed cricket's social life a little too much although his 1,006 first-class wickets still cost only 19 apiece. He quit at 33 to play league cricket.

M.J. HILTON born 2.8.28 (Chadderton, Lancashire). Died 8.7.90. Tests 4 runs 37 average 7.40 wickets 14 average 34.07

ROBIN HOBBS
Essex and Glamorgan 7 Tests 1967-71

ROBIN Hobbs was the last specialist leg-spinner to play for England before Ian Salisbury revived the art in 1992. A good spinner of the ball although he lacked the googly, an inventive batsman and great character, he was an immensely popular cricketer. He went on three tours but, curiously, he played only two Tests overseas where the harder wickets should have suited his bowling. At home in Tests he was considered something of a luxury item. Hobbs quit playing in 1975 but four years later Glamorgan tempted him back as skipper.

R.N.S. HOBBS born 8.5.42 (Chippenham, Wiltshire). Tests 7 runs 34 average 6.80 wickets 12 average 40.08

Robin Hobbs

ERIC HOLLIES
Warwickshire 13 Tests 1935-50

ERIC Hollies was one of cricket's most extraordinary characters, whose meagre 13 Tests in no way reflected his contribution to the game. He was a fastish leg-break bowler who rarely had much use for the googly — except on one auspicious occasion. Don Bradman walked out at the Oval in 1948 for his last Test needing four runs to reach 7,000 and an international career average of 100. The ovation was almost too much for 'The Don' and Hollies' ill-disguised erratic googly certainly was, bowling cricket's greatest batsman second ball for a duck. Stunned silence.

It was not often, apparently, that Hollies was silent. Loquacious, with a rich seam of Black Country humour,

he was an immensely respected and hard-working cricketer. His England career started in the West Indies early in 1935 and he was chosen to make his home debut that summer but a Warwickshire team-mate accidentally sat on him in an hotel room, hurting his neck and forcing him to withdraw. He had to wait 12 years for his next opportunity.

Eric was not the luckiest of fellows, the War robbing him of probably his best years and a dentist depriving him of a trip to the West Indies in 1953-54 because of urgently required repair work. In 1946, however, Hollies did something rather special, taking all 10 Nottinghamshire wickets in an innings without assistance (7 bowled, 3 lbw).

He loved bowling — he was still taking wickets into his sixties in the Birmingham League — and his 2,323 first-class wickets (average 20.94) far outnumbered his runs scored: 1,673

(average 5). Hollies' expertise with the bat was legendary and he revelled in it. When it was time to get his pads on, Eric would prop his bat up in the Edgbaston dressing room window and say to it: 'Now while I'm getting ready, you find out what the ball's doing.'

For illustration see Tom Dollery

W.E. HOLLIES born 5.6.12 (Old Hill, Staffordshire). Died 16.4.81. Tests 13 runs 37 average 5.28 wickets 44 average 30.27

MARTIN HORTON
Worcestershire 2 Tests 1959

A VERSATILE all-rounder who could bat anywhere in the top six and who twice took more than 100 wickets in a season with his off-spin, Martin Horton was possibly fortunate to be elevated to Test status for two matches in 1959. He was, however, a valuable county player and was an important part of Worcestershire's championship successes in the 1960s before he left to become New Zealand's national coach. He is currently coaching at Worcester Royal Grammar School and a committee man at New Road.

M.J. HORTON born 21.4.34 (Worcester). Tests 2 runs 60 average 30.00 wickets 2 average 29.50

Martin Horton

NIGEL HOWARD
Lancashire 4 Tests 1951-52

A SHORTAGE of amateur captains willing and able to lead a weak England party on a gruelling six-month tour of the Indian sub-continent gave Howard his chance. An attractive batsman and enthusiastic leader, he played his four Tests on the tour before pleurisy ruled him out of the last match, which was lost and the series drawn. He became the youngest player to captain Lancashire in 1949 and led them to a share of the championship the next year, but left cricket in 1953 to go into the family textile business.

N.D. HOWARD born 18.5.25 (Gee Cross, Cheshire). Died 31.5.79. Tests 4 runs 86 average 17.20

Dick Howarth

DICK HOWORTH
Worcestershire 5 Tests 1947-48

O NE of the oldest players to make his Test debut at 38 years 112 days, Dick Howorth celebrated with a wicket first ball, only the fifth Englishman to achieve the feat. Howorth was a tremendously versatile left-handed cricketer: a useful batsman anywhere in the order, a spinner who could bowl seam up and an excellent fielder. Before the War, Hedley Verity had restricted his Test chances but Dick was not to be denied, and toured the Caribbean in 1948. Subsequently ignored by England despite good county performances, he gave up disenchanted in 1951 and bought a newsagents just outside the Worcester County Ground.

R. HOWORTH born 26.4.09 (Bacup, Lancashire). Died 2.4.80. Tests 5 runs 145 average 18.12 wickets 19 average 33.42

RICHARD HUTTON
Yorkshire 5 Tests 1971

W HEN people told him he was not as good as his father, Richard Hutton's stock replay was: 'No, and neither were a lot of other players.' Living with the inevitable comparison to Sir Leonard was not easy but Hutton junior, a powerful seam bowler and bold batsman, became a very useful cricketer in his own right and deserved his Test chance when it came in 1971. No sooner had he made a satisfying start to his England career, however, than Tony Greig arrived to claim the all-rounder's role. Currently editor of *The Cricketer* magazine.

R.A. HUTTON born 6.9.42 (Pudsey, Yorkshire). Tests 5 runs 219 average 36.50 wickets 9 average 28.55

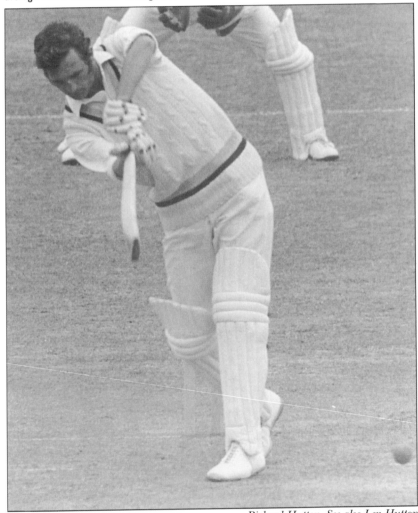

Richard Hutton. See also Len Hutton

NASSER HUSSAIN
Essex 3 Tests 1990-

NASSER Hussain is a precociously talented batsman whose climb to the top was halted abruptly on the 1990 tour of the West Indies. Teenage achievements counted for nothing in the heat of battle and he returned with a bruised reputation and a broken wrist, which he bravely played on with in the final Test in Antigua and spent much of the next summer recovering from. An impetuous streak earned one warning from skipper Gooch in the Caribbean, and a dressing-room fracas during a county match in 1992 was probably born more out of frustration with his own lack of progress than anything else. Time and talent, however, are on his side and he remains one of England's most promising new generation of run-makers.

N. HUSSAIN born 28.3.68 (Madras, India). Tests 3 runs 100 average 20.0

SIR LEONARD HUTTON

Yorkshire 79 Tests 1937-55

LEN Hutton, a slight, quiet man, was a giant among cricketers. Few, if any, batsmen have touched his God-given talent for hitting a cricket ball whatever the conditions, whoever the opponents. His mastery was complete — and yet when he retired from the game in 1955 at 39, many contemporaries believe it was through sheer weariness of the constant scrutiny and criticism. Whatever he did as a batsman, the critics appeared to expect more; as England's first professional captain since Arthur Shrewsbury in 1887, his every move was questioned.

It is perhaps difficult to appreciate today in an era when professionalism is regarded as an attribute, but when Hutton took charge in 1952 it was generally thought only a man with the ideals and diplomacy of an amateur could lead a side. Most counties were captained by amateurs and, indeed, Hutton was never to skipper his county, Yorkshire. Even the other professional players were wary of one of their own in charge, and Hutton was sensitive to having every decision held under suspicion for cross-examination.

In his unobtrusive way, however, Hutton proved himself to be tactically shrewd and sensitive to his players' needs. Despite being criticised for being defensive, England drew only eight of his 23 Tests at the helm, winning 11 and never losing a series. He won back the Ashes in 1953 and held on to them in remarkable style, coaxing the best out of Frank Tyson in 1954-55. He had led England out of some bleak years and had proved himself a great captain as well as a great batsman. A year later it seemed as if the whole country finally appreciated him, once he had retired, when he was knighted.

Buckingham Palace was a long way from Fulneck, near Leeds, for the son of a Yorkshire builder brought up to believe in respect and discipline. As a boy he devoured cricket, and sat in awe as a 14-year-old at Headingley in 1930 watching Don Bradman score 309 on the first day of the Test. Never could he have imagined how sensational a part he was to play in England's revenge against Bradman's Australians eight years later.

It was at the Oval, recalled for his sixth Test, that the 22-year-old Hutton was to amass the highest score made in Test cricket. His 364 — since bettered only by Garfield Sobers' 365 — is still the benchmark for English batsmen. The War interrupted Hutton's sublime progress, and cruelly almost ended it altogether. A gymnasium accident during commando training saw his left arm broken so severely that he required three bone grafts during an eight-month stay in hospital. Discharged and invalided out of the Army, he found his weakened arm was two inches shorter than the other and his game had to be adapted.

The family business... Len Hutton and son Richard

When play resumed after a seven-year break, Hutton always strenuously denied his injury made him more vulnerable, particularly against spinners. He was never one to seek excuses.

He was accused of playing negatively but he often found himself shoring up an unreliable England batting side in the early years after the War. He and Compton were the mainstays, and as opener he had to bear the burden of protecting the order as well as scoring runs. Compton knew Hutton's value only too well and says: 'We were very different characters but very good friends, and he was the greatest opening batsman I have ever seen. I say that because in our day we played on uncovered wickets. His powers of concentration were remarkable, but when he wanted to be, he was one of the best stroke-makers in the game.'

There was no clearer example of Hutton's value than in 1950-51 when England were being beaten 4-1 in Australia. During that series, Hutton averaged 88, 50 more than the next Englishman — and 45 more than the best Australian! When he retired to live in Surrey he developed his golf and a successful business career, returning to the game only briefly for two years as a Test selector in 1975-76.

L. HUTTON born 23.6.16 (Fulneck, Yorkshire). Died 6.9.90. Tests 79 runs 6971 average 56.67 100s 19 wickets 3 average 77.33

Best foot forward... Hutton (right) and Don Smith appearing for the MCC in 1957

For further illustrations see Godfrey Evans, Fred Trueman and Cyril Washbrook

RAY ILLINGWORTH
Yorkshire and Leicestershire 61 Tests 1958-73

WHEN Ray Illingworth strolls on to a Test ground long before play starts on the first morning to inspect the wicket in his capacity as a television commentator and newspaper columnist, England players and management will invariably break off from practice and try to buttonhole him for a gem of advice. No cricket voice is more respected than Ray's flat, forthright Yorkshire tones. Comparisons of England skippers since the War invariably boil down to a debate over the best four: Hutton, May, Brearley and Illingworth. All were as tough as old boots when it came to squashing opponents who were down, and all commanded great loyalty from their men. Unlike the other three, who were all batsmen, Illingworth had the advantage of being an all-rounder and very few tricks escaped him, whether he was playing a Test at Sydney or a Sunday League bash at Hinckley.

Yet his entry as a Test captain arrived when he was 37 and by a curious sequence of events. After 17 years with Yorkshire, Illingworth wanted the security of a contract, which went against the club's policy, and so he quit, moving to Leicestershire, where he was offered the chance to captain a county for the first time. In the summer of 1969 he had led his new county in only eight matches when he was asked to lead England against the West Indies because Colin Cowdrey was suffering from an Achilles tendon injury. 'Illy' thought it was only a temporary move in recognition of his services to the game but he remained in charge for the next 31 Tests, being undefeated in his first 19 and winning series against the West Indies, Australia, New Zealand and Pakistan.

His greatest triumph was regaining the Ashes in 1970-71 when, under intense pressure, he held the squad together and was chaired off at the end of the final Test by his players. England had disputes with umpires (they did not get a single lbw decision in six Tests), John Snow — from whom Illingworth extracted the best — was attacked by a fan on the boundary, and in the final Test, 'Illy' led his players off the field for their own safety when the Sydney crowd started hurling cans and bottles after Snow had been warned for short-pitched bowling.

The responsibilities of captaincy also lifted Illingworth's own game to a higher level than seen previously in his Test career. In his second match as skipper he scored his maiden Test century, which did not come as a total surprise because he had, after all, joined Yorkshire as an all-rounder. In the early days he bowled medium-paced swing but soon converted to off-spin, a job he made his own at Headingley when Bob Appleyard retired. Opportunity, however, was limited. A powerful Yorkshire batting line-up restricted his chances of run-making, and internationally he had to overcome challenges from the likes of Laker, Titmus and Allen. Illingworth was not the biggest spinner of a ball but he bowled with Yorkshire frugality, pinning batsmen down until they snapped. In a run chase on a dusty strip on the last afternoon of a county match with the brilliant hands of Sharpe, Close and Trueman around the bat, he could run through a side.

He played in 30 Tests spread over 13 series before taking on the captaincy, his success patchy and his place rarely assured, while at county level the frustration of not being given a chance to lead Yorkshire grew. When his pay dispute blew up, Leicestershire secretary Mike Turner, who had heard that 'Illy' was the think-tank of Brian Close's leadership at Yorkshire, offered him the chance he had been looking for at Grace Road. It was a fruitful partnership for all concerned although Illingworth's increasingly powerful influence on the England dressing room began to irk some in positions of power. His willingness to speak openly and bluntly also ruffled feathers, and he was dismissed summarily after two heavy defeats at the hands of the West Indies, by chairman Alec Bedser — probably acting under pressure from above — without explanation.

When he left Leicestershire after 10 seasons, Yorkshire immediately took him back as manager to try to resolve their internal mayhem and finally, with lovely irony, in 1982 at the age of 50 he was asked to captain the side. The next summer he led them to the Sunday League title, their first trophy in 14 years. In 1986 he was approached about becoming England's first full-time manager but was unhappy with the amount of control being offered and so continued his work in journalism.

R. ILLINGWORTH born 8.6.32 (Pudsey, Yorkshire). Tests 61 runs 1836 average 23.24 100s 2 wickets 122 average 31.20

For further illustration see John Hampshire

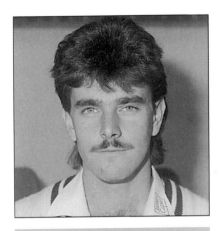

ALAN IGGLESDEN
Kent 1 Test 1989

A CHAOTIC catalogue of injuries and the recruitment for a rebel tour of South Africa led to Alan Igglesden being called into the last Test of a disastrous 1989 Ashes summer at 24 hours' notice. Despite receiving the dubious morale-booster of being described as England's 17th-choice pace bowler by manager Micky Stewart, he made a creditable bow in Test cricket. Igglesden is a good trier, but any ambitions of adding to his one cap had been frustrated by injuries until a recall for the 1993 Ashes series.

A.P. IGGLESDEN born 8.10.64 (Farnborough, Kent). Tests 1 runs 2 average — wickets 3 average 48.66

JOHN IKIN
Lancashire 18 Tests 1946-55

M ANY more gifted players wondered at John Ikin's survival in the Test side. Three half-centuries in 31 innings as a middle-order grafter suggested great belief from the selectors. What Ikin, a calm, popular left-hander who also bowled leg-spin, offered was a touch of defiance if the brilliance of the likes of Hutton, Compton and Edrich did not burn so brightly. There were times when he bailed out England when in trouble and half of his Test appearances were with weak sides sent overseas. But certainly he was one would could never accuse the selectors of southern bias.

For illustration see Bill Voce.

J.T. IKIN born 7.3.18 (Bignall End, Staffordshire). Died 15.9.84. Tests 18 runs 606 average 20.89 wickets 3 average 118.0

RICHARD ILLINGWORTH
Worcestershire 2 Tests 1991

A WICKET with his first ball in Test cricket — only the 11th man to achieve the feat — gave Richard Illingworth understandable delight. A good competitor with his steady left-arm spin, dogged batting and diligent fielding, he was a regular member of England's one-day squad but his Test credentials were questioned. Doubts about Phil Tufnell's attitude gave Illingworth his opportunity against the 1991 West Indians and his memorable first ball bowled opener Phil Simmons, but it proved to be a false dawn.

R.K. ILLINGWORTH born 23.8.63 (Bradford, Yorkshire). Tests 2 runs 31 average 15.50 wickets 4 average 53.25

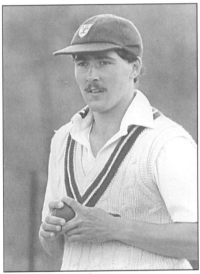

Richard Illingworth

DOUG INSOLE
Essex 9 Tests 1950-57

D OUG Insole learned all he needed to know about being a selector from his own experience of how not to treat a player: his four home Tests were all one-offs in separate summers. Yet when he did get a run in the side, playing five Tests in South Africa in 1956-57, he topped the averages, proving that while his middle-order batting was not pretty, it could be effective. Since then as an influential administrator,

Doug Insole

he has served as selector, tour manager and TCCB chairman. Insole played for Corinthian Casuals in the 1956 FA Amateur Cup Final.

D.J. INSOLE born 18.4.26 (Clapton, London). Tests 9 runs 408 average 27.20 100s 1

ROBIN JACKMAN
Surrey 4 Tests 1981-82

F EW players have made a more dramatic impact on international cricket than Robin Jackman, although his actual playing career was brief and unspectacular. A magnificent trier with a theatrical appeal, Jackman was a fine county fast-medium bowler who finally had his England chance at 35 when Bob Willis broke down in the West Indies in 1981. His arrival in Guyana was universally popular with English players and supporters — but not the local politicians. Married to a South African, Jackman had made several visits to the outlawed Republic and was served with a deportation order. The second Test in the West Indies was cancelled as the whole England party escaped to Barbados, and the rest of the tour was in jeopardy until Jackman's presence was accepted in the politically more relaxed holiday island. Jackman's brief career was never as dramatic as its prologue. He now divides his time between South Africa and Britain, coaching and commentating.

R.D. JACKMAN born 13.8.45 (Simla, India). Tests 4 runs 42 average 7.00 wickets 14 average 31.78

JOHN JAMESON
Warwickshire 4 Tests 1971-74

BORN into the era of Boycott, Edrich and Amiss, John Jameson had precious few opportunities to break into Test cricket. A brave, attacking opener who was at his best trying to hammer fast bowling out of the ground, he played a couple of Tests in 1971 but did not help his cause by being run out in three of his first four innings. Given another chance on the 1973-74 Caribbean tour, he struggled for runs and was dispensed with. After four years on the umpire's list, he coached at Sussex before being appointed MCC cricket secretary in 1989.

J.A. JAMESON born 30.6.41 (Bombay, India). Tests 4 runs 214 average 26.75 wickets 1 average 17.00

John Jameson

LES JACKSON
Derbyshire 2 Tests 1947-63

IT IS one of cricket's great crimes that Les Jackson, a most respected fast bowler on the circuit throughout the 1950s, played only twice for England. It is said that his slingy, hostile action and his blunt opinions did not please the MCC but in an era when Alec Bedser carried England's attack on his own, Jackson's omission was a scandalous loss. He headed the national averages in 1953 and '58 and was as feared as Trueman and Tyson in county cricket, taking his 1,733 first-class wickets at 17.36 apiece. His astonishing England career spanned 12 years from his debut in 1949 to his recall 97 Tests later at the age of 40 in 1961. The youngest of 13 children, he spent his winters in the mines pondering the injustices of cricket and finished his working days as a Coal Board chauffeur.

H.L. JACKSON born 5.4.21 (Whitwell, Derbyshire). Tests 2 runs 15 average 15 wickets 7 average 22.14

Robin Jackman

the bigger spinners of the ball, if not always the most accurate. He took his Test chance well on the 1948-49 South African tour, claiming 16 wickets in a triumphant series. The next summer he took nine wickets against the West Indians at Lord's but could not hold his place, making a brief return in '52.

R.O. JENKINS born 24.11.18 (Worcester). Tests 9 runs 132 average 10.15 wickets 21 average 45.95

JEFF JONES
Glamorgan 15 Tests 1964-68

SOUTH Wales is hardly renowned for fast bowlers but in 1960 a powerfully built left-armer joined the Glamorgan staff and caused undiluted excitement. Unassuming and popular, Jeff Jones introduced a destructive force into Glamorgan's cricket it had never seen before. For a brief period, probably while he was taking 8 for 0 at Leicester in 1965, he was reckoned to be the quickest anywhere. Wickets did not come cheaply, he was erratic, but he could trouble the best. Sadly an elbow injury wrecked it all and, at 26, Jones had to find a job in brewing.

I.J. JONES born 10.12.41 (Dafen, Carmarthenshire). Tests 15 runs 38 average 4.75 wickets 44 average 40.20

Jeff Jones

PAUL JARVIS
Yorkshire 9 Tests 1988-

HAVING wasted three years serving a ban for a rebel trip to South Africa, Paul Jarvis picked up the pieces of his England career impressively in India in 1993. The youngest player to represent Yorkshire (16 years 75 days), Jarvis always had much potential as a well-coordinated pace bowler who skidded the ball through with considerable venom. He played four Tests at 22 but injuries and an unsettled spell at Yorkshire, when he was keen to leave, hampered his progress. The 1990 rebel tour halted it altogether until he was surprisingly chosen for India after a modest county season.

P.W. JARVIS born 29.6.65 (Redcar, Yorkshire). Tests 9 runs 132 average 10.15 wickets 21 average 45.95

ROLAND JENKINS
Worcestershire 9 Tests 1948-52

TRUE to the leg-spinners' image, Roly Jenkins was one of the game's great characters and entertainers whose performances ebbed and flowed with how the mood took him. In an era when wrist-spinners flourished, Roly was one of

Roland Jenkins

BARRY KNIGHT
Essex and Leicestershire
29 Tests 1961-69

IT IS fair to say that Barry Knight enjoyed the Swinging Sixties. A flamboyant cricketer, he was not an armchair-and-slippers man when stumps had been drawn. He was an elegant middle-order batsman and a bowler with a sharp turn of speed who never appeared to run out of energy.

In county cricket he was invaluable — between 1962 and 1965 for Essex he achieved the double (1,000 runs and 100 wickets) — yet for England he failed to convince the selectors that his game had enough substance for international cricket. His longest run in the Test side was the first six Tests he played in India and Pakistan (1961-62). He was recalled no fewer than nine times in a career that was more stop than start.

Occasionally he would blossom: his 240-run partnership with Peter Parfitt against New Zealand in 1963 remains an English sixth- wicket record, and he finished off another Test in that series with a successive 6,4,4. But more often than not he would flatter to deceive and in 38 innings he passed 50 only twice — on each occasion going on for a century.

Off the field, financial problems led to a parting with Essex and a move to Grace Road where he was a popular addition for three seasons. In the winter of 1969 he worked in Australia and telephoned Leicestershire to say that because of a few difficulties in England, he was going to stay put in Sydney, where he opened an indoor cricket school.

B.R. KNIGHT born 18.2.38 (Chesterfield, Derbyshire). Tests 29 runs 812 average 26.19 100s 2 wickets 70 average 31.75

DON KENYON
Worcestershire 8 Tests 1951-55

FEW players demonstrated that results in the county game count for nothing in the heat of Test cricket better than Don Kenyon. A polished batsman who relished taking on fast bowlers, he became the heaviest scorer in Worcestershire's history with more than 37,000 first-class runs to his credit. Yet when his Test opportunities came along, Kenyon could not make it count, falling in single figures in 11 of his 15 England innings. He may feel his opportunities were unfairly sporadic: three Tests on the 1951-52 India tour, two in 1953, three in 1955, but life is tough at the top. A popular and successful county captain, he became a selector and is Worcestershire president.

D. KENYON born 15.5.24 (Wordsley, Staffordshire). Tests 8 runs 192 average 12.80

Barry Knight

ALAN KNOTT

Kent 95 Tests 1967-81

IN MOST lists of England's leading all-rounders since the War there is usually one glaring omission — Alan Knott. The Kent wicketkeeper undoubtedly qualifies as a cricketer who filled two roles — batting and 'keeping — to international standard. Like his Kentish predecessor before the hostilities, Les Ames, Knott added an extra dimension to England Test teams.

Knott's agile 'keeping set new standards in the world game and his batting was full of improvisation and nimble footwork. His 4,389 runs would have been increased substantially had he not been sent in usually at No, 6 or 7. For a decade he made the international ambitions of the 16 other county 'keepers in the country pointless. An automatic choice, he made 65 consecutive appearances — a record since equalled by Ian Botham — until he opted to join Kerry Packer's cricket circus. During much of his time his deputy was Bob Taylor, who, if he was not the best gloveman in the world, was certainly the second best. But Taylor had to bide his time until first Packer and then finally the lure of rebel cricket in South Africa tempted Knott.

In a sport with more than its fair share of eccentrics, the consensus is that 'Knotty' was a standard bearer. He was a health and fitness fanatic who frequently showered and changed kit during intervals, insisted on honey in his tea and was obsessive about his diet. On the field he went through his exercise routines religiously between deliveries to ease a lower-back problem that stayed with him throughout his career. In an era when most cricketers regarded stretching as something you did in the bedroom in the morning, most players viewed his contortions as more proof of eccentricity.

When Knott joined Kent it was as a cricketer who could do a bit of everything, and he was advised by none other than county secretary Les Ames to concentrate on his off-spin ahead of keeping wicket. But his father had been a quality 'keeper in club cricket, and when Kent suddenly found themselves short of glovemen, Knott grabbed his chance. Soon it became apparent it was a sensible move and at 21 he was in the Test team. That winter in the Caribbean he took over from Jim Parks for the fourth Test and the position was his for keeps. His reading of his Kent colleague Derek Underwood facilitated one of the great double-acts in cricket. Knott could nominate exactly which weapon from an armoury of pacey left-arm spin Underwood was about to send down. The anticipation appeared telepathic, and when Underwood was going to let rip with his seamer — a real hazard to unsuspecting close fielders as well as the batsman — Knott would warn his slips.

On his second tour he was within four runs of his maiden Test century when frenzied protesters stormed the outfield in Karachi forcing the match to be abandoned, making him wait until his 25th Test against New Zealand for that first hundred, but his finest hour was his century defying Lillee and Thomson in Adelaide in 1975.

A bad crash during a charity car race at Brands Hatch came close to ending Knott's career. He was injured around the eyes but miraculously his sight was unimpaired although he was left with a neck injury that forced him to discard his favoured cap and adopt a floppy hat, which, with its upturned brim, allowed him to see without

Alan Knott... another victim

bending his neck.

After Packer, he returned to international cricket in 1980 and briefly the following summer, but he did not wish to tour that winter and then opted for the rewards of South Africa. At the time his 269 wicketkeeping dismissals was a world record, since bettered only by Australia's Rodney Marsh (355 in 96

Tests) and West Indian Jeff Dujon (270 in 81). He left Kent and first-class cricket in 1985 but in recent years has been an enthusiastic observer for England's selectors and the team's specialist wicketkeeping coach.

A.P.E. KNOTT born 9.4.46 (Belvedere, Kent). Tests 95 runs 4389 average 32.75 100s 5 dismissals 269 caught 250 stumped 19

Alan Knott... far more than just a wicketkeeper

JIM LAKER

Surrey and Essex 46 Tests 1948-59

JIM Laker did not suffer fools gladly. And in cricket, he would tell you, there were plenty of them about. He was probably the best spinner this country has produced in the past 50 years. One of his successors in the England team, Phil Edmonds, writes: 'In method Laker was the ideal off-spinner... his bowling was of a kind that is effective throughout the ages.' So why, during the span of his international career, did Laker appear in only 46 of the 99 Tests played, and complete only three series? One reason was an impatience and intolerance with others.

Laker was, above all, an intelligent cricketer who cared deeply — deeply enough to tell colleagues home truths. He was a Yorkshireman and he could be blunt. He was not always popular — and it cost him. He also had an idiosyncratic habit of turning away after bowling which could make it look as if he was not that bothered with the business at hand. He had one infamous row with his Surrey and England captain Peter May who accused him of not trying. Laker was so incensed he refused to tour Australia that winter (1958-59) under May; the impasse remained for days until Denis Compton finally arranged a conciliatory meeting.

That winter saw the end of Laker's England career and a year later his words in an acrimonious autobiography shook the foundations of Lord's. He was scathing in his comments, particularly about May and Freddie Brown, another former England captain and chairman of selectors. The fury of the Establishment came down on his head and he was stripped of his honorary life membership of both the MCC and Surrey. Those were the politics of Laker's life. When he played, particularly in tandem with his Surrey colleague Tony Lock, a left-arm spinner, England had the best slow-bowling attack in the world.

Laker grew up playing in the Bradford League as a fast bowler but it was during the War, in Egypt on matting wickets, that he learned how to spin a ball. Tall and poised, he had the perfect action, he could make the ball dip wickedly in flight leaving a batsman stranded, and could find enough turn even on a batting surface. 'You could actually hear the ball hum when it left Jim's fingers,' says his regular England wicketkeeper Godfrey Evans. After the War his employers, Barclays Bank, posted him to Catford and hence the link with Surrey, after they had sought permission to sign him from an uninterested Yorkshire. Within 18 months he was in an experimental England side on its way to the West Indies, and in his first Test innings he claimed 7 for 103. He was the most successful bowler of the tour but the next summer, after taking 8 for 2 in a Test trial, he took some heavy punishment from Australia and began his in-out existence.

He was overlooked for two Ashes tours and it was not until 1956 that he really became a fixture in the side. Earlier that summer he had taken all 10 wickets in an innings to help Surrey defeat the Australians, a taster of that historic Ashes Test at Old Trafford. In the first innings he took 9 for 37, in the second 10 for 53. It is still the only instance of a bowler taking all 10 wickets in an innings in Test cricket and his match figures (19 for 90) have never been approached by anyone else. The most remarkable aspect of Laker's performance was that while he was causing mayhem on a wicket specially prepared for spinners, his partner Lock claimed only one wicket in the Test. On his way home from the match, the national hero stopped in a pub and sat quietly in a corner listening to the other drinkers talk excitedly about his exploits that day. He was not recognised and never identified himself — that was Laker.

He did make his tour of Australia in 1958-59, albeit in a fraught atmosphere under May, but returned home before the New Zealand leg troubled by an arthritic spinning finger which forced him to retire. Three years later he returned to play occasionally as an amateur for three seasons with Essex. Later, the past forgiven, he returned to the Oval where he became cricket chairman and he was admired as an outspoken yet always fair television commentator until his death in 1986.

J.C. LAKER born 9.2.22 (Frizinghall, Yorkshire). Died 23.4.86. Tests 46 runs 676 average 14.08 wickets 193 average 21.24

Jim Laker... in a world, and a class, of his own

For further illustration see Godfrey Evans

ALLAN LAMB
Northamptonshire 79 Tests 1982-

IF THERE was one thing Allan Lamb resented it was to see himself described as South African. The epithet stuck in his throat, particularly after he had just played another gutsy innings to dig England out of a hole against the West Indies. While England became a flag of convenience for Lamb and other southern Africans who followed him, few would question his commitment and courage when he wore the lion on his cap. If England needed a batsman to confront a crisis on some foreign field during the 1980s, there were few better than Lamb. Sturdy and strong, an instinctive stroke-maker, he loved nothing more than to slug it out toe-to-toe with fast bowlers.

With his strong Cape accent and pugnacious Springbok attitude, Lamb was destined to be recognised as imported talent as he blazed a trail for South African players who saw an escape from isolation through qualifying for England. Lamb's parents had come from London and once he realised his talent as a schoolboy, he always wanted to play county cricket. His chance came in 1977 when, in an enterprise initiated by Eddie Barlow, three young Springboks — Lamb, Peter Kirsten and Garth le Roux — were shipped to England to play anywhere they could get a game. Northamptonshire gave them all guest appearances in the second team and Lamb was offered a contract.

He adapted quickly to the slower English wickets and it became obvious that he would be demanding a Test place as soon as his four-year qualifying period was completed. That happened in 1982, the same time that 16 English-born players had made themselves ineligible for England by joining a rebel tour to South Africa. The irony of Lamb, a South African, taking the place of a

banned Graham Gooch could not be avoided. A century in Lamb's fourth innings in Test cricket confirmed his transition and he remained ever-present in the middle of the batting order for a remarkable run of 45 England Tests over four years. His qualities were never more evident than against the West Indies in 1984. As England were being routed by Clive Lloyd's fearsome pace attack, Lamb fought a lone battle scoring three centuries in successive Tests. An excellent fielder, he also became renowned for his one-day innings, frequently holding England together and conjuring last-over victories out of seemingly impossible situations.

The relentless pressure of international cricket, however, began to take its toll on Lamb who, after looking indestructible, fell foul of a series of niggling injuries, including twice tearing calf muscles jogging from a ground to the team hotel on tour. He went through a mid-life crisis of 24 innings without a half-century, often having his defensive technique found out by slower bowlers, but broke the spell in 1988, inevitably against the West Indies, and in 1990 plundered two more centuries off their bowlers in the Caribbean. He enjoyed, if that is the word, the ultimate honour of captaining England three times when Gooch was injured in the West Indies and Australia. Each time England suffered vital defeats, Lamb shouldered the responsibility as acting skipper although he was not wholly to blame. A gregarious character who played his cricket with a blunt edge, he could lack sympathy in the man-management stakes and his days as vice-captain were numbered after he took charge for the first Test in Australia in 1990-91 and made an ill-advised late-night visit to a casino. Not only was the match at a critical stage, but Lamb was in the

middle of an innings on the night of the trip. He was out in the first over the next morning and England suffered a shattering defeat inside three days.

In 1992, dropped from the side and with his Test career seemingly over, Lamb launched an attack on the touring Pakistanis in a newspaper column, accusing their bowlers of cheating by gouging the ball to make it swing. He was fined £2,000 by Lord's with an additional £2,000 suspended. The season did, however, have a happy conclusion with Lamb lifting his first honour, the NatWest Trophy, since taking over as Northamptonshire skipper in 1989.

A.J. LAMB born 20.6.54 (Langebaanweg, South Africa). Tests 79 runs 4656 average 36.09 100s 14 wickets 1 average 23

Lamb (bottom) with Northants team-mates (from top) Richard Williams, Peter Willey, Geoff Cook and Wayne Larkins

Power personified... Allan Lamb

JIM LANGRIDGE
Sussex 8 Tests 1933-46

A GREAT servant of Sussex, Jim Langridge played only one Test after the War in a sporadic England career. As a steady left-handed batsman and patient left-arm spinner, his Test opportunities were greatly limited by the presence of Yorkshire's Hedley Verity. After the hostilities, England turned again to 40-year-old Langridge and took him to Australia in 1946-47 but a groin injury ended his Test days. A captain and then coach at Hove, his 622 appearances are a county record. His brother John and son Richard also played for Sussex.

For illustration see Bill Voce

J. LANGRIDGE born 10.7.06 (Chailey, Sussex). Died 10.9.66. Tests 8 runs 242 average 26.88 wickets 19 average 21.73

WAYNE LARKINS
Northamptonshire and Durham 13 Tests 1980-91

W AYNE Larkins was usually ignored when he should have been selected and selected when he should have been ignored in a career of unfulfilled potential. A destructive opening bat who could demolish any attack if he got going, 'Ned' tired of waiting for England and joined the 1982 rebel tour to South Africa. Recalls in 1986 and '87 were aborted by injuries but the second rebel excursion in 1990 opened the door for him to return after a nine-year absence for tours of the Caribbean and Australia when he was past his best.

For further illustration see Allan Lamb.

W. LARKINS born 22.11.53 (Roxton, Bedfordshire). Tests 13 runs 493 average 20.54

David Larter

DAVID LARTER
Northamptonshire 10 Tests 1962-65

D AVID Larter was a complex character. There were days at Northampton when he just would not fancy bowling. But when the mood took him and his 6ft 7in physique was in perfect working order, he was a frighteningly good fast bowler, as a career record of 666 wickets at 19 apiece suggests. He bagged 16 wickets in his first two Tests but only 21 in the next eight, which were punctuated by injuries and loss of form. It surprised no-one when, at the age of 29, he packed up cricket to work in the family haulage business.

J.D.F. LARTER born 24.4.40 (Inverness, Scotland). Tests 10 runs 16 average 3.20 wickets 37 average 25.43

Wayne Larkins

Eddie Leadbetter

EDDIE LEADBEATER
Yorkshire and Warwickshire
2 Tests 1951

EDDIE Leadbeater's route into Test cricket was somewhat fortuitous. Derbyshire's Bert Rhodes, the leg-spinner in a second-string squad sent to India in 1951, suffered a hernia and Leadbeater was shipped out. Only 5ft 6in but full of spirit, Leadbeater was more of an accurate roller than a traditional leg-spinner and his bowling posed few terrors for the Indian batsmen. While he picked up two England caps in his modest 10-year career, Eddie was never awarded a county cap. The unfortunate Rhodes, meanwhile, never had another Test chance.

E. LEADBEATER born 15.8.27 (Huddersfield, Yorkshire). Tests 2 runs 40 average 20 wickets 2 average 109.0

DAVID LAWRENCE
Gloucestershire 5 Tests 1988-

A SICKENING injury to 'Syd' Lawrence in New Zealand early in 1992 shattered the hopes of this wholehearted fast bowler of establishing himself in Test cricket. A boxer, rugby player and enthusiastic break-dancer, Lawrence had trouble convincing the selectors he also had the control to be a Test bowler. He appeared to be winning the battle when his left kneecap cracked in delivery stride in Wellington, leaving him in agony and his future in doubt. After 13 months of recuperation, he was planning a bold return for the 1993 season when the knee cracked again during a gymnasium work-out.

D.V. LAWRENCE born 28.1.64 (Gloucester). Tests 5 runs 60 average 10 wickets 18 average 37.55

David Lawrence

JOHN LEVER
Essex 21 Tests 1976-86

THE great vaseline smear will always hang over John Lever's proud record. For 23 years he plied his trade with Essex, becoming the finest left-arm pace bowler in the country. Tough, astute, and entertaining in the dressing room, Lever was, as the title of his autobiography suggests, *A Cricketer's Cricketer.*

But whatever his achievements, Lever will always be associated with vaseline and a ball-tampering row which soured England's tour of India in 1976-77. It was JK's first tour and long overdue. He made up for his late start with a sensational debut in Delhi, taking 7 for 46 in the first innings and 10 for 70 in the match — still the best analysis by an Englishman on his debut — which he topped off with a half-century.

England followed up with a second victory in the next Test and then in the third in humid Madras, Lever asked England physio Bernard Thomas for something to stop the sweat running into his eyes. Thomas came up with strips of vaseline-impregnated gauze. They did not work, Lever threw them to the ground only for the umpire to pick them up suspiciously and send away the match ball for analysis amid accusations that vaseline had been used to polish the ball to help it swing.

Lever, who was always in the clear as far as the England authorities were concerned, was never to better his figures — batting or bowling — from that first Test and never commanded an automatic place. He joined the first rebel tour to South Africa in 1982 but in '86 his reliable form in a successful Essex side earned him a farewell Test at the age of 37. He is now passing on his knowledge in the nets as a schoolmaster.

J.K. LEVER born 24.2.49 (Stepney, London). Tests 21 runs 306 average 11.76 wickets 73 average 26.72

John Lever

Peter Lever

Chris Lewis

PETER LEVER
Lancashire 17 Tests 1970-75

PETER Lever's Test career was built on solid virtues rather than eye-catching brilliance. Enthusiastic and well-schooled with a good out-swinger, he was a well-respected fast bowler, and a week before his 30th birthday he was rewarded with a place in England's 1970-71 Ashes party. He had a dangerous bouncer but a gentle nature, both of which were seen when he felled New Zealand's Ewan Chatfield, whose life was saved by mouth-to-mouth resuscitation and heart massage on the pitch at Auckland. Lever fell to his knees in horror and had to be helped off by his team-mates. He never let England down and made a second Ashes tour four years later, which included a memorable 6 for 38 at Melbourne. Coach at Old Trafford for several years, he now works in the sports promotions business.

P. LEVER born 17.9.40 (Todmorden, Yorkshire). Tests 17 runs 350 average 21.87 wickets 41 average 36.80

CHRIS LEWIS
Leicestershire and Nottinghamshire 18 Tests 1990-

A FLUENT century on his 25th birthday in dire circumstances in Madras on England's 1993 tour of India confirmed Chris Lewis has the talent to be a genuine Test-class all-rounder. Whether he has the durability has still to be established.

The son of a preacher man, Lewis came to England from Guyana with his family when he was 10 and attended Willesden High, the same school as Phillip DeFreitas, whom he was to follow to Grace Road. Lissom and affable, Lewis is clearly blessed with natural sporting ability. His bowling can be hostile or thoughtful, he hits the ball cleanly with a natural swing and his fielding is panther-like. But his commitment still worries an England regime that sets great store in the amount of sweat and blood players are prepared to spill for the cause.

Lewis, unfortunately, has a bulging medical file already. He suffers from a rare blood circulation disorder which needs regular hospital treatment, twice he has pulled out of Tests on the morning of the match 'feeling unwell' and he had to return home from the 1990-91 Ashes tour because of a stress fracture of the spine. Lewis, sensitive to aches and strains, concedes that he needs to be totally happy with his physical fitness to be mentally prepared for the rigours of Test cricket.

He had a good tour of New Zealand in 1992 but performances against Pakistan the following summer, after a move to Trent Bridge to give himself the fresh county challenge he felt he needed, again disappointed home supporters — and selectors — yearning for a successor to Ian Botham. England will hope his century in Madras will give him the added conviction to realise his obvious potential.

C.C. LEWIS born 14.2.68 (Georgetown, Guyana). Tests 18 runs 719 average 27.65 100s 1 wickets 50 average 36.60

TONY LEWIS
Glamorgan 9 Tests 1972-73

PLAYERS who bemoan their lot on tour should first talk to Tony Lewis. A few eyebrows were raised — including those of Geoff Boycott — when Lewis was chosen to lead England to India, Pakistan and Sri Lanka in 1972-73 but the Welshman proved an excellent choice. The tour, spread over five months and enormous distances, was not the most appealing. Captain Ray Illingworth had already declined to go, as had senior players John Snow and John Edrich. Lord's asked Mike Smith to be skipper but he was unavailable, and Boycott was also not interested despite the possibility of being vice-captain. So the selectors turned to Lewis, the urbane, popular skipper of Glamorgan, even though he had never sampled Test cricket before.

An elegant batsman and intelligent leader who had first played for Glamorgan when he was at Neath Grammar School, Lewis had led his county to only their second championship success and had enjoyed great success at Cambridge. In his first Test Lewis performed as if he was made for international cricket. On Christmas Day in Delhi he scored an unbeaten 70 that guided England to their first victory on the sub-continent for more than 20 years. England were to lose the next two Tests, however, but they drew

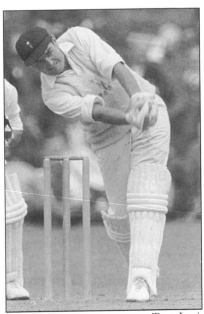
Tony Lewis

the remaining five on tour with Lewis scoring a fine century in Kanpur.

The gratitude and admiration of the selectors was evident the next summer when they picked Lewis to play under Illingworth in the first Test. Knee trouble, which had ended his rugby career at Cambridge, became an increasing problem and when, at 36, he was offered the job of cricket correspondent by a national newspaper, he gave up playing. Tony's work in journalism includes fronting the BBC's Test coverage and recently he stood down as chairman of Glamorgan to concentrate on a new career as chairman of the Welsh Tourist Board.

A.R. LEWIS born 6.7.38 (Uplands, Swansea). Tests 9 runs 457 average 32.64 100s 1

ANDY LLOYD
Warwickshire 1 Test 1984

ANDY Lloyd's Test career lasted just 33 minutes. A competitive left-handed opener, he was chosen in 1984 to face the feared West Indian pace attack, but after scoring 10 runs he turned away from a Malcolm Marshall lifter and was hit a sickening blow on the temple-guard of his helmet. Hospitalised suffering from blurred vision, he did not play again that year. Fully recovered, he returned with 160 for Warwickshire in 1985 but was never in the Test

David Lloyd

reckoning again, diverting his energies instead into the county captaincy at Edgbaston between 1988 and '92.

T.A. LLOYD born 5.11.56 (Oswestry, Shropshire). Tests 1 runs 10 average —

DAVID LLOYD
Lancashire 9 Tests 1974-75

GREAT things were expected when David Lloyd, an attractive left-handed opener, scored an unbeaten 214 in his second Test innings against the touring Indians. It

was, however, the only occasion in 15 Test innings that Lloyd reached 50. 'Bumble' (he loved to talk) had his confidence undermined the following winter in Australia by Lillee and Thomson and never returned to the Test scene. A former Lancashire skipper and umpire, he took over as coach at Old Trafford in 1993.

D. LLOYD born 18.3.47 (Accrington, Lancashire). Tests 9 runs 552 average 42.46 100s 1

PETER LOADER
Surrey 13 Tests 1954-59

A FINE exponent of swing bowling, Peter Loader was at the heart of Surrey's takeover coup of the Championship from 1952 to '58. His new-ball partner was Alec Bedser and when they had finished their work, Laker and Lock took over. Unlike the other three, however, Loader found Test recognition elusive, principally because of the competition from Trueman, Statham and Tyson. His appearances were spread over five years and in two Ashes tours he played only twice. Angular, accurate and with an aversion to breaking down, he emigrated to Australia where he played for Western Australia and set up a transport business.

P.J. LOADER born 25.10.29 (Wallington, Surrey). Tests 13 runs 76 average 5.84 wickets 39 average 22.51

Andy Lloyd

Peter Loader

TONY LOCK

Surrey and Leicestershire 49 Tests 1952-68

TONY Lock, flame-haired, fiercely competitive, was consumed by cricket. He was an aggressive left-arm bowler, a brilliant short-leg fielder, an ever-optimistic No. 9 who lived every minute of every game. His exuberant celebrations when a wicket fell, in the days when a handshake was regarded as somewhat exhibitionist, revealed his passion for his sport. Imagine then his feelings when in 1959 in New Zealand he saw for the first time slow-motion film of his bowling action and the awful truth was confirmed. For years he had bowled under the cloud of suspicion. Everybody suspected — some knew — that he was a 'chucker', the most

damaging accusation a bowler can face. Lock now admitted it for himself but, typical of the man, he rebuilt his action and his career to such an extent that he was still bowling for England nine years later.

'Locky' could never give up cricket. At 14 he was playing for Surrey Colts, by 16 he had turned professional and was in the first team. National Service interrupted and when he returned his success was modest. His flight and gentle spin brought him wickets, but not enough, and he set to work in the indoor nets in Croydon during the winter. A low beam in the hall made it impossible for him to flight the ball so he had to

push it through lower and faster, and discovered, to his delight, that he could turn the ball sharply. He did not realise then what else his reassessment had done for his bowling. Now he became a deadly bowler even on good wickets; on uncovered damp surfaces he was unplayable, and his faster ball was wicked. His partnership with off-spinner Jim Laker was feared and helped bring Surrey seven straight championships (1952 to '58). Lock took 200 wickets in a season twice and in his tenth summer passed 1,500 wickets. How legitimate it is to make comparisons with modern figures can only be guesswork.

Hero worship... Tony Lock arrives at the Oval, 1956

He first played for England in 1952 against India but a few days later, playing for Surrey against the tourists, he was no-balled three times for throwing by former Middlesex 'keeper Fred Price. The selectors' response was to carry on selecting him! The next summer the Australians believed they had been 'thrown out' by Lock and that winter in the Caribbean he was finally called in a Test. It was only the second time in Test cricket history (the first involved Australian E. Jones in 1897-98) that a bowler had been no-balled for throwing. The main concern of umpires was Lock's quicker ball, so he tried to cut it out and continued playing — to much muttering among opponents. In the summer of 1957 he took 34 New Zealand wickets at a cost of 7.47 each. That winter the Kiwis produced their film. The next summer Lock's average almost doubled although he still took more than 100 wickets, he was dropped from the Test side and Surrey surrendered the championship. At 30, struggling with damaged knees, he soldiered on. He was called again in 1960 but the next summer against Australia he won his Test place back with full approval for the new action which produced more loop.

In 1963 he emigrated to Perth to captain Western Australia. He won the Sheffield Shield and became a revered figure in the country that is now his home — but he was not quite finished with England. In 1965, Leicestershire tempted him back for three more seasons as skipper and in the winter of 1967-68 he flew out to the West Indies when Fred Titmus lost four toes in an accident. Lock played in two more Tests at the age of 38 — and scored a career best 89 in his final match to help clinch the series.

G.A.R. LOCK born 5.7.29 (Limpsfield, Surrey). Tests 49 runs 742 average 13.74 wickets 174 average 25.58

Tony Lock... the action that caused a storm

For further illustration see Ken Barrington

FRANK LOWSON
Yorkshire 7 Tests 1951-55

BATTING at the other end to Len Hutton throughout most of his career, Frank Lowson could not help but become a graceful opening batsman. From the boundary, the two men of similar build and style could quite easily be mistaken for one another although the end result was vastly different. It was hoped Lowson would succeed Washbrook in the Test team but after a disappointing tour of India (1951-52) he was dropped. Recalled for one Test in an injury crisis when out of form three years later, he failed again. At 33 he was released by Yorkshire and moved into insurance.

For illustration see Jack Robertson

F.A. LOWSON born 1.7.25 (Bradford, Yorkshire). Died 8.9.84. Tests 7 runs 245 average 18.84

BRIAN LUCKHURST
Kent 21 Tests 1970-74

IN 1969 Colin Cowdrey told Brian Luckhurst he would be a Test player by the end of the next year. As much as he respected Cowdrey, Luckhurst took the prediction with a shovel of salt. He was, after all, past his 30th birthday and had had enough trouble establishing himself as a county batsman.

Originally on the Canterbury staff as a left-arm spinner and tail-end batter, Luckhurst lost his bowling during his National Service days with the Royal Artillery. At the end of 1961 the county were close to letting him go but he was given another one-year contract, forced his way into a team not playing well and steadily worked his way up the order to establish himself as a dependable left-handed opening batsman who shrugged off cracked fingers and bruised hands as occupational hazards.

In 1969 he scored almost 2,000 runs and the next summer was given a Test dress rehearsal playing for England against the Rest of the World. That winter, Cowdrey's prediction came true when Luckhurst was chosen for the tour to Australia and made the transition to Test cricket with consummate ease, scoring two centuries in the series.

Luckhurst is the first to point out that the other major factor in the launching of his international career was the distressing car smash early in 1969 which ended Colin Milburn's Test ambitions just when he looked ready for great things. The pace bowlers of Australia and the West Indies signalled the end of Luckhurst's England days but after he stopped playing in 1976 he continued his work at Canterbury as coach, then manager, and is currently in charge of youth development in the indoor school.

B.W. LUCKHURST born 5.2.39 (Sittingbourne, Kent). Tests 21 runs 1298 average 36.05 100s 4 wickets 1 average 32

Brian Luckhurst

JIM McCONNON
Glamorgan 2 Tests 1954

A LATE starter in county cricket at 27 after a knee injury had curtailed a soccer career which took in Aston Villa and Newport, Jim McConnon looked as if he would threaten Jim Laker's position as England's premier off-spinner. He was tall, had long spinners' fingers and a lovely action but lacked Laker's courage. In the heat of battle nerves let him down. Picked for two Tests in 1954, McConnon was chosen surprisingly ahead of Laker for that winter's Ashes tour but broke a finger and returned home early, never to get another chance.

J.E. McCONNON born 21.6.22
(Burnopfield, County Durham). Tests 2
runs 18 average 9 wickets 4
average 18.50

ARTHUR McINTYRE
Surrey 3 Tests 1950-55

RATED by many the equal to
Godfrey Evans behind the
stumps, Arthur McIntyre was
extremely unlucky not to play more
Test cricket. Originally a
leg-spinner, he kept at the Oval in
an emergency and discovered a new
talent that played a major part in
Surrey's success. For England,
however, he played only twice when
Evans was injured and once in
Australia as a specialist batsman on
his only tour in 1950-51. On other
tours, the selectors frequently tried
younger 'keepers, denying 'Mac' an
opportunity many thought he
deserved. He coached at the Oval
for 20 years after his playing days.

A.J.W. McINTYRE born 14.5.18 (London).
Tests 3 runs 19 average 3.16
dismissals 7 caught 7

Arthur McIntyre

Devon Malcolm

DEVON MALCOLM
Derbyshire 24 Tests 1989-

THE defection in 1989 of Graham
Dilley, Neil Foster and Paul Jarvis to
a rebel team bound for South Africa left
England crying out for fresh, honest fast
bowlers to challenge the West Indies
with a taste of their own medicine that
winter. The selectors opted for two of
their own Caribbean quicks:
Jamaican-born Devon Malcolm and
Ricardo Ellcock from Barbados, both
England-qualified by residence. Their
fortunes were to be vastly different.

Ellcock broke down before the
series started with back trouble which
eventually forced him out of the game;
Malcolm bowled like the wind in
Jamaica as England won the first Test,
took 10 wickets in the second Test and
was the leading wicket-taker in the series
with 19 in four Tests.

Malcolm, incredibly wholehearted
with an easy charm off the field,
became a national hero. Rhythm and
pace is everything for Malcolm. His
radar is sometimes faulty, his run-up
sometimes stutters, but when he gets
it all right, he troubles the very best,
including Viv Richards, with his
inswinging yorker.

Unfortunately, Malcolm's other
ingredient is inconsistency. His county,
Derbyshire, have accused England's
management of filling his head with
too many theories and he had a
difficult tour of Australia in 1990-91
although he was again the leading
wicket-taker, his 16 wickets costing 41
each. The next summer was a disaster
for Malcolm, who soon found himself
out of favour, but he fought his way
back in 1992 against Pakistan to win a
place on the arduous tour of India
where the pitches did not suit him and
success was scarce for the whole squad.

D.E. MALCOLM born 22.2.63 (Kingston,
Jamaica). Tests 24 runs 130
average 5.42 wickets 77 average 37.84

Neil Mallender

GEORGE MANN
Middlesex 7 Tests 1948-49

THE unavailability of several established amateurs for the 1948-49 South Africa tour saw the MCC turn to George Mann as skipper. It was a controversial choice. He was thought to be neither good enough as a batsman nor experienced enough as a captain. As it turned out, he proved a successful leader, and in the final Test of the series he inspired victory with an unbeaten 136. He captained for two Tests the following summer but then stood down, saying he could not play regularly because of the family brewing business. Like his father, Frank, he had been captain in all of his Test appearances. Became TCCB chairman and MCC president.

F.G. MANN born 6.9.17 (Byfleet, Surrey). Tests 7 runs 376 average 37.60 100s 1

VIC MARKS
Somerset 6 Tests 1982-84

IN TYPICAL self-deprecating style, Vic Marks entitled one of his books *Marks out of XI*. He was probably out of the England XI slightly too often. While he was never a fashionable cricketer, he was a determined and highly effective off-spinner cum batsman whose Test figures stand comparison with those often picked ahead of him, such as Geoff Miller and Eddie Hemmings. Oxford-educated, he played 34 one-day internationals and led Somerset before a career as an entertaining broadcaster and writer beckoned.

NEIL MALLENDER
Northamptonshire and Somerset
2 Tests 1992

OCCASIONALLY a county stalwart held in high esteem by his colleagues has a spell of form that coincides with a vacancy in the England team resulting in a Test call-up, and the cricket community is delighted for him. So it was in 1992 for Neil Mallender, who had twice been recruited by England from his winter job with Otago when injuries struck on tours in New Zealand without getting a game. Finally when the chance came, he bowled with pace and guile, as he had done for years, taking 8 for 122 at Leeds to help level the series against Pakistan. He played in the final Test and was disappointed to be rejected for the winter tours, but Mallender will be ever-willing if needed again.

N.A. MALLENDER born 13.8.61 (Kirk Sandall, Yorkshire). Tests 2 runs 8 average 2.66 wickets 10 average 21.50

V.J. MARKS born 25.6.55 (Middle Chinnock, Somerset). Tests 6 runs 249 average 27.66 wickets 11 average 44.0

JACK MARTIN
Kent 1 Test 1947

NOTHING demonstrated the dearth of English pace bowlers immediately after the War more clearly than Jack Martin's call to Test duty to open the attack with Alec Bedser. Martin, a strongly-built, fast-medium bowler, was an insurance man who played club cricket for Catford, turning out for Kent for a handful of games each summer during his holidays. In a 15-year career, he played just 44 first-class matches, one of which, at Trent Bridge in June 1947, was very special indeed.

J.W. MARTIN born 16.2.17 (Catford, Kent). Died 4.1.87. Tests 1 runs 26 average 13 wickets 1 average 129

Jack Martin

MATTHEW MAYNARD
Glamorgan 1 Test 1988

MATTHEW Maynard's reaction to some crass handling by the selectors was to join the 1990 rebel tour to South Africa, incurring what became a three-year Test ban. An excitingly talented batsman, Maynard was called into the maelstrom of England's series against the West Indies in 1988 for the final Test amid an injury crisis. He made a nervy debut, was dropped for the easier task against Sri Lanka three weeks later and then not selected for the aborted tour to India. Ignored again the next summer, he turned to South Africa and both he and England have missed out.

M.P. MAYNARD born 21.3.66 (Oldham, Lancashire). Tests 1 runs 13 average 6.5

Matthew Maynard

117

PETER MAY
Surrey 66 Tests 1951-61

THE most startling aspect of Peter May's rich playing career was the end of it. He retired from the international stage at the age of 31 with the flame of talent still burning bright. 'PBH' was unquestionably one of the post-War greats. His name can be mentioned in the same breath as Hutton and Compton, while others — Cowdrey, Barrington, Graveney, Boycott, Gower, Gooch — have to bide their time, their membership applications for the Batting Legends Club left in the pending tray.

May was also captain of England a record 41 times, with a healthy balance sheet of 20 wins against 10 defeats, and was still in control in 1961 when he announced he had had enough. The reason has never been clear cut. Illness, which had forced him home from the West Indies early the previous year, had taken its toll; he had grown weary of the inevitable criticism that goes with the job; he had achieved everything; and as an amateur and family man, he had a future in the City to think about. In essence, the cricket of May's era was coming to an end and he was less comfortable with the modern game and modern players.

This was never more obvious than in his less than successful term as chairman of selectors from 1982 to '88. He was well-meaning but spoke a different language from most of the modern professionals. His disenchantment after Mike Gatting's troubles led to the choice of Chris Cowdrey as captain. Cowdrey, his godson, was patently not good enough as a Test player although he was an adventurous, successful and eloquent captain of Kent. It was an appointment at odds with the thinking of the team's professional manager Micky Stewart. Cowdrey was hurtfully shunted aside after one Test, and May stepped down at the end of that year.

May's cricket ideals were forged in the public schools of Britain were he blazed a trail. He played for the Public Schools at Lord's at 15 and for Berkshire during the school holidays. From school he joined the Royal Navy and in 1949, aged 19, playing for the Navy and Combined Services, he finished third in the national averages with 63.18, behind Joe Hardstaff and Hutton. At Cambridge he won Blues at soccer and rugby fives as well as cricket, and went into the Test side at 21, scoring 138 in his first innings against South Africa.

The foundations of a monumental career were laid. Tall and raw-boned, May played straight and with power. He had no discernible weakness. He had the grit to battle it out when required, he had the polish to dismantle an attack if the chance arose. He learned the first-class game from the taciturn Hutton with England and the audacious Surridge at Surrey to become an amateur with a professional outlook. He was a ruthless and determined captain, a good tactician and a caring man, but not always a great communicator. Some players found him aloof, others dogmatic and difficult to warm to. In truth, he was just showing the world the stiff upper lip expected of his generation.

Nevertheless May's glorious batting was universally admired. In 1953 Lindsay Hassett's Australians paid the 23-year-old May the compliment of setting out to get him, which they did to devastating effect against Surrey. May played only two Tests that summer but still he displayed the maturity to return for the last Test and play an important part in an English victory. Hutton was named as captain for the South African visit of 1955 but when he withdrew because of back trouble, May, still only 25, took charge. England won a thrilling series 3-2, and so began the longest unbroken reign of any England captain — 35 Tests over six years.

His greatest innings came in 1957 at Edgbaston against the West Indies when Ramadhin was destroying England with his slow bowling. Sonny took 7 for 49 in the first innings and

Peter May... a great player and famous captain

had already taken two more in the second innings when Colin Cowdrey joined May. The pair played out until close and that evening, so says cricket folklore, former Test bowler Bill Bowes, then a journalist, advised them to play everything from the 'mystery bowler' as if it were off-spin. May has no recollection of the 'Bowes advice' but whatever their inspiration, they went on to add 411, an English record for any wicket, with May's unbeaten 285 the highest score by an England captain until Gooch's 333 against India in 1990.

Although May stopped playing in 1963, he has remained one of the most influential men in the game on various committees with Surrey, the MCC and the TCCB.

P.B.H. MAY born 31.12.29 (Reading, Berkshire). Tests 66 runs 4537 average 46.77 100s 13

Peter May... on the boat train at Paddington bound for Avonmouth and the Caribbean, 1959

119

Another bloody tour... Geoff Miller (right) and Geoff Boycott. Antigua, 1981

GEOFF MILLER
Derbyshire and Essex
34 Tests 1976-84

GEOFF Miller concedes that he probably enjoyed cricket too much. He did not take it as seriously as some. And when it became a rigorous, grim-faced business, he was not sorry to bow out of an eight-year Test career that never reached the peaks many expected. Despite his powerful 6ft 2in build, 'Dusty' was not an aggressive cricketer. His off-spin was flighted, his batting was easy and correct. But on a turning wicket or against fast, hostile bowling, the killer instinct rarely emerged from this Chesterfield Grammar School boy.

He was a Young England player and made modest strides as the selectors toyed with the idea of giving him a run. Then Kerry Packer's recruiting of established stars opened the door for him as it did for several others. Under Mike Brearley, Miller was at his happiest, and in Australia in 1978-79, he showed signs of exploiting his ability at last. He took 23 wickets at 15 apiece and scored useful runs as England romped through the series. It was also a pretty

entertaining tour with David Gower, Ian Botham, John Lever and his Derbyshire colleague Mike Hendrick in the party for good company.

Miller never claimed a regular place again until England's return to Australia four years later when he took 13 wickets, but those two Ashes tours were the only occasions in 14 series that his wicket tally reached double figures. In 51 innings, his highest score was an unbeaten 98.

At Derbyshire he tried the captaincy but it affected his form and he thought about leaving more than once before joining Essex for three years. In 1990 he returned to the Racecourse Ground for a final bow before concentrating on his sports shop business and a nice line in after-dinner speaking.

G. MILLER born 8.9.52 (Chesterfield).
Tests 34 runs 1213 average 25.80
wickets 60 average 30.98

GEOFF MILLMAN
Nottinghamshire 6 Tests 1961-62

A NEAT, unobtrusive wicketkeeper and gritty batsman, Geoff Millman was a reliable county performer called up by his country as No. 2 to John Murray for the 1961-62 trip to India.

After three poor Tests, Murray was dropped and Millman performed impressively to keep his place the next summer. But in the second Test against Pakistan, he played when ill and was criticised for not stepping down. It was to be his last appearance. After three years as Nottinghamshire skipper, he quit at 30 to return to the family jewellery business.

G. MILLMAN born 2.10.34 (Bedford).
Tests 6 runs 60 average 12.00
dismissals 15 caught 13 stumped 2

ARTHUR MILTON
Gloucestershire 6 Tests 1958-59

ARTHUR Milton was the last man to play cricket and soccer for England. His lone soccer cap came as a right winger with Arsenal against Austria in 1952, and six years later he became a double international when he opened against New Zealand, achieving the rare feat of scoring a century in his first Test innings. Despite that initial success, this stylish, relaxed run-maker did not enjoy opening and in his remaining eight Test innings he did not get beyond 36. Arthur was always happier in the middle-order playing with his county chums and he spent 27 summers with Gloucestershire before becoming a postman. Now retired, he is an England 'observer', a regional adviser to the selectors.

C.A. MILTON born 10.3.28 (Bristol).
Tests 6 runs 204 average 25.50 100s 1

HUGH MORRIS
Glamorgan 3 Tests 1991-

A TALENTED, easy-going cricketer, Hugh Morris has to convince the selectors he has the steel to succeed at the highest level. A left-handed opener, he played three Tests in 1991, finding it difficult to adjust against the West Indies. He did, however, have every right to feel aggrieved about being overlooked for the subsequent tour of New Zealand. Glamorgan's youngest skipper at 22 in 1986, he resigned after three years to work on his batting but was reinstated in 1993 and remains a strong Test candidate. Played first-class rugby union for Aberavon.

H. MORRIS born 5.10.63 (Cardiff).
Tests 3 runs 115 average 19.16

Arthur Milton

Hugh Morris

COLIN MILBURN
Northamptonshire 9 Tests 1966-69

CRICKET does not have a more cruel story to tell than that of Colin Milburn, a lovely man and a marvellous cricketer. Self-deprecatingly he called himself a 'slogger' but he was far more than that. He was a clean, natural hitter of the ball who had an infectious zest for the game and life. Both were savagely cut short for Milburn. 'Ollie' was fat because he enjoyed good food, good beer and good company too much to diet. Yet despite his 18 stone padded around a 5ft 10in frame, he was agile and alert on his feet. He hit the ball with the strength of a lumberjack and he had the courage of a lion but he was no neanderthal clubber. He was a sensitive cricketer who, when he tried to bat at No. 3, had to switch back to opening because waiting to go in made him sick with nerves. When a car accident robbed him of his left eye — his sighting eye — England's doubting selectors were about to give him an overdue extended run in the team. He was 27 and probably at his peak. When he died in 1990, aged 48, even those who never saw him bat felt a sad sense of waste and loss.

Milburn's roots were deep in County Durham where his father was a big-hitting professional in the Tyneside League, and news of the boy's potential quickly spread south. As a schoolboy he scored a century against the 1959 Indians in what was his first and only game for Durham. Warwickshire wanted him and offered him £10 a week; down the M1 Northamptonshire secretary Ken Turner offered him £10.10s. (£10.50p) and Milburn signed. 'It was the best ten bob I ever spent,' said Turner.

Early in 1960 a series of colossal scores for the second team took him into the championship side but there were still complaints about his size. It was claimed he was vulnerable against off-spin, partly because of his bulk which inevitably kept his bat away from his pads and left a gap. He tried to diet one year, depriving himself and training hard, but when he could not get below 16 stone, he gave up the unequal battle. Several times his mighty shots resulted in burst trousers — it happened once in a Test — and 'Ollie' would smile, hugely enjoying the joke with the crowd. And how they loved him. He came on to the scene when English cricket was so desperately short of excitement and suddenly everyone wanted to see him do well. He did not disappoint them, scoring runs with the gusto of a big man simply having fun.

His first Test came in 1966 against the powerful West Indians and he was run out for a duck in the first innings. In the second he went from 88 to 94 with a six off spinner Lance Gibbs, then was out next ball trying to repeat the feat. In the next Test he went on the rampage with an undefeated 126 but after some modest scores in the next two, he was dropped for the last of the series. The selectors could never come to terms with his size and there was a tendency not to take his ability seriously. They complained about his lack of mobility in the field but his 43 catches in a summer, mainly at short leg, remains a Northamptonshire record.

He played two Tests in each of the next two summers but if England did not want him, Australia did, and he was an enormous success with Western Australia. He was in Perth when he was called into the 1969 tour of Pakistan and scored 139 in his only Test innings on foreign soil before the match in Karachi was abandoned after a riot.

Milburn... smiling through adversity

Milburn... on the rampage

The next summer started explosively for Milburn. He helped Northants beat the touring West Indians and that fateful evening he joined the victory celebrations. The crash saw him thrown through the windscreen, he lost his left eye and damaged the right. He tried to play again in 1973 and '74 but it was no good. He continued to turn out in charity matches and make occasional appearances at Test matches as a commentator. He was ever-cheerful, but it was a brave front and his heart gave out on him on a cold February evening in an inhospitable pub car park in Newton Aycliffe in his beloved County Durham. He is commemorated at the Northamptonshire County Ground where they have named the players' favourite bar after him. 'Ollie' would have appreciated that.

C. MILBURN born 23.10.41 (Burnopfield, County Durham). Died 28.2.90. Tests 9 runs 654 average 46.71 100s 2

JOHN MORRIS
Derbyshire 3 Tests 1990-

A FLY-PAST in a Tiger Moth on the 1990-91 Australian tour grounded John Morris' Test career. A talented and potentially destructive middle-order batsman, he finally achieved Test status with limited opportunities against India in 1990. Morris' inclination to enjoy life, however, did not impress the England management, who saw the pleasure flight with David Gower during an up-county game in Queensland as confirmation of their doubts about his application. Since that tour he has seen others move ahead of him on the waiting list for Test places.

J.E. MORRIS born 1.4.64 (Crewe, Cheshire). Tests 3 runs 71 average 23.66

JOHN MORTIMORE
Gloucestershire 9 Tests 1959-64

T ALL, lean and composed, John Mortimore was a notable member of Gloucestershire's stable of post-War spinners. While fellow off- spinner David Allen turned the ball more, 'Morty' coaxed batsmen to their downfall with accuracy and cunning. Also a resolute lower-order batter, he was unfortunate to be born into an era blessed with world-class slow bowlers and most of his Test cricket was restricted to appearances on tour. During his 26-year

John Mortimore

career at Bristol he captained the county for three seasons, scored more than 15,000 runs and took more than 1,000 wickets.

For further illustration see Mike Smith

J.B. MORTIMORE born 14.5.33 (Bristol). Tests 9 runs 243 average 24.30 wickets 13 average 56.38

ALAN MOSS
Middlesex 9 Tests 1954-60

T HE product of a London newspaper's find-a-player scheme, Alan Moss was a thoughtful, enthusiastic swing bowler who, given the right conditions, could run through a team. During his National Service he saved up his RAF leave so he could play for Middlesex and his keenness was rewarded in 1954 with

Alan Moss

the first of two tours of the Caribbean. A pillar of Middlesex's side throughout the 1950s, he sparred with a Test career without ever looking totally convincing at the highest level. Appropriately, he went into the printing trade after he stopped playing.

A.E. MOSS born 14.11.30 (Tottenham, London). Tests 9 runs 61 average 10.16 wickets 21 average 29.80

MARTYN MOXON
Yorkshire 10 Tests 1986-

T HE Yorkshire captaincy, far from being the millstone that many predicted, has been the making of Martyn Moxon, who has emerged as a candidate for the England leadership. Despite limited Test opportunities, the ability and temperament of this thoughtful opener, who learned much from Geoff Boycott, has rarely been in doubt. Bad luck has dogged his career at vital stages: a broken arm delayed his Test debut for two years, his first tour was curtailed by the death of his father, his first tour as England 'A' captain was ended in the first week by injury. Moxon remained very close to a Test return in the winter of 1992-93 when he led England 'A' to Australia and was on stand-by for the senior tour of India.

M.D. MOXON born 4.5.60 (Barnsley, Yorkshire). Tests 10 runs 455 average 28.43

Martyn Moxon

TIM MUNTON
Warwickshire 2 Tests 1992-

CONSISTENT county performances had their reward for Tim Munton when he was called up for a brace of Tests against Pakistan in 1992 as England struggled to find the right fast bowling combination. At 6ft 6in, with an ability to make the ball swing, Munton is at his best in English conditions and was overlooked for both the tour to India and the 'A' team trip to Australia during the 1992-93 winter.

T.A. MUNTON born 30.7.65 (Melton Mowbray, Leicestershire). Tests 2 runs 25 average 25.0 wickets 4 average 50.0

JOHN MURRAY
Middlesex 21 Tests 1961-67

MIDDLESEX tried to persuade John Murray that his batting technique was good enough for him to open the innings, but he would not have it. He loved his wicketkeeping too much and did not want to do anything that might detract from his work behind the stumps. His attitude was that if the runs came they were a bonus. He paid little attention to his elegant batting and paid the price at Test level.

As an athletic, poised 'keeper, Murray was the high-class gloveman

John Murray

England had been looking for since Godfrey Evans' departure. And his batting was good enough to bring him 1,000 runs in a season six times with Middlesex and a century in Test cricket against the West Indies in 1966 having gone in at No. 9. Throughout the 1960s he was on the England scene, selected for six major tours, yet he frequently missed out because of injuries early in his career and later because the selectors favoured the sounder batting of Jim Parks.

When Murray suffered a 'pair' against Pakistan at Lord's in 1967, the selectors tried a young Kentish player named Alan Knott and from that moment job opportunities with England for the rest of the wicketkeeping fraternity became distinctly limited. Murray set a world record with his 1527 first-class dismissals which was surpassed in 1983 by Bob Taylor. He served as a selector in 1977 and '78.

J.T. MURRAY born 1.4.35 (North Kensington, London). Tests 21 runs 506 average 22.0 100s 1 dismissals 55 caught 52 stumped 3

PHIL NEWPORT
Worcestershire 3 Tests 1988-

PHIL Newport, one of the most effective swing bowlers in county cricket, has failed to convince the selectors that he can be effective at Test level. Seven wickets on his debut against Sri Lanka in 1988 earned him a place on the subsequent India tour, which was cancelled. He struggled in one Test in 1989 and then had to wait until 1991 for another chance, being summoned from the 'A' tour of Sri Lanka for the final Test in Australia. He was in the squad again in 1992 but seemed destined to remain in the wings.

P.J. NEWPORT born 11.10.62 (High Wycombe, Buckinghamshire). Tests 3 runs 110 average 27.50 wickets 10 average 41.70

Phil Newport

CHRIS OLD

Yorkshire and Warwickshire 46 Tests 1972-81

WHEN the mop-haired bank clerk from Middlesbrough turned up in the Headingley nets, Yorkshire were convinced they had discovered England's next great all-rounder. He made his first-class debut at 17 and by the time his 6ft 3in, 14 stone frame had matured, he had all the credentials. He was a big-hitting left-hander with a straight blade and lovely timing, and his right-arm pace bowling was beginning to show real promise. Somewhere it went wrong, although 46 Tests in nine years hardly represents failure. Some days, Chris Old could be too good, his out-swingers and in-cutters consistently doing too much to find the edge of the bat. His steady approach and good action in harness with his height extracted life from the dullest of pitches and he was a master of control, as he demonstrated with his 4 for 41 in 41 overs against Pakistan at Leeds in 1978. They were good days. The bad days for 'Chilly' were frustratingly too frequent.

In 1970 and '71, before he had broken through into the Test side, he had surgery on both knees, and injury was to dominate his career. 'You didn't dare ask how he was in the morning,' says one former skipper, 'because he would run through the medical dictionary.' Possibly the major surgery so early in his career made Old fearful of every ache and pain, and his departures from the field to the physio's couch became part of cricket lore. Old's maladies were such that he inspired one of the bowling impersonation routines that Graham Gooch sometimes ran through on the dullest of final days. Gooch's send-up of 'Chilly' involved agonised back-clutching half-way through the run-up.

It is a sad fact that of the 10 series Old played abroad, he never completed one of them. At home the only summer he was an ever-present was in 1974 when he appeared in all six Tests against India and Pakistan, taking 25 wickets at 22 apiece. Against Pakistan four years later he had another memorable summer, taking 13 in three Tests including a burst of four wickets in five balls in an over at Edgbaston. Old was unfortunate that, with Snow's career on the wane and Willis just emerging, he often found himself cast as the new-ball spearhead and probably tried to bowl too fast when his natural pace was best suited to coming on first change.

His batting drifted and he rarely appeared above No. 8 for England. While he could belligerently dispatch medium pacers and spinners in the county game, he was uncomfortable against pace, particularly the short stuff which he never learned to master. A Test average of 14 with the bat was a travesty for someone with so much ability. He showed how destructive he could be, albeit against occasional bowlers, when he hit a century in 37 minutes — the second 50 took nine minutes — for Yorkshire against Warwickshire in 1977. His brother Alan played once for Warwickshire, as well as regularly for Durham before they achieved first-class status, but was better known as a rugby union international, collecting 16 caps as a fly half with England.

'Chilly' took over the captaincy at Yorkshire in difficult times when the Headingley blood-letting was in full flow, and it was a brief and unhappy tenure. The next summer personal problems affected his performances and he was sacked half-way through the season, manager Ray Illingworth taking over at the age of 50. By this time Old had consigned his Test days to the record books by joining the first rebel tour to South Africa and incurring a three-year international ban. He spent three summers with Warwickshire as a curtain call to a career that achieved much but had promised even more.

C.M. OLD born 22.12.48 (Middlesbrough, Yorkshire). Tests 46 runs 845 average 14.82 wickets 143 average 28.11

Chris Old... getting it all right

days. Nimble, happy anywhere in the order, he was a great technician and one of the best batsmen of his era on a bad wicket. He failed, however, to convert good starts into big scores, reaching 50 129 times in his first-class career but going on to a century on only 32 occasions. That was why England's selectors never thought he warranted more than a fleeting Test opportunity in 1960.

D.E.V. PADGETT born 20.7.34 (Dirk Hall, Yorkshire). Tests 2 runs 51 average 12.75

Charles Palmer

ALAN OAKMAN
Sussex 2 Tests 1956

ALAN Oakman's fleeting acquaintance with Test cricket barely gave him the opportunity to show off his free-flowing batting or off-spin bowling in an era when competition was tough. Sussex's 6ft 6in former Grenadier Guardsman replaced Tom Graveney for two Ashes Tests in 1956 but England victories by an innings meant he had only two knocks. He made more of an impact with his close catching, holding on to five of Jim Laker's 19 victims at Old Trafford. A first-class umpire for a year, he became coach and then cricket administrator at Edgbaston.

A.S.M. OAKMAN born 20.4.30 (Hastings, Sussex). Tests 2 runs 14 average 7

DOUG PADGETT
Yorkshire 2 Tests 1960

MUCH was expected of Doug Padgett when in 1951 he became the youngest player to represent Yorkshire at 16 years 320

Doug Padgett

Ken Palmer

CHARLES PALMER
Worcestershire and Leicestershire
1 Test 1954

CHARLES Palmer's brush with Test cricket involved 22 runs and five wicketless overs but his influence on the game has been considerable. An all-rounder, he made his sole appearance as player-manager on Len Hutton's 1953-54 tour of the West Indies, a trip beset by troubles which Palmer did much to soothe. His input as a softly-spoken diplomat was to reach far and wide. He enjoyed much success as captain-secretary of Leicestershire, served as MCC president and TCCB chairman (1983 to '85) and remains a respected voice.

C.H. PALMER born 15.5.19 (Old Hill, Staffordshire). Tests 1 runs 22 average 11

KEN PALMER
Somerset 1 Test 1965

KEN Palmer owes his Test cap to being in the right place at the right time. A steady county bowler and useful batsman, he was coaching in Johannesburg when England faced an injury crisis before the last Test of their 1964-65 South Africa tour. Pace bowlers John Price, David Brown and Tom Cartwright were crocked, and Palmer was drafted in for an honour he never expected. He has gone on to make many more Test appearances as an umpire, as has his brother Roy.

K.E. PALMER born 22.4.37 (Winchester, Hampshire). Tests 1 runs 10 average — wickets 1 average 189

PETER PARFITT
Middlesex 37 Tests 1961-72

PETER Parfitt is convinced he was picked by England before he was ready and ignored when he was at his best. Between the summers of 1966 and '72, he made just four Test appearances but was good enough to be asked by chief selector Peter May if he would tour India in 1972-73 under Tony Lewis. By that time, however, 'Parf' had already decided he needed more security and at 35, he quit the game. It is a decision he now regrets.

Parfitt, of Norfolk farming stock,

Peter Parfitt

was a fine sportsman, playing wing-half for Norwich City reserves and in Minor Counties cricket before Middlesex offered him a contract. He was a stocky, powerful left-handed batsman, happy to take on the quicks, and he made a dramatic impact in Test cricket despite his misgivings. In his fourth Test in Pakistan he scored a century and followed that with three more off the Pakistan attack when they visited England the next summer, to record four centuries in five Test innings.

That summer, however, was to be one of only two occasions when Parfitt was to play in a full series, the other being in South Africa in 1964-65. He suffered from a reputation of being a bad starter — he was out in single figures one innings in three during his Test career — and from the competition of the more stylish Graveney and Dexter.

When Fred Titmus stood down at Middlesex, he took over the captaincy but was disappointed to be allowed only two full seasons in charge before Mike Brearley was installed. Confident and convivial, he decided on a publican's life at 35 and took over an inn on the Yorkshire moors, combining the work with speaking engagements before setting up a highly successful business supplying hospitality suites at sporting events.

P.H. PARFITT born 8.12.36 (Billingford, Norfolk). Tests 37 runs 1882 average 40.91 100s 7 wickets 12 average 47.83

JIM PARKS
Sussex and Somerset 46 Tests 1954-68

JIM Parks must have bent down to tie his bootlace whenever fate swung a cruel blow his way. Jim, a cheerful companion, had the happy knack of being in the right place at the right time. Luck, however, may bring one England appearance but it will not get you through a 46-Test career. Parks was a gifted batsman and a most effective wicketkeeper, and few of his contemporaries will complain about his contribution. Although he never suggested he was in the same class as Godfrey Evans before him or Alan Knott after, Parks had safe hands and was a good stopper.

For a while Parks wondered if, like his father Jim senior before the War, he would be a one-Test wonder. He was called up as a 22-year-old batsman in 1954 to face Pakistan, made 15 and drifted away from the scene until the winter of 1956, when he was included in Peter May's squad for South Africa. He was soon to return home, however, after being hit on the head during fielding practice and suffering a recurrence of the double-vision he had first been troubled with when he was kicked on the head playing Sussex League soccer with Haywards Heath. Back at Sussex he carried on scoring fluent runs but the next England chance looked elusive.

In 1958, Sussex captain Robin Marlar made a momentous suggestion. The county were struggling for a 'keeper and Marlar proposed Parks should have a go. This was quite a turnaround for a player who had first broken through as a leg-spinner batting at No. 10 in 1949, been picked by England as a batsman and was now being asked to keep wicket, something he had done only a couple of times before in emergencies. He gave it a go and, in his first full season as a 'keeper, made 93 dismissals and scored 2,313 runs.

The next opportunity was to open up early in 1960 while England were touring the Caribbean. May, the

captain, had to fly home because of illness and, with Ken Barrington also on the sick list, England needed a replacement fast. Parks, coaching in Trinidad, acclimatised and fit, was the perfect choice and joined the party. Although England had two specialist 'keepers with them in Roy Swetman and Keith Andrew, they decided to pack the batting for the final Test and go for the draw that would clinch the series. Parks was drafted in and, batting at No. 7, scored an unbeaten century. His reputation as a batsman-wicketkeeper was made and through the mid-1960s Parks was to become a permanent member of the side. Twice, when illness ravaged the England team in India in 1963-64, he played as a specialist batsman but for the rest of the time, he rarely had the opportunity to let his batting blossom as it had once promised.

At Sussex the Parks name was something of an institution. Before the War his father and uncle, Harry Parks, had been prominent, but sadly it turned a little sour for Jim.

Appointed captain in 1967, he quit mid-way through the next summer because he felt he did not have the support of the players or the backing of the committee. In the winter of 1973, Sussex were looking to groom a younger 'keeper and a dispute with cricket chairman Eddie Harrison led to Parks leaving, so ending an unbroken 46-year association between the Parks family and Hove. The tradition could have gone on longer because there was another generation, Bobby, Jim's son, in the pipeline. Jim, already in a good job with Whitbread, moved on to Somerset for four seasons to play out his days and Bobby joined Hampshire, himself keeping once in a Test at Lord's after coming on as a substitute fielder in 1986. Happily, Jim Parks was to return to Hove where he became marketing manager.

J.M. PARKS born 21.10.31 (Haywards Heath, Sussex). Tests 46 runs 1962 average 32.16 100s 2 wickets 1 average 51 dismissals 114 caught 103 stumped 11

Taking guard... Jim Parks

For further illustration see Mike Smith

Paul Parker

Gilbert Parkhouse

PAUL PARKER
Sussex and Durham 1 Test 1981

PAUL Parker, an elegant middle-order batsman and athletic fielder, never found the right form at the right time. When England were in need of new talent, Parker was not scoring the runs to back up his claims. His one chance came in the final Test of 1981 with the Ashes already won. He took David Gower's place but his first innings lasted only three deliveries, his second not much longer, and his hopes of a tour place were gone. He left Sussex after four years of captaincy to join Durham's adventure into first-class cricket.

P.W.G. PARKER born 15.1.56 (Bulawayo, Zimbabwe). Tests 1 runs 13 average 6.50

GILBERT PARKHOUSE
Glamorgan 7 Tests 1950-59

THE feeling that Glamorgan cricketers have to do something extra to convince the England selectors may well have been born out of the experiences of Gilbert Parkhouse. A self-centred approach did not make him the easiest of team-mates, but his contemporaries agree that this nimble, stylish middle-order batsman should have won many more caps. He went on the 1950-51 tour of Australia when England were crushed and was then ignored for eight years. He returned against India with scores of 78,17 and 49 only to be discarded for good. Played rugby union with Swansea.

W.G.A. PARKHOUSE born 12.10.25 (Swansea). Tests 7 runs 373 average 28.69

TONY PIGOTT
Sussex 1 Tests 1984

TONY Pigott, a promising fast bowler, was playing for Wellington in New Zealand during the winter of 1983-84 when the SOS came from an injury-stricken touring England side. Could he cancel his forthcoming wedding — England had a more pressing engagement in Christchurch? 'Lester' put off his bride and took a wicket with his seventh ball in Test cricket — but the honeymoon did not last long. England lost inside 12 hours of actual play, being bowled out twice for fewer than 100. Pigott's Test aspirations have since been hampered by injuries rather than marital plans.

A.C.S. PIGOTT born 4.6.58 (Fulham, London). Tests 1 runs 12 average 12 wickets 2 average 37.50

Tony Pigott

WINSTON PLACE
Lancashire 3 Tests 1948

WINSTON Place was entitled to wonder at the injustice of life, having been dropped by England after scoring a century. A dependable rather than destructive opener, Place went with an under-strength England team to the West Indies in 1947-48, taking the place of his Lancashire colleague Cyril Washbrook, who was not available. Place failed in his first five innings but scored 107 in the last Test batting at No. 3, only to be ignored by the selectors as they tried all sorts of batting combinations against Australia the following summer.

W. PLACE born 7.12.14 (Rawtenstall, Lancashire). Tests 3 runs 144 average 28.80 100s 1

PAT POCOCK
Surrey 25 Tests 1968-85

THE selectors never really trusted Pat Pocock, although he was one of the most authentic spin bowlers of his generation. Pocock's action was

Pat Pocock

textbook high; he spun the ball, varied his angles and had a sweet loop. But when it came to Test cricket, 'Percy' was considered something of a luxury. Far safer to go in with the more reliable Underwood, Illingworth or Emburey. Pocock bubbled with enthusiasm for cricket whether asked to play it or talk about it. Patience was not one of his assets and he loved to experiment if the batsman was getting on top. Full of theories, particularly in his formative years at Surrey, he never played the percentages game.

Pocock's joy for cricket survived some brutal treatment by the selectors. Taken on the 1967-68 tour of the Caribbean to learn, he found himself playing Test cricket after Fred Titmus lost four toes in a boating accident. The next summer he played in the first Test against Australia, took 6 for 79 in their second innings — and was dropped for Underwood. It

was to be his only Ashes appearance and, although he went on three subsequent England tours, he had to wait another eight years for his next home Test in 1976, when he made two appearances against the West Indies.

His next recall was eight years and 86 Tests later — only Derek Shackleton (103 Tests) and Les Jackson (96) have had a longer wait between international duties. The captaincy of David Gower provided Pocock with a happy sign-off to his England days with three Tests in 1984 and a place on that winter's tour of India, on which he formed a successful partnership with Phil Edmonds. He captained Surrey in 1986, his final season, but found the responsibility took the fun out of playing, and fun was 'Percy's' stock in trade.

P.I. POCOCK born 24.9.46 (Bangor, Caernarvonshire). Tests 25 runs 206 average 6.24 wickets 67 average 44.41

DICK POLLARD
Lancashire 4 Tests 1946-48

DICK Pollard probably reached his peak as a swing and seam bowler of great stamina in 1938, when he took 149 wickets before having to swap his whites for Army khaki. When peace returned, Pollard, still in the Army, played his first Test in 1946, taking 5 for 24 against India on a damp Old Trafford wicket. He toured Australia with scant success but his enthusiastic efforts brought two more Tests in 1948 and despite his feat of removing Bradman in successive games, the selectors were already looking for a younger partner for Alec Bedser.

For illustration see Bill Voce

R. POLLARD born 19.6.12 (Westhoughton, Lancashire). Died 16.12.85. Tests 4 runs 13 average 13 wickets 15 average 25.20

CYRIL POOLE
Nottinghamshire 3 Tests 1951-52

CYRIL Poole, an enterprising left-handed batsman, could be a thrilling destroyer of attacks but his attention to defence often left something to be desired. His Test chance came when John Ikin withdrew from a second-string MCC squad bound for India in 1951. One of seven new caps on tour, Poole made two half-centuries on his debut but when he returned home he never convinced the selectors he deserved another chance. Played football for Gillingham and Mansfield.

For illustration see Allan Watkins

C.J. POOLE born 13.3.21 (Mansfield, Nottinghamshire). Tests 3 runs 161 average 40.25

GEORGE POPE
Derbyshire 1 Test 1947

GEORGE Pope was a gifted all-rounder with a cantankerous streak who would have played much Test cricket if the War had not rudely interrupted. Chosen for the abandoned 1939-40 India tour, he refused to play in one unofficial Test at the end of the War because it meant missing a profitable league

match. His sole appearance came against South Africa in 1947, but he was sacked the next season by Derbyshire after another disagreement, later returning to cricket as an umpire. Brothers Harold and Alf also played for Derbyshire.

G.H. POPE born 27.6.11 (Tibshelf, Derbyshire). Tests 1 runs 8 average — wickets 1 average 85

JOHN PRICE
Middlesex 15 Tests 1964-72

COMING in off a long, curved run that started somewhere near deep mid-off, John Price made rapid strides after a late start in county cricket at 24. A great trier who generated pace and swing, he claimed his place on the 1963-64 tour of India and was a Test regular for two years. Injuries, particularly to his back, disrupted his progress but he was recalled by England after a six-year absence in 1971, continuing to do a job that was dependable but never destructive.

J.S.E. PRICE born 22.7.37 (Harrow, Middlesex). Tests 15 runs 66 average 7.33 wickets 40 average 35.02

ROGER PRIDEAUX
Kent, Northamptonshire and Sussex 3 Tests 1968-69

THE biggest impact Roger Prideaux made on Test cricket happened when he did not play. A gutsy, powerfully-built opener, Prideaux scored a debut 64 in the fourth Test of 1968 but withdrew from the final Test because of a cold, allowing Basil D'Oliveira to make a sensational return. It sparked a chain

Roger Prideaux

of events which became the 'D'Oliveira Affair' and led to South Africa's isolation. Prideaux, elected the first chairman of the Cricketers' Association when it was formed in 1967, made two more undistinguished Test appearances in Pakistan.

R.M. PRIDEAUX born 13.7.39 (London). Tests 3 runs 102 average 20.40

DEREK PRINGLE
Essex 30 Tests 1982-

DEREK Pringle has become something of a cult figure in English cricket. A line in T-shirts emblazoned with 'I saw Derek Pringle's comeback Test' would be a big seller. Not only has Pringle made enough comebacks but also now he has enough fans. From being sneered at by the Headingley hardcore as an educated southern softie with an earring, he is now welcomed with affection on every ground in the country. 'Pring' takes the adulation with the same shrug of his massive shoulders he used to reserve for the hecklers.

George Pope

John Price

At 6ft 5in and hovering about 16 stone, Pringle looks like he should be the most explosive cricketer since Ian Botham. That was part of his trouble: in his early days he was compared ludicrously with Botham. Pringle neither bowls very fast nor hits the ball very hard but he is a fine technician and a great trier.

Pringle's late father Don, based in Nairobi, played for East Africa in the 1975 World Cup. Seven years later Derek had to forgo the honour of captaining Cambridge to play for England, the last time a university student was summoned to play Test cricket. A great deal was expected, the results were modest.

England had to wait another two years for Pringle's maiden half-century and first five-wicket haul, but both achievements came against the West Indies, proving his ability. The great frustration was that he could never demolish the weaker opponents. So often effective in typically English conditions of the sort found at an overcast Headingley, Pringle rarely toured. After going to Australia in 1982-83, he had to wait 10 years for his next tour to Australasia, playing in the World Cup to claim a unique father-son double. Interested in archaeology, photography, writing, real ale and the more obscure musical trends, Pringle rarely wastes his winters fretting over the next recall.

D.R. PRINGLE born 18.9.58 (Nairobi, Kenya). Tests 30 runs 695 average 15.10 wickets 70 average 35.97

Derek Pringle

GEOFF PULLAR
Lancashire and Gloucestershire
28 Tests 1959-63

WHEN Geoff Pullar heard he was going to open the batting for England he thought the selectors must have made a mistake. A calm, stylish left-hander settled in the Lancashire middle-order, he had never opened before in his life. But on the recommendation of his skipper Cyril Washbrook when England were facing a crisis at the top of the order against India in 1959, the selectors pushed him in for the third Test.

It was an inspired move. A partnership of 146 with Gilbert Parkhouse, recalled after eight years, was an English record against India. In the next Test, Pullar became the first Lancashire player to score a Test century at Old Trafford when he rattled up 131, and for the next four years his name was virtually an automatic inclusion. All but one of his 49 Test innings were at the top of the list — the exception was when injury forced him down to No. 11 — and a Test average of 43 made him one of England's most successful post-War openers. Yet Pullar confesses he never felt comfortable going in first.

He was 'Noddy' to everyone in cricket, not because of his penchant for dozing in the dressing room, but after the Enid Blyton character his team-mates once caught him watching on TV. An arthritic knee forced him home from a tour of Australia in 1962-63 and brought an end to his Test days, but still he plundered runs for Lancashire until a clash with chairman Tommy Higson, who accused him of being a bad influence on younger players, saw him leave in 1968 to finish his career with two summers for Gloucestershire. When he stopped playing he carried on opening... as proprietor of a shoal of fish and chip shops.

G. PULLAR born 1.8.35 (Swinton, Lancashire). Tests 28 runs 1974 average 43.86 100s 4 wickets 1 average 37.00

Geoff Pullar

NEAL RADFORD
Lancashire and Worcestershire
3 Tests 1986-88

NEAL Radford took a circuitous route to Test cricket. Born in Zambia, educated in South Africa, he spent five unsuccessful years at Old Trafford before being sacked and moving to Worcester in 1985. Then, at 28, his career was transformed and his bustling, enthusiastic fast-medium bowling made him the most successful bowler in the championship. Qualified for England by residence, he made his debut in 1986 and toured New Zealand in 1988, and while his lack of pace denied him success at the top level, it was never for want of effort.

N.V. RADFORD born 7.6.57 (Launshya, Zambia). Tests 3 runs 21 average 7 wickets 4 average 87.75

CLIVE RADLEY
Middlesex 8 Tests 1978

CLIVE Radley's crab-like stance was never pretty but it was effective, and there was no more determined batsman on the circuit during his 24 summers at Lord's. Tutored by former Middlesex favourite Bill Edrich at Norfolk, Radley scored heavily — many of his runs were uncannily quick singles — which won him Test recognition at 33

Clive Radley

on the 1978 tour of New Zealand. He made a confident start, and his second innings was an 11-hour vigil for 158. After a successful summer, he toured Australia but could not break into the side again, retiring with a Test average the envy of many a more stylish batsman. Currently MCC head coach.

C.T. RADLEY born 13.5.44 (Hertford). Tests 8 runs 481 average 48.10 100s 2

MARK RAMPRAKASH
Middlesex 9 Tests 1991-

THE intensity Mark Ramprakash invests in his elegant batting spilled over too often for England's selectors in 1992. He was left at home to ponder where his immensely promising career was going while England teams travelled to India and Australia early in 1993 without him. A tough debut series full of resolve, if not runs, against the West Indies in 1991 had marked Ramprakash out as a batsman of precocious talent, but clashes with opponents and supporters brought a fine, suspension and warnings from his county and a cooling off period from England.

M.R. RAMPRAKASH born 5.9.69 (Bushey, Hertfordshire). Tests 9 runs 241 average 17.21

Mark Ramprakash

Dermot Reeve

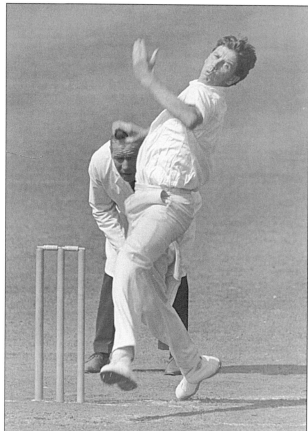

Harold Rhodes

DERMOT REEVE
Sussex and Warwickshire
3 Tests 1992-

DERMOT Reeve was summoned for the 1992 New Zealand tour when Angus Fraser withdrew through injury. An innovative nudger of runs and teasing swing bowler, Reeve is at his most effective in the one-day game but he played in all three Tests. His eagerness to succeed has been known to rub opponents up the wrong way but that makes him a good tourist, and he was selected again for the 1993 trip to India. A former Hong Kong sports personality of the year for his cricketing exploits in the colony, he was prompted by ambition to leave Sussex and he took over the Warwickshire captaincy in 1993.

D.A. REEVE born 2.4.63 (Hong Kong). Tests 3 runs 124 average 24.80 wickets 2 average 30.00

HAROLD RHODES
Derbyshire 2 Tests 1959

HAROLD Rhodes' promising England career as a fast bowler was blighted by doubts about his action. He played two Tests in 1959 but the next year umpire Paul Gibb no-balled him six times for throwing in one innings. Rhodes' loose-jointed arm bent backwards from the elbow, giving the impression that he threw.

Dick Richardson

Most umpires were happy but he was still called occasionally and only after enquiries and filmed evidence was he cleared by Lord's in 1968. By then it was too late for Rhodes, who quit the first-class game the next year.

H.J. RHODES born 22.7.36 (Hadfield, Derbyshire). Tests 2 runs 0 average — wickets 9 average 27.11

DEREK 'DICK' RICHARDSON
Worcestershire 1 Test 1957

DICK Richardson's Test career was brief but historic. When he played in the same team as his more famous brother, Peter, at Trent Bridge in 1957 against the West Indies, it was the first and, to date, only instance this century of siblings appearing in the same team for England. The selectors, however, saw little future in his free-flowing left-handed batting in the middle order and the family ties were swiftly broken.

D.W. RICHARDSON born 3.11.34 (Hereford). Tests 1 runs 33 average 33

DEREK RANDALL

Nottinghamshire 47 Tests 1977-84

IT IS very difficult to say Derek Randall without smiling. The Retford imp was, and still is, one of the most fondly admired figures in the game. His is a figure that is unmistakable, from his coat-hanger shoulders down to those flapping size elevens. The rolling gait and big, sad eyes make him Chaplinesque — and like all clowns, there is pathos behind the public image. Randall is a serious batsman, whose failures wound deeply and fill him with gnawing self-doubt. Much of the perpetual malarky masks a shy man.

He came into cricket late, perhaps that is why he questions himself. The love of cricket first played in his backyard in Retford, imagining he was his hero Tom Graveney, with his mother bowling unchanged from the scullery end, has not been dulled by 20 years in the professional game. He is still refreshingly excited in a fresh-scrubbed sort of way each day he turns up at Trent Bridge. Randall obviously had an exceptional eye as a young player. He may have shuffled and twitched at the crease as the bowler ran in, but he played natural shots, mixing impudence with a sound idea of preserving his wicket. And no-one should be fooled into thinking that Randall does not have a shrewd cricket brain. His constant talking to himself at the crease — 'Come on 'Rags', get forward, watch the ball, nothing stupid 'Rags'' — is his way of training the mind.

'Rags' is one nickname which suits the chaotic mess of his hotel room perfectly. The other, given him by his England colleagues, is 'Arkle', after the racehorse, because of his galloping grace in the field. Most captains believe that Randall's cover fielding is worth at least 20 runs, and there is always the possibility of a spectacular run out and cartwheel celebration to follow.

His England career was launched in India when Tony Greig told him to just be himself in the field or at the crease. The crowds loved his antics of hurling his floppy hat in the air, catching it on his head and finishing with an exaggerated swagger. Soon, bowlers were paying him attention too. It took just one remarkable innings in Melbourne at the end of that Indian tour to make Randall a world figure. The scene was the Centenary Test, England were heading for defeat at the hands of a snorting Dennis Lillee and in came the wide-eyed country boy from Nottinghamshire. He played the innings of his life, and the more eccentric he became the more infuriated were the hard-nosed Australians. Lillee came back time and time again to try to bounce him out. One snorter flicked the Randall cap, but as he fell backwards he turned it into an acrobatic tumble, landing on his feet again and doffing his cap in one movement to Lillee with: 'No point in hitting me there, mate. There's nothing in it.' In front of the Queen he scored 174 that failed to save the match but made Randall a hero even in Australia.

Inevitably, the next 42 Tests of Randall's career were always going to be a case of 'after the Lord Mayor's Show.' His fervent patriotism sometimes did Randall few favours because he would unhesitatingly bat wherever England asked him, which ranged from No. 1 to No. 7. A shade more selfishness may have brought that extra consistency for which the selectors were always looking. Randall, it seemed, was made a regular scapegoat for the team's failings, and he deserved better. He was always available, always loyal, and his Test average in no way flattered him. He has, after all, appeared in more Tests than any Nottinghamshire cricketer — Simpson, Larwood, Voce, the Hardstaffs, Shrewsbury; he tops the lot. And that 174 in Melbourne is the highest Test score by any Nottinghamshire batsman. Against Middlesex in 1979 he scored 209 and 146, another feat unequalled at Trent Bridge. At times, genius sat on Randall's shoulder — the only trouble was it would not stop fidgeting.

D.W. RANDALL born 24.2.51 (Retford, Nottinghamshire). Tests 47 runs 2470 average 33.37 100s 7

The imp at play... Derek Randall

JACK RICHARDS
Surrey 8 Tests 1986-88

AN ABILITY to rub people up the wrong way counted against Jack Richards, England's most gifted wicketkeeper-batsman since Alan Knott. Always competitive, often outspoken and sometimes disruptive, Richards was alert and agile with the gloves although prone to the odd lapse. He worked so hard on his batting that he became good enough to score a Test century. Those talents sparkled on the 1986-87 Ashes tour but after playing the last two Tests of 1988, he split with Surrey, walking out of cricket at 30 and moving to Holland.

C.J. RICHARDS born 10.8.58 (Penzance, Cornwall). Tests 8 runs 285 average 21.92 100s 1 dismissals 21 caught 20 stumped 1

PETER RICHARDSON
Worcestershire and Kent
34 Tests 1956-63

PETER Richardson was one of cricket's great characters although you would never have guessed it watching him bat. As a left-handed opener he was a great fighter, a nudger and a pusher rather than a fluent hitter. He was feared by slow bowlers for his lap to leg. Yet off the field he was a one-man entertainment show, particularly when the troops were stuck in some up-country billet in India. His sense of humour and sharp mind enlivened many a dull official function to the delight of his team-mates. His love of a prank continued after his playing days with outrageous letters from fictitious Colonel Blimps to the *Telegraph*.

Yet on the field he was a sober, dependable sort. For three years he was an automatic choice opening the England innings home and abroad. He was particularly successful against the 1957 West Indians with Ramadhin and Valentine, averaging almost 60 in the series and scoring two centuries. He played as an amateur for ten summers at Worcestershire, doubling up as captain and assistant secretary in his latter days, before taking a year out to qualify for Kent as a professional, becoming a more expansive run-maker and winning back his place in the Test side. He toured the sub-continent in 1961-62 and then returned for a one-off appearance against the 1963 West Indians.

His brother Derek (better known as Dick), another left-handed batsman, also played at New Road and in 1957 they appeared together in the third Test against the West Indies. It is the only instance of brothers playing in the same England Test side this century. A third brother, Bryan, yet another left-hander, had five seasons with Warwickshire.

For further illustration see Ken Barrington

P.E. RICHARDSON born 4.7.31 (Hereford). Tests 34 runs 2061 average 37.47 100s 5 wickets 3 average 16

Peter Richardson

Fred Ridgeway

FRED RIDGEWAY
Kent 5 Tests 1951-52

IN THE days when leading performers often declined to tour India, many fringe players were given the chance to wear the cap. One such player was Fred Ridgeway, a shortish fast bowler who skimmed the ball through with some hostility. Having had a Test trial in 1949 and been 12th man at Lord's in 1951, Ridgeway was one of seven players to make Test debuts in the first three Tests that winter. He opened the bowling with Brian Statham throughout the series but with little success and returned to county cricket.

F. RIDGEWAY born 10.8.23 (Stockport, Cheshire). Tests 5 runs 49 average 8.16 wickets 7 average 54.14

Jack Robertson (left) going out to bat for the MCC, New Delhi 1951, with Frank Lowson

JACK ROBERTSON
Middlesex 11 Tests 1947-52

JACK Robertson, an elegant, masterful opener, must have been one of the most unfortunate players of the 1950s. The dominance of Hutton and Washbrook limited his Test chances to tours of the Caribbean and India when leading players opted out. He played two home Tests only when injuries allowed and discovered in 1949 that even a century at Lord's could not keep him in the side. England's batting was so strong that space could not be found for him down the order but, despite a Test average the envy of most, Robertson was never heard to complain.

For further illustration see Allan Watkins

J.D.B. ROBERTSON born 22.2.17 (Chiswick, London). Tests 11 runs 881 average 46.36 100s 2 wickets 2 average 29.0

TIM ROBINSON
Nottinghamshire 29 Tests 1984-89

TIM Robinson modelled himself unashamedly on Geoff Boycott and for one glorious year it looked as if England had found a chip off the old blocker. The softly-spoken Nottinghamshire lad with a degree in accountancy from Sheffield University slipped into Test cricket with the calm assurance of the genuine article. His county opening colleague Chris Broad had stood up commendably to the West Indian pace onslaught during the summer of 1984, but out of the blue that autumn the selectors switched horses and named the right-handed Robinson to open in India.

Their choice was inspired and in his second Test, 'Robbo' played a match-winning eight-and-a-half-hour innings of 160. Patient and with the full range of strokes, Robinson used to mutter to himself when weariness struck: 'Boycott wouldn't get out now, I mustn't get out.'

Of his four Test centuries, the lowest was 148. There was more run-plundering with two centuries against Australia, and in his first 11 Tests he had scored close to 1,000 runs at an average of 62.

Then came the West Indies.

Tim Robinson

Brutally the Robinson technique and temperament were stripped bare. He came home from the Caribbean in 1986 shell-shocked by Marshall, Garner and Patterson. He had scored 72 runs in eight innings and all but two of his scores were in single figures.

He returned to Test cricket a year later with 166 against Pakistan, but all too frequently he was being found out by the new ball and a hostile attack before he had set out his stall. Robinson was recalled for the fourth Test against Australia in 1989 but before the match was over it had been revealed that he was one of 16 players signed up for a rebel tour of South Africa that winter.

R.T. ROBINSON born 21.11.58 (Sutton-in-Ashfield, Nottinghamshire). Tests 29 runs 1601 average 36.38 100s 4

Graham Roope

run in 1977. He toured Pakistan and New Zealand that winter and kept his place the following summer against the same opponents until the selectors decided enough was enough — and reinstated Geoff Boycott.

When Roope finished at the Oval in 1982, with almost 20,000 runs from his first-class career, he returned to Berkshire, where it had all started for him in the Minor Counties League 20 years earlier.

G.R.J. ROOPE born 12.7.46 (Fareham, Hampshire). Tests 21 runs 860 average 30.71

BRIAN ROSE
Somerset 9 Tests 1977-81

EYE trouble in the glaring light of the Caribbean forced Brian Rose home early from the 1981 tour and ended his Test career, although he carried on playing in glasses. After a moderate tour of Pakistan and New Zealand in 1977-78, this handsome left-handed batsman was recalled to face the West Indies in 1980 but he never relished the battle against hostile bowling. While he failed to convince in the Test arena, as an astute Somerset captain he led the county to their first five titles in six years, and is currently cricket chairman at Taunton.

B.C. ROSE born 4.6.50 (Dartford, Kent). Tests 9 runs 358 average 25.57

Brian Rose

GRAHAM ROOPE
Surrey 21 Tests 1973-78

GRAHAM Roope was one of those cricketers who thrilled spectators and frustrated selectors. Tall and stylish, there was a touch of class about his middle-order batting. He could make the ball swing at medium pace and his slip fielding was what you would expect from a Corinthian Casuals goalkeeper. He was also a highly competent stand-in wicketkeeper and as a former selector said: 'He looked the part — but never played it.'

In 21 Tests, Roope passed 50 seven times but never travelled further than 77. He had a run of eight Tests in 1973 before the selectors lost patience. They felt this gregarious, easy-going character lacked the steel for international cricket but his continued good form for Surrey won him another extended

FRED RUMSEY
Worcestershire, Somerset and Derbyshire 5 Tests 1964-65

BUILT like a battering ram with finesse to match, Fred Rumsey crashed on to the Test scene for a few vividly entertaining performances of left-arm fast bowling when England were hit by injuries. His opening bursts were distinctly hostile but a girth that would horrify the modern fitness-orientated English regime took its toll in later spells. For such a *bon viveur* who spread his career around three counties, it was natural that Fred should go into the travel business when he stopped playing.

F.E. RUMSEY born 4.12.35 (Stepney, London). Tests 5 runs 30 average 15 wickets 17 average 27.11

ROBERT 'JACK' RUSSELL
Gloucestershire 31 Tests 1988-

JACK Russell has had to take other people's failures stoically on the chin. England's struggle to find a genuine all-round replacement for Ian Botham and the batting frailty of others have often drawn the selectors to the same conclusion: jettison the wicketkeeper.

Russell appeared destined to join England's dynasty of great post-War 'keepers — Evans, Knott and Taylor — during his early days at Gloucestershire. Like most stumpers, Russell was cheerfully independent in his lone occupation. His dedication to his cause, safe hands and nimble reactions made him stand out and, once the selectors had conquered their nerves about his batting, he grabbed his place in the final Test of 1988 against Sri Lanka. Jack's batting was quirky, he was susceptible to the quick stuff, but, aware of the selectors' concern, he worked feverishly at improving his defences. The result was 94 in his first Test innings.

The next summer against Australia, England had a disastrous time but Russell, with the bravest of centuries at Old Trafford, finished the series third in the England averages. He thought he had proved his point. He remained ever-present for the next three series but whenever England found themselves in a corner, Russell was under pressure. The arrival of Alec Stewart as a batsman who could keep well enough, gave the selectors the option of handing him the gloves, which they did with increasing frequency to strengthen the batting or the bowling.

Russell was depressed to find himself out of the 1992 World Cup despite a good all-round tour of New Zealand but worse was to come the following winter in India when England dispensed with a specialist 'keeper altogether. As a sop to Russell, he was made vice-captain of the 'A' tour to Australia and left to wonder if his special skills would ever be called upon again.

R.C. RUSSELL born 15.8.63 (Stroud, Gloucestershire). Tests 31 runs 1060 average 27.18 100s 1 dismissals 83 caught 75 stumped 8

Jack Russell

ERIC RUSSELL
Middlesex 10 Tests 1961-67

A SMOOTH, assured opening batsman, Eric Russell suffered from never getting a settled sequence in the England team. His 10 Tests were spread over seven series and five countries, and two half-centuries in 18 innings did not do his ability justice. The presence of Edrich and Boycott for much of his career did not improve Russell's chances and, say colleagues, neither did a dour nature which did not make him the easiest of dressing-room companions. He had reason to be unhappy on the 1965-66 Ashes tour when hand injuries sabotaged his series in the first Test.

W.E. RUSSELL born 3.5.36 (Dumbarton, Scotland). Tests 10 runs 362 average 21.29

Ian Salisbury

IAN SALISBURY
Sussex 4 Tests 1992-

THE selection of Ian Salisbury against Pakistan in 1992 made cricket romantics rejoice. When he played at Lord's he became the first specialist leg-spinner selected for England since Robin Hobbs in 1971. Although a novice at his chosen art who had originally started life as a seamer, Salisbury showed an impressive temperament in that first series and added to his credentials with a half-century in his second Test. He finished the summer as the leading English wicket-taker and was added to the squad in India after the tour had started.

I.D.K. SALISBURY born 2.1.70 (Northampton). Tests 4 runs 136 average 19.42 wickets 8 average 67

MIKE SELVEY
Surrey, Middlesex and Glamorgan 3 Tests 1976-77

A POWERFUL, intelligent — and, at times, very hairy — swing bowler, Mike Selvey was unfortunate to be at his peak when the queue of pace bowlers waiting to get into the England side was not short of class. A collection of injuries to rivals in 1976 gave him his chance against the West Indies and within 20 deliveries he had put Fredericks, Richards and Kallicharran back in the pavilion. In India that winter, however, John Lever's astonishing entry into Test cricket restricted Selvey to just one more Test on his only tour. After a brief waltz with the Glamorgan captaincy, he turned his astute thoughts to cricket journalism.

M.W.W. SELVEY born 25.4.48 (Chiswick, London). Tests 3 runs 15 average 7.50 wickets 6 average 57.16

Mike Selvey

cricket this century with 8 for 4 against Somerset, had earned his retirement, becoming a coach and an umpire for a few seasons.

D. SHACKLETON born 12.8.24 (Todmorden, Yorkshire). Tests 7 runs 113 average 18.83 wickets 18 average 42.66

PHIL SHARPE
Yorkshire and Derbyshire 12 Tests 1963-69

PHIL Sharpe is possibly unique in that he was selected by England for his exceptional catching ability in the slips. An accomplished but inconsistent middle-order batsman, he was called up to an England side suffering from an attack of 'dropsy' in 1963. After six in-and-out performances he was discarded but in 1969 he returned, again to bolster the fielding. He took his catching tally to 17, batted well (scoring a maiden Test century), and was unlucky there was no tour that winter. Has served recently as an England selector and observer.

For further illustration see Mike Smith

P.J. SHARPE born 27.12.36 (Shipley, Yorkshire). Tests 12 runs 786 average 46.23 100s 1

DEREK SHACKLETON
Hampshire 7 Tests 1950-63

DEREK Shackleton was the forerunner of the bowling machine. There has been no-one more reliable or more accurate in county cricket this century. Sparingly built with a well lubricated right shoulder, 'Shack' wheeled away tirelessly with his right-arm medium-paced bowling over 22 summers for Hampshire. His bowling, like his hair, always seemed immaculate.

No-one has approached Shackleton's record of taking 100 wickets a season on 20 successive occasions. Wilf Rhodes reached 100 wickets 23 times but not consecutively. 'Shack' finished in 1969 with 2,857 first-class wickets, the eighth highest aggregate, at an average of 18.65. And he did all this with sight in only one eye.

He became a bowler by accident, having been signed as a batsman. In 1948, his first season, Hampshire were so short of fire-power that everyone was ordered into the nets and told to bowl fast. Shackleton tried a bit of 'seam-up', discovered he could swing it, and never had to rely on his run-making again.

At Test level his lack of pace would have been found out by the best batsman but it is difficult to understand why he did not play more often when conditions cried out for a specialist English bowler who could make it wobble. He played three Tests in the early 1950s, went on one tour to the sub-continent and then endured a wait of 12 years and 103 Tests, the longest break on record, before being recalled.

In 1963 and rising 39, 'Shack' returned at slow-medium pace to face the West Indies and England rejoiced when the old trooper polished off the opposition with three wickets in four balls. Shackleton, who posted the most remarkable figures in county

Phil Sharpe

RT. REV. DAVID SHEPPARD
Sussex 22 Tests 1950-63

IT **IS** difficult to imagine just what the Australians thought when England arrived at Freemantle for their 1962-63 series with David Sheppard the only member of Ted Dexter's squad not wearing an MCC touring tie. Instead he was sporting his clerical 'dog collar'. These days promoted up the order as the Bishop of Liverpool, the Rt. Rev. David Sheppard remains the only ordained minister to have played Test cricket.

A strong, stylish back-foot player, he could have been one of the leading figures in English cricket through the 1950s but sport was rarely more than a part-time occupation. He broke all manner of university records at Cambridge,

playing for Sussex between studies. As soon as he graduated, Sussex made him skipper and they were transformed from stragglers to title contenders, finishing second.

That was his last summer of full-time cricket but that did not dissuade the MCC the next year, when Len Hutton was unfit, from putting 25-year-old Sheppard in charge of England for two Tests against Pakistan. Sheppard was, however, anything but an Establishment man, being one of the first and most vociferous voices opposed to South Africa's apartheid laws. He refused to tour there in 1956-57 and was still fighting the cause 25 years later as MCC members tried to maintain sporting links with South Africa.

His church work, primarily in London, kept him busy until the latter half of most summers, when he

would play for Sussex and England during his holidays. He never appeared in more than two Tests in any home series. His final summer was 1962 but that winter he took a sabbatical and ended his playing days with eight consecutive Tests in Australia and New Zealand. He became Bishop of Liverpool in 1975.

D.S. SHEPPARD born 6.3.29 (Reigate, Surrey). Tests 22 runs 1172 average 37.80 100s 3

ARNIE SIDEBOTTOM
Yorkshire 1 Test 1985

TALL, talented and dedicated, Arnie Sidebottom probably came closer than anyone to being the first double international since Arthur Milton in the 1950s. He never quite made it in soccer during five years as a defender at Manchester United; he just made it in cricket as a wholehearted swing bowler and capable batsman. He replaced an unfit Neil Foster against Australia in 1985 but an injured toe and a lifeless Trent Bridge wicket did not help Arnie, who might well have played before then but for a three-year ban as one of the 1982 South African rebels.

A. SIDEBOTTOM born 1.4.54 (Barnsley, Yorkshire). Tests 1 runs 2 average 2 wickets 1 average 65

Ken Shuttleworth

Reg Simpson

KEN SHUTTLEWORTH
Lancashire and Leicestershire
5 Tests 1970-71

WHEN Ken Shuttleworth turned up in the Old Trafford nets as a youngster, his magnificent action reminded observers of Fred Trueman. At 6ft 3in with an aggressive streak, 'Shut' had everything going for him — but he could not convert it into results at Test level. He was a great worrier; when things went wrong he fretted endlessly about his technique, which had originally looked second nature. Injuries did not help and his only taste of success came on the 1970-71 tour of Australia and New Zealand.

K. SHUTTLEWORTH born 13.11.44 (St Helens, Lancashire). Tests 5 runs 46 average 7.66 wickets 12 average 35.58

REG SIMPSON
Nottinghamshire 27 Tests 1948-55

REG Simpson was arguably the finest player of fast bowling in his era but his strength was also his weakness. He was essentially a back-foot player, swaying back with the bowler in delivery stride and playing fearless, handsome shots with cool assurance. If the bowler dug it in short, he would simply sway away from danger, not a hair on his immaculate unprotected head out of place.

His style, however, left suspicions about his vulnerability against spin and he was never taken on a tour of India or Pakistan. Len Hutton, in particular, was dubious about Simpson's ability at a time when he was looking for a natural successor to Cyril Washbrook to open the batting with him. Simpson and Hutton did open several times together but nowhere near often enough for Simpson's supporters, who believed he was criminally neglected by England.

It may also be relevant that when Hutton was made England's first professional captain this century, it was Simpson who was the one to miss out, being the senior amateur county captain in the England side at the time, and who might have expected to be offered the job. The pair were never to get on. Simpson was, like Hutton, a dogmatic character who, while he amassed 30,000 first-class runs, had a fairly unsuccessful time in 10 years as skipper at Trent Bridge, but his devotion to the county could not be questioned. A former managing director of bat-makers Gunn and Moore, Simpson has been on the county committee since 1961, serving as chairman and recently as president.

R.T. SIMPSON born 27.2.20 (Sherwood Rise, Nottingham). Tests 27 runs 1401 average 33.35 100s 4 wickets 2 average 11

Gladstone Small

WILF SLACK
Middlesex 3 Tests 1986

WILF Slack's sudden death from a heart attack while batting on a private tour of The Gambia stunned cricket. Few players had been as popular as this self-effacing, dedicated left-handed opener. Slack had suffered three black-outs while playing the previous summer but doctors could find nothing wrong. His England chance came in his native West Indies when Mike Gatting had his nose smashed and Wilf was summoned from the 'B' tour of Sri Lanka, but he was exposed as a fine county player out of his depth in the Test arena.

W.N. SLACK born 12.12.54 (St Vincent, Windward Islands). Died 15.1.89. Tests 3 runs 81 average 13.50

FRANK SMAILES
Yorkshire 1 Test 1946

FRANK Smailes, a captain in the Royal Artillery, surrendered his best years as a cricketer to the War. A swing bowler and left-handed batsman, he played a major part in Yorkshire's pre-War success and was selected for the washed-out Old Trafford Test of 1938. As if to put the record straight, the selectors gave him his cap eight years later — at Lord's against India in England's first Test after the conflict — at the age of 36, shortly before he ended his playing days.

T.F. SMAILES born 27.3.10 (Ripley, Yorkshire). Died 1.12.70. Tests 1 runs 25 average 25 wickets 3 average 20.66

GLADSTONE SMALL
Warwickshire 17 Tests 1986-91

GLADSTONE Small overcame a hunched physique to become a remarkably effective fast-medium bowler and one of the most popular characters on the county circuit. He was on the England scene for six years, playing in two World Cup campaigns in 1987 and '92 but injuries cropped up to prevent him enjoying a long run in the Test side.

G.C. SMALL born 18.10.61 (St George, Barbados). Tests 17 runs 263 average 15.47 wickets 55 average 34.01

Frank Smailes

ALAN SMITH
Warwickshire 6 Tests 1962-63

THE last amateur to play for England before the status was scrapped by the MCC, Alan Smith played all his Tests on a tour of Australasia. Not the most stylish of 'keepers, he went as second choice to John Murray but batted well in the state games and played in the first two Tests. Murray returned but injured a shoulder and Smith took over for the rest of the tour. An enterprising Warwickshire captain and then county secretary, 'AC' has become one of the most influential administrators in the game. A former selector and tour manager, his diplomacy is now put to good use as TCCB chief executive.

A.C. SMITH born 25.10.36 (Hall Green, Birmingham). Tests 6 runs 118 average 29.50 dismissals 20 caught 20

David Smith

Chris Smith

CHRIS SMITH
Glamorgan and Hampshire
8 Tests 1983-86

CHRIS Smith paved the way into English cricket for his more talented younger brother, Robin. Seeing no future in South Africa, Smith qualified for England in 1983 and his resolute batting was soon recognised, although his first Test innings was ended traumatically, first ball, by Richard Hadlee. He kept his place as opener that winter in New Zealand and Pakistan but played only one more Test after that, in 1986, despite consistent performances for Hampshire. Smith emigrated to Australia in 1991 and is currently chief executive of the Western Australian Cricket Association.

C.L. SMITH born 15.10.58 (Durban, South Africa). Tests 8 runs 392 average 30.15

DAVID MARK SMITH
Surrey, Worcestershire and Sussex
2 Tests 1986

DAVID Smith, a powerful 6ft 4in left-hander, made himself into one of the most dominant openers in the country, but a volatile nature and susceptibility to injuries held him back. Smith was sacked and re-employed three times by Surrey and it was with Worcester that he won a place on the 1986 West Indies tour and played two Tests. Called to the Caribbean again in 1990 to replace the injured Graham Gooch, Smith broke a thumb before he could re-state his Test case. Runs a decorating business when not pasting the bowling.

D.M. SMITH born 9.1.56 (Balham, London). Tests 2 runs 80 average 20.00

MIKE SMITH
Leicestershire and Warwickshire 50 Tests 1958-72

MIKE Smith baffled cricketers of his day. 'MJK' was an outstanding middle-order batsman in county cricket. He topped 1,000 runs 19 times, for six consecutive summers (1957 to '62) he scored 2,000 runs, and in 1959 went past 3,000 runs. That year and in 1963 he topped the national averages. Yet on the Test field he struggled to make class tell. He was not a failure — but in 78 innings for England he would have expected many more than three centuries. Perhaps that was why the public never took this scholarly-looking player with his shatter-proof specs to heart, even when he stepped into the breach and captained England 25 times. He was unfortunate that his term in office coincided with some pretty uninspiring Test years and, while England lost only three times under his leadership, they won only five matches, three of them on a roll against a weak New Zealand in 1965.

But if the public did not respond to Smith, his players did. A relaxed, cheerful and caring leader, he was immensely popular with those who played under him, particularly on tour. He was laid back well before the phrase was pigeon-holed for David Gower. Players were allowed to enjoy a social life as long as it did not get in the way of their cricket. His determined yet unflappable attitude was that of a player with a well-rounded perspective on life. He had played for Leicestershire during his National Service days before moving to Oxford University, where he collected a host of Blues for cricket and rugby union. A fly-half, he played for England against Wales in 1956, which makes him cricket's last double-international. Smith moved to Warwickshire that summer and broke through into Test cricket two years later as an opener. He was a brilliant player of spin but there was a suspicion he was suspect against quality pace bowlers (who isn't?), and he lost his place until the next year when he returned in a more

accustomed middle-order position and scored a century in his first match back against India. He was made captain for the 1963-64 tour of India when Ted Dexter was unavailable. Dexter resumed control the next summer against the Australians, Smith missing out on the whole series, but he returned again that winter to lead the team to South Africa when again Dexter's position was uncertain because he was contesting a seat (unsuccessfully, in Cardiff against Jim Callaghan) in the general election. England won the series — their last in the Republic — 1-0 and Smith was finally established, holding on to the job for the next two years. It was a happy time in the camp, as Geoff Boycott, never one to gloss over a criticism, acknowledges: 'Mike Smith was a superb captain for me as a young player in the side. If he lacked anything tactically compared to men like Close and Illingworth, he more than compensated for that in terms of his personality and attitude.'

Smith suffered a heavy defeat at the hands of the West Indies in the first Test of 1966 and was deposed by

Colin Cowdrey, also losing his place in the side. It was not quite the end of the road, however. He was recalled solely as a player against the Australians in 1972 but his top score in three Tests was 34. His playing days finished in 1975 but he has since become a widely respected administrator as president of the National Cricket Association and county chairman of Warwickshire.

M.J.K. SMITH born 30.6.33 (Westcotes, Leicestershire). Tests 50 runs 2278 average 31.63 100s 3 wickets 1 average 128

Opposite: Fine judgement as usual from 'MJK'

Below: Mike Smith (second from right) on the way to India in December 1963 with (from left) Don Wilson, John Price, Phil Sharpe, Fred Titmus, Jim Parks and John Mortimore

ROBIN SMITH
Hampshire 40 Tests 1988-

BEFORE Robin Smith had become a twinkle in the selectors' eyes, his elder brother Chris had put a hefty wager down with an unsuspecting bookmaker that the young man would collect 50 caps for England. Chris, who played eight Tests before Robin appeared on the scene, should be able to collect — fitness permitting — early in 1994. Little brother Robin has become an automatic choice in the Test batting line-up since his debut in 1988, and an average hovering around 50 is the best of any current England player.

Yet along the way Smith has had a few obstacles to overcome to become England's most consistent young batsman. He was one of a cluster of players from southern Africa who, deprived of Test cricket in their homeland because of political isolation between 1970 and '92, came to England to find a flag of convenience under which to launch international careers. Their presence caused some resentment among English-born players and supporters but Robin Smith, nicknamed 'The Judge' at Southampton because of his carpet of curly hair, has been accepted more than any. An easy-going, open character, he cut off playing links with South Africa and set up a family home with his English wife in Hampshire, where he is enormously popular.

Smith, supremely fit and powerful, was a sporting phenomenon at school in Natal. He set 28 school athletics records inside three years, set national junior records in the shot putt and 100m hurdles, and broke rugby and cricket scoring records. His 1,525 runs in one summer bettered the South African schools record once held by one of his heroes, Barry Richards. As a 17-year-old he followed his father, John, into the Natal side but soon decided to follow brother Chris to England to begin a four-year qualifying period. Nottinghamshire and Gloucestershire tried to tempt him but his home was always going to be at Southampton with Chris, who became something of a guiding light.

In his first full season in 1985 he matched up to his promise, finishing as the county's second-highest run scorer behind his brother, but their dream of playing Test cricket together never materialised. Chris had already been discarded a couple of years earlier when Robin produced an eye-catching 38 in a very low-scoring Benson and Hedges Cup Final at Lord's in 1988. That summer England were being routed by the West Indies and 12 days later, Smith was pushed into the Test team and did not let anyone down. He was picked to tour that winter but the trip was cancelled when the Indian

government refused visas to half the squad because of their links with South Africa. The next summer, with England struggling again against Australia, Smith confirmed his arrival, posting centuries in his sixth and seventh Tests. He topped the England averages and his future looked assured.

Yet despite his tenacity and power, epitomised by a savage cut, Smith's form could be erratic, Once set, he could murder any attack but occasionally he lacked discipline under pressure early in an innings. A tendency to fret about failures made him more anxious at the crease where he exposed his nerves by continually stretching and walking between deliveries. This surfaced on tour where he failed to repeat his performances at home and the more tirelessly he worked at his game the more he struggled for the really big scores. On his first three tours to the West Indies, Australia and New Zealand, Smith averaged 35 and while he scored seven centuries in his first 31 Tests, a prodigious striking rate, none of them had come on foreign soil. He finally broke his barren overseas spell with a century in Sri Lanka early in 1993.

R.A. SMITH born 13.9.63 (Durban, South Africa). Tests 40 runs 2954 average 49.23 100s 8

Robin Smith... pent-up power

DON SMITH
Sussex 3 Tests 1957

SRI Lanka's historic first victory over England early in 1993 will have given at least one English Test player a certain amount of satisfaction. Don Smith, a steady left-handed opener capable of some useful swing bowling, became Sri Lanka's national coach in the late 1980s. His own Test experience was confined to a wholly unsuccessful three matches against the touring West Indians when he could muster only 25 runs in four innings. After a happy Sussex career he coached schoolboys before emigrating to Australia and then moving on to Sri Lanka.

For illustration see Len Hutton

D.V. SMITH born 14.6.23 (Broadwater, Sussex). Tests 3 runs 25 average 8.33

DAVID ROBERT SMITH
Gloucestershire 5 Tests 1961-62

DAVID Smith was one of three wholehearted county pace bowlers — his partners were Alan Brown (Kent) and Butch White (Hampshire) — given their chance on the gruelling eight-Test, five-month tour of India and Pakistan in 1961-62. While more celebrated performers gave it a miss, the trio performed the stock bowling job in the heat and the dust before the spinners got to work. A bundle of energy and a good tourist, Smith did not do enough to convince the selectors to give him a chance at home. He also played soccer as a winger for Bristol City and Millwall.

D.R. SMITH born 5.10.34 (Bristol). Tests 5 runs 38 average 9.50 wickets 6 average 59.83

PETER SMITH
Essex 4 Tests 1946-47

IN 1933 Peter Smith, a young leg-spin bowler, reported to the Oval excitedly clutching a telegram telling him he was selected for the third Test against the West Indies. It was a cruel hoax. Some 13 years later, Smith, an extravagant, enterprising wrist spinner, put the record straight on the same ground against India and that winter he toured Australia

David Smith

but could not reproduce his Essex form for England. He scored an astonishing 163, a world record for a No. 11, against Derbyshire at Chesterfield in 1947. Peter died from a brain haemorrhage after a fall while on holiday in France.

For illustration see Bill Voce

T.P.B. SMITH born 30.10.08 (Ipswich, Suffolk). Died 4.8.67. Tests 4 runs 33 average 6.60 wickets 3 average 106.33

GERALD SMITHSON
Yorkshire and Leicestershire
2 Tests 1948

THE selection of 20-year-old Gerald Smithson, a bold left-handed batsman, for the 1948 West Indies tour caused questions in the House of Commons. Smithson had been conscripted to the mines as a 'Bevin Boy' and needed Government dispensation to join the tour. As was common, most of England's leading players opted out of the Caribbean trip, and Smithson was one of seven players in a grossly under-strength team to make their debuts in the first two Tests. Injured on tour, he never interested the selectors again.

G.A. SMITHSON born 1.11.26 (Spofforth, Yorkshire). Died 6.9.70. Tests 2 runs 70 average 23.33

Gerald Smithson

DICK SPOONER
Warwickshire 7 Tests 1951-55

DICK Spooner, like so many of his wicketkeeping contemporaries during the reign of Godfrey Evans, had to content himself with rare opportunities on tour. When Evans, with most other leading lights, opted out of the 1951-52 India tour, Spooner took his chance alongside seven other new caps. A capable 'keeper and sound left-handed batsman whose technique was good enough for him to open in Test cricket, Spooner played again in the Caribbean two years later but in his only home Test in 1955 he suffered a 'pair'.

For illustration see Tom Dollery

R.T. SPOONER born 30.12.19 (Stockton-on-Tees, County Durham). Tests 7 runs 354 average 27.23 dismissals 12 caught 10 stumped 2

DAVID STEELE
Northamptonshire and Derbyshire 8 Tests 1975-76

IN THE glorious summer of 1976 England had a new folk hero, and bank clerks everywhere played out their dreams. It was the summer of endless sunshine, parched outfields, hard wickets and Clive Lloyd's new-look West Indies with the fearsome Holding, Roberts, Daniel and Holder making sure it was Tony Greig who did the grovelling. And it was David Steele's summer.

The bespectacled 34-year-old Steele with his neat mat of grey hair did not project the aura of a sporting hero. His day-job scoring runs for Northampton-

shire normally attracted adjectives such as staunch, courageous and steady. He was the epitome of an English county pro. Perhaps that was why when the muck and bullets were flying against Australia's Lillee and Thomson in 1975 and the West Indies a year later, Greig wanted Steele's steel in his side.

Steele, overlooked in previous summers, thought his chance had gone when the call came for him to play at Lord's. So anxious was he that on his way out for his first innings he lost his way in the pavilion and ended up in the Gents. Relieved to be in the middle, he scored 50, 45, 73, 92, 39 and 66 that summer. Nothing spectacular, just careful and reliable.

The next year Steele faced the more hostile West Indians and, his cap firmly in place, he confronted the barrage again, opening the series with a century at Trent Bridge. He was, almost callously after his sporting heroics, ignored for that winter's tour to India on the theory he could not play spin. His national service over, Steele returned quietly to county life to go about his everyday business of scoring championship runs without fuss or demur. His career finished back at Northampton in 1984 with 22,000 runs in the book, of which 673 held a special memory for the everyday hero who went to war.

D.S. STEELE born 29.9.41 (Bradeley, Staffordshire). Tests 8 runs 673 average 42.06 100s 1 wickets 2 average 19.50

David Steele

ENGLAND have not produced a better fast bowler in the 50 years since the War than John Snow. Before Fred Trueman chokes on his pipe or Brian Statham raises a quizzical eyebrow, it must be recorded that that assessment is offered by Ray Illingworth — and as they will tell you for miles around Headingley, what 'Illy' doesn't know about cricket is not worth knowing.

Snow was the archetypal hero for schoolboys: mean and moody, rebellious towards authority and ruthless towards opposing batsmen, with a mop of hair and the demeanour of a gunslinger. Just the sort of attributes you would expect of a public school-educated only son of a Worcestershire country rector! He was not a Larwood or a Trueman escaping a life in the mines, but a member of the comfortable class who trained as a teacher and was part of the Swinging Sixties era.

For Sussex, who signed him originally as a batsman, he rarely purveyed more than fast-medium, seeing little point in busting a gut in a match destined to be drawn. County cricket has its tedium which Snow alleviated by contemplating poetry — he had two volumes published — and eventually at Sussex he found himself dropped for lack of effort.

That was one John Snow. The other was poetry in motion. In the Test arena he became the most hostile bowler in world cricket from the late 1960s until Dennis Lillee arrived on the scene. When he bowled for England, and in particular for Illingworth, the blood coursed and he hunted batsmen with a predatory instinct. Illingworth pays this testimony: 'He had a wonderful action. Fred could swing the ball more but with Snow's height he had the ability to bounce the ball into the batsman from just short of a length. He also made it swing and seam and when he was firing for me in the early '70s he was as good as any of them.'

Snow's 27 wickets in four Tests, which is an English record in the

A fast bowler's favourite sight... Snow flattens Andy Roberts' middle stump at Headingley, 1976

Caribbean, helped England to their last victorious series in the West Indies in 1967-68 and four years later he helped Illingworth bring home the Ashes with 31 wickets in the series. But through it all, the obvious headline — 'Snow Storm' — was regularly being dusted off by newspaper sub-editors. In Illingworth's first Test as captain, Snow would not bowl when required and found himself dropped; in Australia he was on the carpet again this time, as Illingworth put it, 'for buggering about in the field and upsetting other bowlers.'

But the pair had mutual respect and Snow knew that under Illingworth he would be used as a thoroughbred, not a packhorse. During the last Test of that series, Snow, who had felled Australian batsman Terry Jenner with a sharp

lifter, was attacked by a spectator as he fielded on the boundary and Illingworth led his team off until the outfield had been cleared of debris thrown at Snow. But even Illingworth's protection could not save Snow the following summer when India were the visitors at Lord's. In an incident frequently replayed on newsreels, Snow barged over Sunil Gavaskar as the little Indian opener attempted a quick single off his bowling. The response on the field was laughter all round — including from Gavaskar — but when the players went off for lunch MCC secretary Billy Griffith stormed into the England dressing room and shouted at Snow: 'That was the most disgusting thing I've ever seen on a cricket field.' Illingworth evicted Griffith and official apologies were sent to Gavaskar, but despite the

captain's protests, Snow was dropped for the next Test.

A few years later he found himself out of favour again and his omission from the 1974-75 Ashes tour was one of the selectorial sins of a decade that ended with John joining the Packer circus and — three years after being released by Sussex — Warwickshire, with whom he made his point by helping them win the Sunday League in 1980. After his playing days, England failed to utilise his talent in the coaching field but Snow stayed in touch with the game by ferrying supporters and journalists around the world in his new occupation as a travel agent.

J.A. SNOW born 13.10.41 (Peopleton, Worcestershire). Tests 49 runs 772 average 13.54 wickets 202 average 26.66

BRIAN STATHAM

Lancashire 70 Tests 1951-65

IT MUST have been like facing a police cross-examination, batting against Brian Statham and Fred Trueman. It was the archetypal nice guy-bad guy routine. Statham, cajoling his victim and offering the occasional encouraging 'Good shot', Trueman coming in like a bull stung by a bee, snorting aggression and oaths. One way or the other, the pair usually got their man to come quietly. An honest, straightforward fast bowler, Statham became used to living in the shadow of his more demonstrative partners. If it was not Trueman, it was likely to be Tyson. But Statham's worth would never be undervalued by his team-mates. So often his rhythmic, high action would have to cope with bowling from the 'wrong end', more often than not into the wind. Accurate, unrelenting and sharp, he hit the seam at will, most balls nipping into the right-hander, the odd one cutting away. Statham was never sure himself when or why it happened. And the batsman could never relax because the Statham bouncer was not to be trifled with.

He was called the 'Greyhound' because of his sleek lines and 'Gentleman George' because of his manners. It is said that as a young bowler he almost hit a few opponents and did not enjoy it, so he generally pitched the ball up. Regularly he would pop into the opponents' dressing room for a chat before play while Trueman pawed the ground. Part of Statham's flexibility was down to the fact that he was loose-jointed; indeed to take off his sweater he would reach down over his shoulder to the waistband and pull it up over his head.

Sport came naturally to the young Statham. He had a trial as a winger with Manchester United but the other Old Trafford was where he made his home. He was picked prematurely, at 20, to fly out to join the 1950-51 tour of Australasia and made a modest Test debut in New Zealand. Because of a shortage of fast bowlers in England at the time, he went on four tours by the age of 24 and in the West Indies was asked to do the work of the main strike bowler, which he had the pace to do. He was relaxed about whatever role he was expected to fill and when Tyson burst on to the scene the next year, they made a great double act in Australia.

But it was for his work at the other end to Trueman that Statham will be remembered. Together they played 31 Tests in the late 1950s and early '60s and the race was on for Alec Bedser's world record of 236 wickets. Statham made it first in Australia early in 1963 but a few weeks later in Christchurch, New Zealand, Trueman raced ahead with nine wickets, never to be caught by his colleague and friend. Statham did have the last say over Trueman, however, when after a two-year break he was recalled for a final Test of 1965 a few weeks after Trueman had played his last game for England.

Possibly the most telling fact about Statham's worth is his record with Lancashire, where he was entitled to the choice of ends. His 2,260 first-class wickets came at an average of 16.36, the lowest of any recognised pace bowler since the Great War. He was Lancashire captain for three summers before he stopped playing in 1968 but he was involved with the county until recently, helping with coaching and as a committee man.

J.B. STATHAM born 17.6.30 (Gorton, Manchester). Tests 70 runs 675 average 11.44 wickets 252 average 24.84

Brian Statham... the badge on the heart is England's

ALEC STEWART

Surrey 26 Tests 1990-

LIFE as an England player was never going to be straightforward for Alec Stewart. When your father is the boss there are bound to be questions, remarks and insinuations. Stewart had to win over the doubters in the only way open to him, on the field with performances, but once he had established himself as a Test player in 1992, he was facing another dilemma. The selectors wanted him to be a batting wicketkeeper to give them more options; he wanted to concentrate on his run-making. By the end of a depressing and revealing 1993 trip to India and Sri Lanka, he was at the crossroads and needed to make the right decision about which way he was heading.

Alec was always going to be a sportsman. His father Micky was a respected Surrey captain and an England opener who did not enjoy the best of luck. He was also an England amateur footballer, a fit, tough midfielder who ended up playing professionally for Charlton. The two boys, Alec and brother Neil, grew up in their south London home with sport as the all-abiding passion. Cricket by summer, soccer by winter. Alec used to turn up at the Oval, to see his dad, wearing his beloved Chelsea kit. Cricket won the day and he was soon on the Surrey books, a confident, combative batsman and, like his father, a superb fielder. He was so good he could take over the wicketkeeping gloves whenever asked and look totally at home. It was this ability to keep wicket that eventually won Alec England recognition — but

then threatened to undermine his career.

He went with a rebuilt team to the West Indies in 1990 as a batsman who could also provide back-up for Jack Russell if necessary. For several seasons Stewart's positive stroke-play had impressed in county cricket but naturally, his father, now England's first full-time manager, was reluctant to push him forward. He offered to leave selection meetings whenever Alec's name cropped up, only too aware that unfounded accusations of nepotism lurked in every county committee room if his boy failed.

Alec had a tendency to be flashy outside the off-stump, and his competitive streak, which saw him through that initial tour, was too strident for some who felt he was in danger of crossing the line between enthusiasm and gamesmanship. He failed to consolidate his position, losing his place in 1991, but his wicketkeeping talent, seen generally only in one-day matches at Surrey, was to earn him a reprieve. Faced with defeat in the final Test that summer against the visiting West Indians, England recalled him as wicketkeeper-batsman to help balance the side, and he grabbed his chance. In the subsequent Tests he played as a specialist batsman against the weaker opposition of Sri Lanka and New Zealand, blossoming as Gooch's opening partner and now vice-captain in the absence of an injured Mike Atherton. He scored three centuries in four Tests and made that four in five in the first Test

of 1992 against Pakistan.

His energy was boundless and his willingness to take on any job would probably have seen him driving the team bus if asked. But it was also Stewart's Achilles heel. Once again in 1992 against Pakistan, he took over behind the stumps and once again his form with the bat slumped. In India that winter he tried to combine the jobs of opening, keeping wicket and being the skipper's right-hand man, and it proved too much. History argues that the physical and mental demands of keeping wicket and opening the batting are not compatible and so it proved again.

In India, Stewart gave up the gloves to keep his opening position, and when Gooch fell ill he had to run the team as well. In charge again in Sri Lanka, with Gooch departed, Stewart kept wicket but slipped himself down the batting order. Having suffered the indignity of being the first England captain to lose a Test to Sri Lanka, Stewart was faced with his dilemma: as a specialist batsman he had averaged 46 in 19 Tests, as a wicketkeeper in seven Tests his batting average had been 20, well below the specialist wicketkeeper he had replaced, Jack Russell. With Gooch's retirement approaching, the England captaincy beckoned Stewart — but first he had to make sure he was on the ship.

A.J. STEWART born 8.4.63 (Merton, Surrey). Tests 26 runs 1705 average 38.75 100s 4 dismissals 21 caught 19 stumped 2

Alec Stewart... doing what he does best

JOHN STEPHENSON
Essex 1 Test 1989

BY THE time John Stephenson was picked in 1989, England's selection policy resembled one of those bingo machines in which numbered balls are blown up a tube at random. Stephenson, an intelligent, useful all-round cricketer, became player No. 29 used by England in a shambolic series — a post-War record. That was hardly his fault and he acquitted himself adequately, out-scoring his more illustrious opening partner from Essex, Graham Gooch, in both innings, but his England opportunities since have been limited to 'A' tours.

J.P. STEPHENSON born 14.3.65 (Stebbing, Essex). Tests 1 runs 36 average 18.0

GRAHAM STEVENSON
Yorkshire and Northamptonshire 2 Tests 1980-81

A BELLIGERENT pace bowler who could be a real handful when the mood caught him, Graham Stevenson replaced an injured Mike Hendrick on the 1979-80 tour of Australia and made his debut on the way home in the Jubilee Test in India. He toured again the next winter in the West Indies, making another solitary appearance, but his most auspicious performance came for Yorkshire when he became only the eighth No. 11 to make a first-class century, hitting an unbeaten 115 in a partnership of 149 with Geoff Boycott at Edgbaston in 1982.

G.B. STEVENSON born 16.12.55 (Ackworth, Yorkshire). Tests 2 runs 28 average 28 wickets 5 average 36.60

Micky Stewart

MICKY STEWART
Surrey 8 Tests 1962-64

THERE are not enough days in the week for Micky Stewart, even with his 60th birthday behind him. His jaunty enthusiasm for cricket remains as boundless as ever as he undertakes his latest assignment for the TCCB, co-ordinating the development of youth cricket. A

Graham Stevenson

staunch patriot and the toughest of opponents, he stamped his mark on Test cricket as England's first full-time manager far more emphatically than he did as a player.

A neat opening batsman and superb close fielder, Stewart was unfortunate to play in only eight Tests. Competition for batting places was tough in the early 1960s but just as he appeared to be establishing himself, illness struck Stewart down. He went to India in 1963-64 as Mike Smith's vice-captain but was able to play only one innings before dysentery forced him home.

Although Stewart impressed as the Surrey captain for the next 10 years until he finished playing in 1972, he was never to get another Test chance.

He was an outstanding all-round sportsman, having been an England amateur international soccer player. Before he played professionally with Charlton Athletic as an inside-forward, he had hoped to compete in the 1956 Olympic soccer tournament but was barred because of his pro status as a cricketer.

Stewart returned to the Oval in 1979 as manager and in 1987 was put in charge of the England team. He forged his most successful partnership with Graham Gooch and, while his methods were not universally admired, he achieved new levels of fitness in the players and a much-needed continuity in team selection. At Lord's in 1988, he also had the pleasure of seeing his son Alec score the Test century that had eluded him.

M.J. STEWART born 16.9.32 (Herne Hill, Surrey). Tests 8 runs 385 average 35

RAMAN SUBBA ROW
Surrey and Northamptonshire
13 Tests 1958-61

AN ASTUTE left-handed batsman who sold his wicket dearly, Raman Subba Row had no sooner posted his highest Test score (137) than he gave up cricket to devote himself to his public relations business. His valuable run-making, usually as opener, established him in the England team in 1960, and against Australia in 1961 he scored two centuries and averaged 46 — and then signed off prematurely. A prominent administrator, he has been a tour manager, TCCB chairman, MCC and Surrey committee man and ICC referee.

R. SUBBA ROW born 29.1.32 (Streatham, Surrey). Tests 13 runs 984 average 46.85 100s 3

Roy Swetman

ROY SWETMAN
Surrey, Nottinghamshire and Gloucestershire 11 Tests 1959-60

A BUBBLY character, Roy Swetman never quite fulfilled the potential he showed as a wicketkeeper after replacing Godfrey Evans. He played 11 Tests in 14 months, was replaced by John Murray and quit the game a year later in 1961, somewhat disillusioned. Slight, nimble and confident, he had no trouble, however, making a comeback with Nottinghamshire five years later. After two seasons he took another five-year sabbatical, running a pub before returning with Gloucestershire for three seasons.

R. SWETMAN born 25.10.33 (Westminster, London). Tests 11 runs 254 average 16.93 dismissals 26 caught 24 stumped 2

BOB TAYLOR
Derbyshire 57 Tests 1971-84

WHEN Bob Taylor's unwavering patience was rewarded, the cricket world quietly rejoiced. For years it seemed one of the game's rather special talents would remain buried deep in county cricket. The Staffordshire stalwart merely sucked on his pipe philosophically and waited his chance. Taylor was a superb, soft-handed wicketkeeper, some suggest the best of his day, but there was Alan Knott in front of him in the queue. Knott, five years ahead of Taylor into the England team and five years his junior, kept wonderfully himself, was a Test-class batsman and a fitness fanatic who looked as if he would go on forever.

In the days when England took two specialist 'keepers on tour (as opposed to none) Knott and Taylor were constant companions and competitors, but inevitably the man from Kent got the nod. In New Zealand, early in 1971, Taylor did play one Test but he was to have a six-year wait for the next. For three tours he had to be content with carrying the drinks and giving Knott a breather in the odd district game; for countless summers in England he kept immaculately for Derbyshire while Knott was compiling a record sequence of 65 consecutive Test appearances.

Kerry Packer's chequebook changed all that. Knott was one of the stars tempted to join the cricket circus and, at the end of 1977, Taylor was first choice at last. Knott made a brief return in 1980-81 but was enticed away again, on a rebel tour to South Africa, and Taylor was reinstated to confirm his rightful place in the dynasty of great English 'keepers since the War that includes Knott and Evans before him.

Taylor was one of cricket's universally liked players. He would stop to talk to committee man, journalist or supporter alike on his ambles around the Racecourse Ground. He deserved his nickname 'Chat'. There were no airs about the amiable Taylor. As a schoolboy he learned his cricket on the cinder car park behind Stoke's football ground near his home, and at 15 he was able to play for Staffordshire in the Minor Counties championship once he had finally convinced the gateman at Norton that he was a player. Compact, light on his feet, Taylor was the ideal build for a 'keeper and appeared instinctively in the right position to take the ball, By the time he was 21 he was established at Derbyshire but received a jolt when he picked up an ankle injury playing soccer for Port Vale and lost his early season place, having told the club he had slipped on an escalator while out shopping!

The football career subsided when Taylor realised cricket was his calling and the winters would be busy with either England or on invitation tours. He also worked on his batting so that he became a respectable lower-order contributor with a sound defence if needed. He got to within three runs of a Test century once in Adelaide in 1979 and two years later scored his maiden century in 20 years of first-class cricket, against Yorkshire. It was to be the only century in his 639-match career.

His 'keeping statistics, however, are more impressive: his 1,649 dismissals are a world record ahead of John Murray (1,527), his 10 dismissals (all caught) against India in 1979-80 a world record in Tests, and his 1,222 dismissals a county championship record. He took the last of those catches for Derby in 1984 but had a bizarre opportunity to add to his total two years later in a Test against New Zealand at Lord's. Bruce French had been injured while batting and during the lunch interval an urgent call went out to Taylor, who was working for the sponsors and helping to supervise the meals in the hospitality area. Taylor — of course — had his gloves in the boot of his car and took his place behind the stumps. For the rest of the day it was as if 'Chat' had never been away. Taylor remains involved in the game, coaching and representing a sports goods company.

R.W. TAYLOR born 17.7.41 (Stoke-on-Trent, Staffordshire). Tests 57 runs 1156 average 16.28 dismissals 174 caught 167 stumped 7

More chat... Bob Taylor

ROY TATTERSALL
Lancashire 16 Tests 1951-54

TALL, lean Ray Tattersall did not enjoy the best of luck in his cricket career. His one insuperable problem was that he was a contemporary of England's best post-War off-spinner Jim Laker. From a great height — he was 6ft 3in — Tattersall could produce pace and bounce allied to his off-spin, and in 1950 he was a sensation for Lancashire, heading the national averages with 193 wickets at 13 apiece.

That winter, when injuries struck in Australia, he was summoned from England to make his Test debut and kept his place for 14 consecutive matches. The next summer proved to be the summit for 'Tatts'. On a rain-affected wicket at Lord's, the South Africans found him virtually unplayable on the second day as he claimed nine of the 14 wickets to fall. He finished with match figures of 12 for 101, inspiring England who levelled the series mid-way through the third day.

That winter in India, however, he was asked to do the donkey work and was never quite the same bowler again. Originally a medium-pacer, he could push it through, and on the sub-continent he bowled a gruelling 246 overs in eight innings, double the contribution of any other bowler.

At Old Trafford, Cyril Washbrook was never a great admirer of off-spin and used to hammer Tattersall in the nets, and during matches he was often under-employed. He played one Test in 1953 and another in 1954, retiring in 1960 with hip trouble.

R. TATTERSALL born 17.8.22 (Bolton, Lancashire). Tests 16 runs 50 average 5 wickets 58 average 26.08

CHRIS TAVARE
Kent and Somerset 31 Tests 1980-89

CONVINCING the mass of English cricket supporters that somewhere deep inside Chris Tavare lurks a fluent, graceful stroke-maker is not easy. All that most spectators remember from his 31 Tests is sombre-faced defence and batting that Insomniacs Anonymous wished they could bottle and send to their members.

Appearances can be so deceptive. This Oxford University zoologist had performed with such great promise for England Schools, with his university and in the early days at Canterbury that Test selection was inevitable. Unfortunately, when it came he was asked to fill the troublesome No. 3 position against the rampaging 1980 West Indians and was given the job of sheet anchor to protect the rest of the brittle batting.

This he did and he survived only two Tests. When he was selected again the next summer against Australia he performed the same role, and so Tavare's vocation in life was determined. He kept his place doggedly for the next 25 Tests but never appeared to be able to relax and play his natural game when wearing the lion on his cap. His batting landmarks revolved inevitably around stints of great patience, including the second-slowest half-century in the history of the English game: 5 hours 50 minutes against Pakistan in 1982.

The selectors — and public — finally lost patience in 1984 when Tavare scored a wretched 14 against Sri Lanka, and he was consigned to county cricket where the outlook was no brighter. After two years and two unsuccessful cup finals in charge of Kent, Tavare was shamefully elbowed out by a faction of the county committee who wanted a Cowdrey, this time Chris, in charge.

Tavare bit his lip and stayed for another five years before joining Somerset in 1989, winning an unexpected England recall for one Test in a summer of crises against Australia.

C.J. TAVARE born 27.10.54 (Orpington, Kent). Tests 31 runs 1755 average 32.50 100s 2

Chris Tavare

KEN TAYLOR
Yorkshire 3 Tests 1959-64

IF KEN Taylor, a graduate of the
Slade School of Fine Art, were to
produce a picture representing his
career, it would surely be an abstract.
A fine straight-hitting batsman and
brilliant fielder, he was also a skilful
footballer with Huddersfield and
Bradford. Yet he never made full use
of his bounteous abilities and was
affected by nerves when the stakes
were high. In two Tests, in 1959 and
1964, he failed to make an
impression. 'A total enigma,' was how
one former team-mate described him.
Son Nick, a fast bowler, played briefly
with Yorkshire, Surrey and Somerset.

*K. TAYLOR born 21.8.35 (Huddersfield,
Yorkshire). Tests 3 runs 57
average 11.40*

LES TAYLOR
Leicestershire 2 Tests 1985

LES Taylor, a powerful, cheerful
ex-miner, appreciated every
moment of his cricket career, which he
started late at 23. His seam bowling was
not pretty but it was hostile and
effective, while his flailing batting was
pure entertainment. Ignored by
England, he joined the 1982 rebel tour
to South Africa but after his ban he
played in the two Tests which won the
1985 Ashes series. Chosen for the
winter trip to the West Indies, so little
was seen of him he was dubbed 'Lord
Lucan' — and there *was* a passing
resemblance to the missing peer.

*L.B. TAYLOR born 25.10.53 (Earl Shilton,
Leicestershire). Tests 2 runs 1 average —
wickets 4 average 44.50*

PAUL TAYLOR
Derbyshire and Northamptonshire
1 Test 1993-

A SPELL of 0 for 92 off 12 overs put
Paul Taylor on the road to India in
1993. The burly left-arm pace bowler,
released by Derbyshire after four
fruitless summers, was playing for
Staffordshire in the NatWest Trophy
against Northamptonshire in 1990
when he clocked up those unflattering
figures. Northamptonshire, however,
were so impressed with Taylor's
potential that they offered him a
second chance in county cricket.
Taylor's rapid progress brought a
surprise selection for India, where he
won his first cap.

Paul Taylor

*J.P. TAYLOR born 8.8.64
(Ashby-de-la-Zouch, Leicestershire). Tests 1
runs 34 average 17 wickets 1 average 74*

Les Taylor

167

FRED TITMUS
Middlesex and Surrey 53 Tests 1955-75

A PHONE call to Fred Titmus while England were touring in India in January 1993 went something like this: 'Hello Fred,' said the caller. 'Hello,' replied Titmus. 'And before you ask — no, I'm not available if they need an extra spinner out in India.' He was joking — well, probably. Though past his 60th birthday, Titmus gives the impression that if he laid down his pipe and stopped chattering about cricket for a few minutes, he could still go out and, off a few easy paces, float the ball on to the spot.

Titmus played first-class cricket over five decades from 1949 to '82 and few players can say that. Brian Close is one. Titmus was a classy off-spinner unluckily born into an era when good slow bowlers were two-a-penny, and an old penny at that. He had first to contend with the superb Laker and Lock, then Illingworth, Allen, Gifford, and, later in his career, Underwood and Pocock. But still he managed to play 53 Tests and it would have been more but for an argument his left foot had with the propeller of a boat while on tour in the West Indies in 1968. Titmus lost four toes but little sleep over the accident.

He had the perfect spinner's temperament: that of a cunning pacifist. He made his debut at 16 for Middlesex, then did his National Service and tried his hand at bowling seamers as many spinners tended to do. But spinning was his trade, it suited the stream of banter that used to flow from him. In the slips he fielded usually on the end of the cordon because he was deaf in his right ear and did not want to miss out on the chat.

In 1955 he claimed 191 wickets and did the double (1,000 runs and 100 wickets) for the first of eight times. He was a more than useful lower-order batsman who had a defensive technique that made captains have no fear about pushing him up the order. That summer, at 22, he played his first two Tests and

was put back on the shelf for seven years, during which time he honed his skills of flight and pace. His successors at Middlesex, Emburey and Edmonds, are convinced that Titmus bowled much slower than modern spinners who have to cope with the one-day game. Titmus strongly denies this. He says that he and his contemporaries made the ball fizz when they wanted, but he had no doubt slowed down a little when he was playing county cricket a few months away from his 50th birthday.

His powers were at their peak in the early 1960s and much of his success came on tour. In 1962-63 in Australia, so often an off-spinner's graveyard, he claimed 21 wickets including a career best 7 for 79. The following winters in India and South Africa brought more success but a tour of the West Indies brought an abrupt halt to his progress. It was in Barbados where Titmus and some team-mates were enjoying a swim when they spotted the captain's wife, Penny Cowdrey, in a motorboat. Titmus swam over to the front of the boat to keep well away from the propeller and allowed his feet to drift under the craft — not realising the propeller was in the middle of the hull. It cost him four toes and a place on the rest of the tour (Tony Lock replaced him) for which he received £90 compensation from the MCC's insurance policy. It was a paltry pay-out that led to a revision of insurance for England cricketers abroad.

Titmus, typically, was not fussed. He was back bowling and captaining Middlesex within three months, untroubled by his loss.

Thinking of the future he took over a Hertfordshire sub-post office but cricket would not let go. In 1976 he moved to the Oval as manager-coach but it was an unhappy liaison and he left after playing one match. Afterwards he happened to mention to Middlesex skipper Mike Brearley on a walk around Lord's that if he was ever short, to give him a

ring. The Titmus phone was forever busy. He carried on playing until 1982, creating a Middlesex record of 642 appearances and taking 2,361 wickets, another county record, as well as scoring more than 20,000 runs. Fred remains actively involved in the game having been a selector and currently serving his country as an observer (non-playing).

F.J. TITMUS born 24.11.32 (St Pancras, London). Tests 53 runs 1449 average 22.29 wickets 153 average 32.22

Not just a bowler... Fred Titmus wins the Cricket Society's award for 'the best all-rounder in English cricket', 1968

For further illustration see Mike Smith

FRED TRUEMAN
Yorkshire 67 Tests 1952-65

MYTHS about Fred Trueman became a cottage industry in Yorkshire when the great man was in his prime. He never downed gallons of ale as if prohibition was being introduced the next day, he never told a West Indian dignitary to 'pass the salt Gunga Din,' and he never scraped coal out of t'pit with his bare hands before joining Yorkshire. But something the publicists did not have to tart up was his phenomenal ability and hostility as a fast bowler. Belligerence and bravado filled every menacing step of his beautifully balanced gallop to the crease. The black mane waved, the shirt billowed and the back arched as he delivered from a perfect sideways-on position. If the ball didn't get you the expletive would. He was not the fastest but he was the most ruthless and cunning, he had a wicked late away-swinger, intimidated with the bouncer, and had a cricket brain that did not understand the meaning of mercy. In his inimitable way he believed he was 'the finest bloody fast bowler to ever draw breath' — and he may have been right.

Trueman was the first bowler to take 300 Test wickets and he did so at a strike rate only the likes of Lillee, Marshall and now Waqar Younis can match. But for Fred's confrontational, uncompromising nature, he would have played a lot more Tests and taken many more wickets. While the public loved the larrikin image that Ian Botham was later to inherit, Lord's did not. The Establishment did not like a bowler who turned away and walked back to his mark after felling an opposing batsman, a cricketer who could not give a stuff about rocking the diplomatic boat.

Over the 13 years of Trueman's international career, he figured in barely more than half of the Tests played by England: 67 out of 121. He toured for England only four times — twice to the Caribbean, twice to Australasia — sometimes out of choice, sometimes because he was not wanted.

On his first tour to the West Indies in 1954 his wilful attitude made life uncomfortable for skipper Len Hutton, his Yorkshire colleague, and he never played in any of Hutton's remaining 11 Tests. When Peter May, an man of protocol, succeeded Hutton, Trueman played in only three of his first 15 Tests in charge. Forgiveness was not freely handed out, particularly at a time when there were plenty of fast bowling options, even if none were quite as good as 'Fiery Fred'.

The perfect cartwheel... Trueman in full flow

Trueman was always a handful from the moment his grandmother delivered him into the world in Stainton weighing a mighty 14lb 1oz. He was an outstanding, natural young bowler yet when he first appeared for Yorkshire Seconds he was far from the broad-beamed charger he was to become. Among other jobs, he worked briefly on the tubs at Maltby Colliery and played soccer for Lincoln before National Service in the RAF finally matured his bowling frame.

He introduced himself to Test cricket with three wickets in eight balls on his debut to reduce India to 0 for 4 in their second innings. His bowling, his rugged looks, his flamboyant batting and his reputation made him an instant public hero. His finest hour was probably in 1963 when he set a series record between England and West Indies by taking 34 wickets, 12 in one Test, 11 in another. Flickering black-and-white film suggests Trueman had slowed down considerably by then and, despite his assertions to the contrary, he had — but he still swung the ball prodigiously. He left Test cricket two years later and Yorkshire in 1968, but his controversial contribution to the game did not diminish one iota as he continued to tear into the world's best as a pungent commentator and journalist.

Well wrapped up for a Caribbean winter... Trueman (second left) bound for the West Indies in 1953 with his Yorkshire colleagues (from left) Watson, Wardle and captain Hutton

F.S. TRUEMAN born 6.2.31 (Stainton, Yorkshire). Tests 67 runs 981 average 13.81 wickets 307 average 21.57

Paul Terry

GREG THOMAS
Glamorgan and Northamptonshire
5 Tests 1986

ENGLAND turned to Greg Thomas, a gently-spoken Welsh schoolteacher, when they wanted some hostility to counter the West Indies in the Caribbean in 1986. While his county success had been limited, Thomas had shown bursts of destructive fast bowling when the mood took him, although too often his control went off the radar. A difficult first tour was followed by one home Test, disruptive injuries, an unsuccessful move to Northampton, and then a decision to join the 1990 rebel tour to South Africa.

J.G. THOMAS born 12.8.60 (Trebanos, Glamorgan). Tests 5 runs 83 average 13.83 wickets 10 average 50.40

PAUL TERRY
Hampshire 2 Tests 1984

PAUL Terry was one of many prolific English county batsmen who have had their Test careers mown down by the West Indies' attack. Two Tests after Andy Lloyd was put out of action for the summer by a blow to the head, Terry, a tall, correct opener, was drafted in. Unable to cope with the extra pace, he had his left arm fractured by a rising Winston Davis delivery in his third innings, although he reappeared in plaster at No. 11 to allow Allan Lamb to score the two runs he needed for a century. It was Terry's last act of bravery for England.

V.P. TERRY born 14.1.59 (Osnabruck, Germany). Tests 2 runs 16 average 5.33

Ian Thomson

IAN THOMSON
Sussex 5 Tests 1964-65

IAN Thomson was only a few weeks short of his 36th birthday when he won Test recognition, a reward for dutiful county performances. A tall, medium-paced bowler in the Alec Bedser mould, Thomson took 100 wickets in 12 successive seasons before being called up for the 1964-65 tour of South Africa. He did a steady job on a victorious trip before returning home for a final season with Sussex. His 10 for 49 against Warwickshire at Worthing in 1964 is the last occasion of a bowler taking all ten wickets in an innings in this country.

N.I. THOMSON born 23.1.29 (Walsall, Staffordshire). Tests 5 runs 69 average 23.00 wickets 9 average 63.11

ROGER TOLCHARD
Leicestershire 4 Tests 1977

ROGER Tolchard was an enthusiastic wicketkeeper but it was his determined batting which earned him his four caps on the 1976-77 tour of India. Alan Knott kept wicket but 'Tolly' was brought in to bolster the batting and justified Tony Greig's selection with his first innings, a six-hour 67 on a crumbling Calcutta wicket which helped set up victory. He looked destined to play again as a batsman on the 1976-77 Australia tour but a fractured cheekbone forced him home. He captained Leicestershire for three years before moving into teaching.

R.W. TOLCHARD born 15.6.46 (Torquay, Devon). Tests 4 runs 129 average 25.80

MAURICE TREMLETT
Somerset 3 Tests 1948

MAURICE Tremlett made such an impact in his first season in 1947 that he found himself in an experimental England team sailing for the West Indies that winter. His high, smooth action impressed captain Gubby Allen, who took him to open the attack, but looks were deceptive and Tremlett had an unrewarding tour. After a fruitless South Africa trip, Tremlett lost his bowling altogether, but developed his batting and became a successful captain at Taunton. His son Tim played for Hampshire and is now coach at Southampton.

M.F. TREMLETT born 5.7.23 (Stockport, Cheshire). Died 30.7.84. Tests 3 runs 20 average 6.66 wickets 4 average 56.50

Maurice Tremlett

Roger Tolchard

PHIL TUFNELL
Middlesex 13 Tests 1990-

PHIL Tufnell has been cast as England's *enfant terrible* and at times he appears determined to live up to his reputation. He emerged on the 1990-91 tour of Australia as a player of genuine match-winning potential but also one with a finger that toyed with the self-destruct button.

A left-arm spinner who mixed aggression and inventiveness into his bowling cocktail, he set up victories for England in three of his first seven Tests, but there was a dark side to Tufnell, too. If things went wrong for the Middlesex spinner, he could be moody and truculent towards umpires, opponents and even team-mates.

The son of a London silversmith, Tufnell revealed his rebellious nature in his schooldays and, for a while during his teenage years, lost interest in cricket altogether. He was persuaded back to Lord's, chopped off his pony-tail, worked hard and emerged as the most exciting slow bowling talent in the country.

England took him to Australia but on his Test debut he remained wicketless and clashed with an umpire. In his second match he foolishly refused his captain's handshake when he took his first wicket. It was too much for Gooch, who left him out the next summer until England were on the brink of

Phil Tufnell

defeat against the West Indies. Tufnell returned with a devastating 6 for 25 spell as England levelled the series. A five-wicket return helped win the next Test against Sri Lanka and an incredible 7 for 47 performance conjured victory from nothing for England in the first Test that winter in New Zealand.

A burst appendix ruined the summer of 1992 for Tufnell, but he was included in the 1993 tour of India only for his frustrations to spill over again in an up-country clash with an umpire. That earned him a £500 fine from the management and posed more doubts about his attitude and ability to cope with the demands of being an England cricketer.

P.C.R. TUFNELL born 29.4.66 (Barnet, Hertfordshire). Tests 13 runs 53 average 6.62 wickets 45 average 33.48

FRANK TYSON

Northamptonshire 17 Tests 1954-59

IN 1955 John Arlott wrote of Frank Tyson: 'He is what Hollywood calls box office.' Few cricketers have had the magnetic effect of drawing spectators into a ground just to see one man perform — Grace, Compton, Trueman, Botham, spring to mind as being among the few Englishmen who have been box office. And so too, for a few gloriously unexpected years, was Tyson, 'The Typhoon'. When Arlott wrote those words, Tyson was back from a winter in the southern hemisphere where he had destroyed Australia, and in the first Test of the summer against South Africa at Trent Bridge had taken eight wickets to give him 52 victims in nine appearances for England.

While most modern cricketers agree that Australia's Jeff Thomson has been the fastest bowler of modern times, few of the previous generation would argue that Tyson wore that mantle in his era. Denis Compton, who saw Tyson in his pomp from close range says: 'For two or three years, Tyson was the fastest I ever saw. He was never the greatest fast bowler but, by God, he was the fastest.' 'The Typhoon' blew itself out inside five years but during that time Tyson was a fearsome sight. Tall and bulky with a beer barrel for a chest, he hurled himself in off a vast run-up and wrenched the ball down the track. He had a good bouncer, developed the yorker, but defeated batsmen principally by sheer speed.

Yet unlike the widely-held image of the thick-set, thick-skulled quickie, Tyson was an academic. He completed a degree course at Durham University but found himself rejected by his native Lancashire because of his lack of technique, and had to spend a year qualifying for Northamptonshire by residence. As he prepared for first-class cricket, he applied his scholarly mind to his sport. He analysed his assets and worked out logically how to make maximum use of them. He fine-tuned his run-up, put everything into six deliveries and then would slump back to his fielding position, body dropping, to conserve energy like a boxer heading for his corner waiting for the next round of combat. It was wonderful drama unless you

The Typhoon is on its way

happened to be standing 22 yards away with a bat in your hand.

His zenith came on his first tour to Australia in 1954-55, though few of the home crowd were particularly worried by Tyson when he finished with 1 for 160 in the first Test which England lost by an innings and 154 runs. In the next Test at Sydney, England levelled the series with Tyson taking 10 for 130. Reverting to a slightly shorter run-up after the first Test humiliation, Tyson took 27 wickets in the remaining four Tests at 15 apiece and England won the series 3-1. No English bowler, with the exception of Harold Larwood, has caused such mayhem to Australian batting.

Tyson became the most talked-about cricketer in the country which did not suit a man who was basically publicity-shy. Sadly, he was soon to fade from public consciousness, anyway. Leg problems restricted his appearances, and the re-emergence of Fred Trueman as the exciting and more reliable spearhead saw Tyson disappear from the scene almost as dramatically as he had appeared. He quit county cricket in 1960 and, like Larwood, emigrated to the country where he had enjoyed his greatest moments. He made a career in teaching in Australia, also writing and broadcasting on cricket before a spell as coach to the Victorian Cricket Association.

F.H. TYSON born 6.6.30 (Farnworth, Lancashire). Tests 17 runs 230 average 10.95 wickets 76 average 18.56

Underwood... which trick next?

DEREK UNDERWOOD
Kent 86 Tests 1966-82

DEREK Underwood was unique. He developed a style of bowling that no-one could categorise — let alone hit. Was he slow-medium or fastish slow? Was he a spinner or a cutter? Or was he a swing bowler? Two things are unchallenged: he was a left-armer and he was a terrific bowler. The nickname 'Deadly' fitted him beautifully. His unceasing accuracy and indefatigable desire to bowl and turn the screw made him deadly to batsmen who rarely encountered anything like him except when they played Kent or England. But for his pragmatic decisions to accept the money on offer, first from Kerry Packer and then from South Africa, Underwood could have become the first, and probably only, English bowler to reach 400 Test wickets.

A quiet, courteous man, he shunned the attention and notoriety that went with being a 'rebel', just as he did not enjoy the internal manoeuvring that went on at Canterbury in his latter days as his long-standing colleague Alan Knott and captain Chris Tavare were levered aside. He slipped quietly out of the game at 42 in 1987, having claimed 2,465 wickets at a whisker over 20 apiece, yet a year later, when England were scouring the country for a left-arm spinner with whom to confront the West Indies, there were many who believed he could have done a good job.

He learned his cricket bowling on matting at his Kent home where, in his mind's eye, he was a fast bowler. His first efforts in the Canterbury nets were as one of several seam-up merchants but, with few slow bowlers around, Underwood adapted. Still running in smartly in his splay-footed style but with a slow arm action, he found he could impart cut on the ball with great control and produce awkward bounce. In his first season of county cricket in 1963 this rogue spinner so confounded

batsmen that he became the youngest player, at 17, to take 100 wickets at the first attempt. By 25 he had harvested his first 1,000 with only turn-of-the-century bowlers George Lohmann and Wilf Rhodes achieving the feat at a younger age.

In the days when wickets were left uncovered once a match had started, Underwood became virtually unplayable on a damp surface. The sight of rain clouds made him as happy as a mudlark but sometimes on dry turning wickets, he would disappoint, still pushing the ball through, not wanting to risk being hit back over his head, which he hated. Curiously, Underwood rarely completed a whole series as England captains would often turn to a bigger spinner of the ball, such as Norman Gifford, to prise out the opposition, particularly as pitches grew drier in the 1970s and after full covering was introduced in 1979. But give Underwood a 'sticky dog' and there was no more destructive bowler in the world.

His most memorable success was at the Oval in 1968 when he ran through

the Australians with just five minutes to spare to level the series in the last Test. At lunchtime on the final day, Australia looked safe, particularly when a freak storm hit the ground and flooded the square, but the sun reappeared and the groundstaff, supported by an army of spectators and armed with blankets, mopped up the mess so play could resume with Australia 86 for 5 and 75 minutes to play. They were 110 for 6 with 36 minutes left when Underwood was brought back to bowl and he mesmerised them on a mudheap.

Underwood the batsman should not be forgotten either. He was an awkward, dour tail-ender and towards the end of his career in 1984 at Hastings — one of his favourite bowling haunts — having gone in as nightwatchman, he scored a century in his 618th first-class innings. There was no more popular century that summer.

D.L. UNDERWOOD born 8.6.45 (Bromley, Kent). Tests 86 runs 937 average 11.56 wickets 297 average 25.83

Deadly combination... Clive Lloyd c Knott b Underwood again

THE FARLEY STAND
ERECTED 1931

BILL VOCE
Nottinghamshire 27 Tests 1930-47

BILL Voce took only one wicket in Test cricket after the War but his place in any book of England cricketers warrants more than a passing reference. When he played his three post-War Tests he was overweight and medium-paced, a sad reminder of the force he had once been with his Nottinghamshire colleague Harold Larwood.

Voce was in the mines at 14 but his left-arm spin bowling provided an escape to a better life. He soon discovered he could swing the ball at a sharp pace and at the age of 20 was on his way to the Caribbean as the MCC staged simultaneous inaugural tours in the West Indies and New Zealand.

Tall and powerfully built, Voce was to prosper overseas, playing only five of 27 Tests at home. In 1932-33 Douglas Jardine devised his famous 'Bodyline' tactics and while Larwood was by far his most hostile weapon, Voce, bowling around the wicket and with his extra bounce, was said to be equally unpleasant to face. He took 15 wickets in four Tests on that tour.

The next summer when the smarting Australians toured England, Voce took 8 for 66 in the first innings of their county match at Trent Bridge and was 'rested' for the second innings. Like Larwood, he was not picked for the Tests that summer. While Larwood always refused to apologise for following his captain's instructions on that 'Bodyline' tour, Voce voiced his regret and was reinstated for the 1936-37 Antipodean tour, and showed he could be equally effective pitching the ball up, taking 17 wickets in the first two Tests.

Bill Voce (seated right) ready for his last tour to Australia in 1946 with team-mates: Back (l to r) J Langridge, D Compton, L Hutton, G Evans. Middle (l to r) C Washbrook, D Wright, J Ikin, A Bedser, P Smith, R Pollard, R Howard (Manager). Front (l to r) J Hardstaff, L Fishlock, N Yardley, W Hammond, B Edrich, P Gibb, Voce.

In his latter days, the hefty Voce tended to be over-bowled by Nottinghamshire and knee trouble became an increasing problem. After the War he played briefly, becoming coach at Trent Bridge and bowling occasionally, reverting to his original nippy spinners.

W. VOCE born 8.8.09 (Annesley Woodhouse, Nottinghamshire). Died 6.6.84. Tests 27 runs 308 average 13.39 wickets 98 average 27.88

PETER WALKER
Glamorgan 3 Tests 1960

PETER Walker was a victim of English success. He played his part in three resounding victories over South Africa and was then dropped so the selectors could enjoy the luxury of looking at other talent. It would never happen now. Walker was similar in many ways to Tony Greig: brought up in South Africa, he was tall, batted with a flourish, could bowl left-arm seam up or spin, was a wonderful close fielder and hated boring cricket. If he had played for a more fashionable county it may have helped his cause. Now runs a video company and works in television.

P.M. WALKER born 17.2.36 (Clifton, Bristol). Tests 3 runs 128 average 32.00

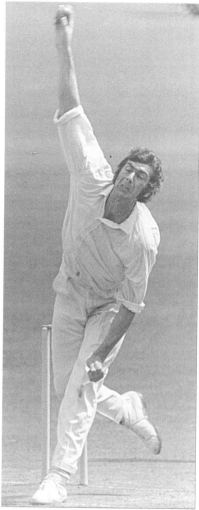
Alan Ward

Peter Walker

ALAN WARD
Derbyshire and Leicestershire 5 Tests 1969-76

WHEN Alan Ward's body was functioning perfectly he was a superb fast bowler. He was seen as the partner for John Snow to give England the best new-ball attack in the world. It was not to be. Ward's lean 6ft 3in frame proved too fragile and his lack of motivation often exasperated captains. His Derbyshire skipper Brian Bolus once sent him off when he refused to bowl in a championship match. He came home from his only tour, to Australia in 1970-71, injured before the Tests had started, and his sporadic England career spluttered out.

A. WARD born 10.8.47 (Dronfield, Derbyshire). Tests 5 runs 40 average 8 wickets 14 average 32.35

JOHNNY WARDLE
Yorkshire 28 Tests 1948-57

JOHNNY Wardle's story is as unorthodox as his bowling. He was a remarkable bowler and a cantankerous character who found it difficult to win over the selectors. The fact that England never got the best out of him in 28 intermittent Tests is another example of intolerance clouding judgement. His Yorkshire days ended in an acrimonious sacking which prompted England to throw him out of a tour party and led to him quitting the first-class game in his prime.

Originally Wardle was an orthodox left-arm spinner but he learned to switch to wrist spin without any discernible alteration in his action, which started behind his back. He had the talent to toss in that rarest of beasts, the chinaman (the left-armer's ball that darts back into the pads) and the googly. A few tried the art but none bowled it at the highest level like Wardle, who took more than 100 Test wickets at 20 apiece, the lowest average of any recognised spinner since the First World War. His unorthodoxy, however, bred a mistrust among the selectors, who leaned towards Tony Lock much of the time despite the persistent doubts about the Surrey man's action. The debate about who has been England's best legitimate left-arm spinner since the War is not, though, in doubt north of St John's Wood.

Wardle reflected his upbringing: tough and uncompromising. During the War he was a fitter down the mines, and cricket offered him an escape which he grabbed. He was given his chance by Yorkshire in June 1947 and by the end of the season had done enough to be included in Gubby Allen's experimental side headed for the West Indies. He played in one Test, bowled just three overs and had to wait two years for his second opportunity, and then another 12 months for his third.

For much of his early career at Yorkshire he was expected to be a stock bowler and his ventures into wrist-spinning were more profitable on harder wickets, which he found, to his delight, overseas. He was a regular tourist and was at the height of his powers in South Africa in 1956-57 when he took no less than 90 first-class wickets on the tour at 12 apiece. In four Tests he claimed 26 victims, including 12 at Cape Town, at an average of 13.

A year later Yorkshire were looking for a new captain and many of the professionals thought Wardle, with his sharp cricket brain and unflagging determination to win, should be given the job but, of course, he was a professional and the committee would have nothing to do with that idea. They turned instead to Ronnie Burnet, captain of the Second XI and also a skipper in the Bradford League, but who knew little about the wiles of the first-class game and who struggled to justify his place. The committee asked Wardle as senior pro to support Burnet, and resentment between the pair soon developed. At Sheffield the antagonism erupted when Burnet accused Wardle of not trying for him. Brian Close remembers: 'He could not have made a more false accusation. Johnny Wardle not trying? He could as soon stop breathing as stop trying like hell to win every match he played in.' Wardle accused Burnet of not listening to advice and making the professionals look like fools to the spectators. During an afternoon session the committee met to choose the next side and Burnet left the field to sit in as usual, leaving Wardle in charge. He bowled 33 overs and took 6 for 46 but when he came off he was ordered to the committee room and told he had been sacked. He retaliated with a series of newspaper articles 'telling all'. And Lord's responded by withdrawing his invitation to tour Australia that winter. England lost that Ashes series 4-0 and Lock, with the left-arm spinner's job, took 5 for 380.

Wardle moved with great success into League cricket and played until 1969 for Cambridgeshire. Yorkshire and the MCC finally forgave him his sins — both making him an honorary life member — but it was scant consolation to a great bowler unfulfilled.

J.H. WARDLE born 8.1.23 (Ardsley, Yorkshire). Died 23.7.85. Tests 28 runs 653 average 19.78 wickets 102 average 20.39

Johnny Wardle... what was it this time?

For further illustration see Fred Trueman

CYRIL WASHBROOK
Lancashire 37 Tests 1937-56

HUTTON and Washbrook — they went together like Flanagan and Allen or Marmite and toast in post-War Britain. While the pair were there at the top of England's batting order the Empire was in safe hands. For five years after the War, they played together in 31 Tests, two dapper characters walking out side by side to open the innings a record 51 times, Hutton always taking the first ball. If England did not enjoy a century partnership to start the innings, people felt cheated, and their 359 on the first day of the second Test against South Africa in 1948 remains an England first-wicket record against any opposition. Hutton, the Yorkshire half of the famous Roses partnership, was the star turn, but Washbrook was also a formidable performer. His contribution is sometimes overlooked outside Lancashire, but around Old Trafford they will point out that their man's England career actually outlasted that of Sir Len.

Washbrook was of good Lancashire stock but the county had to move smartly to make sure they did not lose him. Born in Barrow, he was brought up in Shropshire, where his father ran a calico-printing business, and was playing for Warwickshire Seconds and considering an offer from Edgbaston when Lancashire signed him up in 1933. Washbrook, with another promising young batsman named Denis Compton, made his England debut against New Zealand in 1937 but had to wait another nine years for his second cap because of the War.

There was an air of control about Washbrook. Stocky, well-balanced, he moved like a middleweight and hit with clean power, particularly against the quicks. He did not much care, though, for leg-spinners or left-arm spinners who tried their tricks. His was a forthright uncomplicated game. He loved to hook, and his Roses battles with Fred Trueman were famous. When Trueman started to goad him, Washbrook could be heard to actually growl back down the wicket. He was a superb cover fielder and was worshipped by Old Trafford's faithful, but in a crowd he was shy to the extent that some thought him aloof. Put him in the nets with some young hopefuls, however, and, remembers Geoff Pullar, he would talk all day.

Against Australia, New Zealand and the West Indies at home, he had marvellous summers, his Test average never dropping below 50, but inexplicably it all went wrong on the 1950-51 tour against the triumphant Australians. Washbrook's top score in 10 innings was 34 and it seemed his England days were over. He lost his Test place after the tour and contentedly continued his work at Lancashire where, in 1954, he became the county's first professional skipper.

In 1956 he was elected an England selector and when he sat down with his colleagues to choose the side for the third Test that summer, after Peter May's side had been routed by Australia in the second, chairman Gubby Allen asked him to leave the room. Allen felt it was time to inject some experience into a flaccid middle-order and wanted Washbrook, at 41 and five years out of international cricket, in the side. May had his reservations but was talked round and Washbrook — himself reluctant — was called back into the room and told he was back in the Test team. He batted as if he had never been away, going in at No. 5 and scoring 98 to help set up an innings victory. In the remaining two Tests, Washbrook failed to reach double figures but England won the series and it provided a fitting postscript to his career. He stopped playing in 1959 and a brief spell as team manager at Lancashire in 1964 was not successful, but Washbrook remained a big influence at Old Trafford on committees and as county president.

C. WASHBROOK born 6.12.14 (Barrow, Lancashire). Tests 37 runs 2569 average 42.81 100s 6 wickets 1 average 33

Together again... Washbrook (right) and Hutton

ALLAN WATKINS
Glamorgan 15 Tests 1948-52

SHORT and tubby, Allan Watkins hardly looked like a full-time athlete but that was what he was, with Glamorgan by summer and by winter with Plymouth Argyle and Cardiff City as a soccer player. It was cricket at which he excelled. A left-hander, he loved to cut and hook, preferring to take the fight to the bowlers, but he could also battle it out, as a nine-hour unbeaten 137 in Delhi proved. A useful swing bowler and excellent close catcher, he saved his best for tours, never scoring a half-century in five home Tests.

A.J. WATKINS born 21.4.22 (Usk, Monmouthshire). Tests 15 runs 810 average 40.50 100s 2 wickets 11 average 50.36

Out of India... Watkins (left), Jack Robertson (centre) and Cyril Poole sign off after their ship docks at Tilbury in 1952

JOHN WARR
Middlesex 2 Tests 1951

AN EXTREMELY humorous after-dinner speaker, John Warr makes great play of his position as the most expensive wicket-taker in the history of English Test cricket (1 for 281) — 'and the batsman walked for that one,' he says. 'JJ' was a tall and tireless fast bowler who could be extremely hostile and enjoyed much success with Middlesex. His Test opportunity, however, came while he was still at Cambridge University. A youthful back-up bowler for the 1950-51 Ashes series dominated by Australia, he played when injuries depleted the squad.

J.J. WARR born 16.7.27 (Ealing, London). Tests 2 runs 4 average 1 wickets 1 average 281

John Warr (right) autographing postcards with Alec Bedser during the voyage to Australia in 1950

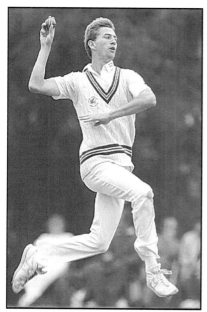

left-hander playing his first Ashes match and better known as a footballer. Watson, as a rugged Sunderland left-half, had played in four internationals but was still trying to tackle an England cricket career.

On a spiteful, worn pitch against Lindwall, Miller and a battery of spinners led by Benaud, Watson and Bailey batted for over four hours for a partnership of 163 that is regarded as one of the classic rearguard actions of Test cricket. They saved the Test with Willie scoring 109, his maiden century for England. Watson was regarded as one of the sweetest left-handers in the country during the early 1950s but his Test career was a series of false starts, and, despite that epic effort at Lord's, he typically found himself dropped for the last

Test which clinched the Ashes for England.

He was a taciturn Yorkshireman who wearied of the Headingley maelstrom and moved to Leicestershire for the latter days of his career. 'Silent Willie' he became known as because, as skipper of Leicestershire, he liked to lead by example rather than expletive, but he was a popular captain and won back his England place. At Grace Road he also doubled up as assistant secretary and became an England selector (1962-64) before emigrating to South Africa.

For further illustration see Fred Trueman

W. WATSON born 7.3.20 (Bolton upon Dearne, Yorkshire). Tests 23 runs 879 average 25.85 100s 2

STEVE WATKIN
Glamorgan 2 Tests 1991

A GRADUATE of the England 'A' team system, Steve Watkin found the step up to Test cricket a difficult one. He made an unexpected debut in the first Test of 1991 against the West Indies when Chris Lewis cried off unwell on the morning of the match. Watkin's seam bowling was ideally suited to the helpful Headingley conditions, and he made a useful contribution of five wickets towards an English victory, but at Lord's a fortnight later his lack of pace and penetration on a good batting wicket was exposed.

S.L. WATKIN born 13.9.64 (Maesteg, Glamorgan). Tests 2 runs 8 average 2.66 wickets 5 average 30.60

WILLIE WATSON
Yorkshire and Leicestershire 23 Tests 1951-59

WILLIE Watson will always be remembered — as a cricketer, at least — for one innings at Lord's on the last day of June in 1953. No-one gave anything for England's chances. Set 343 to win by Australia, they started the day at 20 for 3 with the old ground virtually deserted. Denis Compton was soon out and Trevor Bailey arrived in the centre to join Willie Watson, a tall, poised

Willie Watson

ALAN WHARTON
*Lancashire and Leicestershire 1 Test
1949*

ALAN Wharton, a lively left-handed batsman and right-arm pace bowler who could open both the batting and bowling for Lancashire, still wonders why he was discarded after one Test. Picked for the first Test of 1949 against New Zealand, he helped Cyril Washbrook score a century as his runner then followed orders and went out to throw his bat. Selected for the second Test, he had to withdraw through injury, and never heard from England again. After a productive county career and five years in Rugby League with Salford, he took up teaching full-time and early in 1993 retired as England's longest serving JP.

A. WHARTON born 30.4.23 (Heywood, Lancashire). Tests 1 runs 20 average 10

JAMES WHITAKER
Leicestershire 1 Test 1986

JAMES Whitaker finished the 1986 summer as the leading English batsman with 1,526 runs (average 66) and went on the winter tour of Australia as an uninhibited stroke-maker of considerable potential. He returned home confused by theories on technique and finished the 1987 season with an average of 36 and placed 64th in the national list. Since then he has never looked like adding to the solitary cap he collected in Adelaide when Ian Botham was injured.

J.J. WHITAKER born 5.5.62 (Skipton, Yorkshire). Tests 1 runs 11 average 11

DAVID WHITE
*Hampshire and Glamorgan 2 Tests
1961-62*

WHEN eight of the 29 players asked about their availability for a five-month tour of India and Pakistan ticked the 'No' box, opportunity knocked for untried hopefuls such as 'Butch' White. Built like a bull with a heart to match, he was a tearaway fast bowler who came snorting in off an enormous run. A great character and a good tourist, injury spoiled his England chance, restricting him to the first and last Tests in an eight-Test schedule on the sub-continent's dead wickets.

D.W. WHITE born 14.12.35 (Sutton Coldfield, Warwickshire). Tests 2 runs 0 average — wickets 4 average 29.75

David White

James Whitaker

186

Peter Willey

PETER WILLEY
Northamptonshire and Leicestershire
26 Tests 1976-86

WHEN the land was being scoured for an England captain to pick up the pieces of a disastrous 1989 and take England to the Caribbean that winter to confront the full force of the West Indies again, almost half the county captains in the country were nominated from one quarter or another. Also thrown into the hat by none other than Mike Brearley, in his role as a journalist, was Peter Willey.

Willey, by then, was not even a county captain, he would have been 40 when the tour started and had not played a Test for three years. Yet it made more sense than some suggestions. In the end, the selectors opted for Graham Gooch but the similarities with Willey went deeper than the stubble on their gnarled chins.

A tall, intimidating Geordie, Willey was a hardened pro down to the spikes in his boots. He did not waste words, he detested frippery and anyone prepared to accept defeat. It is said he was the only player whom Ian Botham made sure he did not cross. In fact, 'Will' enjoyed and cultivated the mean, moody image.

With an extraordinary stance so open that his left shoulder was pointing at the square-leg umpire, Willey quite literally squared up to the fastest of bowlers, but his off-spin was used only in emergency at Test level. The selectors continually turned to him when things were getting nasty and all but two of his 26 Tests were against the pace attacks of the West Indies or Australia. When the going got easy, Willey found himself discarded for more attractive run-makers.

He was the youngest player, at 16 years 180 days, to appear for Northamptonshire but quit after a clash with the committee in 1983 and joined Leicestershire, where he had one difficult season as captain before leaving in 1991 to pursue a career in umpiring. Heaven help a player who disputes one of his decisions.

For further illustration see Allan Lamb

P. WILLEY born 6.12.49 (Sedgefield, County Durham). Tests 26 runs 1184 average 26.90 100s 2 wickets 7 average 65.14

NEIL WILLIAMS
Middlesex 1 Test 1990

NEIL Williams' selection for the final Test of 1990 against India could hardly have been put in the category of 'forward planning'. At 28, Williams was a skilful, reliable fast-medium county bowler whose only sniff of international recognition had been when he had been put on stand-by for the 1983-84 tour of New Zealand and Pakistan. A safety-first choice, he was due to be 12th man at the Oval but Chris Lewis felt ill just before the start and Williams felt what it was like to be a Test cricketer.

N.F. WILLIAMS born 2.7.62 (St Vincent, Windward Islands). Tests 1 runs 38 average 38 wickets 2 average 74.0

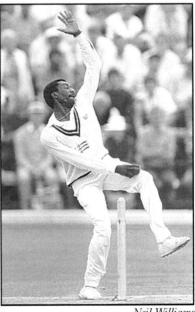

Neil Williams

DON WILSON
Yorkshire 6 Tests 1963-71

DON Wilson was always surprised when a batsman survived the cunning of his flighted left-arm spin. Each delivery was completed with a jump in the air in anticipation of a wicket. He was a fine fielder, bold hitter and an eternal enthusiast, but his Test chances suffered behind Lock and then Underwood, both bigger spinners, and his only chances came on tour, first in India and seven years later in New Zealand. Disillusioned by Boycott's captaincy at Leeds, he quit the game prematurely but rediscovered his enthusiasm as MCC head coach from 1977 to '90.

For further illustration see Mike Smith

D. WILSON born 7.8.37 (Settle, Yorkshire). Tests 6 runs 75 average 12.50 wickets 11 average 42.36

BARRY WOOD
Yorkshire, Lancashire and Derbyshire 12 Tests 1972-78

NOT one of life's shrinking violets, Barry Wood would be the first to admit he did not do justice to his ability as a rugged opening batsman at Test level. He suffered from not having a good run in the side, which was caused principally by the presence of Boycott, Edrich and Amiss. A tremendous hooker and gutsy competitor, he was vulnerable to top-quality spin and scored only two half-centuries in 21 attempts. His son Nathan, a left-handed opener, is a budding star with Lancashire and England Under 18s.

B. WOOD born 26.12.42 (Ossett, Yorkshire). Tests 12 runs 454 average 21.61

DOUG WRIGHT
Kent 34 Tests 1938-51

MOST bowlers are happy to take one hat-trick in their career. They will happily recount every treasured moment of that rare occasion. For Doug Wright hat-tricks became almost routine. The bounding leg-spinner took a world record seven: six for Kent, one for the MCC in South Africa. And it is no freak statistic because when Doug decided it was his day, there was no more dangerous spin bowler in the world. He would charge in off 15 paces in a series of hops and, with a final leap, send the ball fizzing through, delivered either with leg-spin or as a googly. If the batsman dared think about advancing down the pitch, he had a nasty bouncer, and if the ball found the edge, it would frequently fly over the slips for four. Unfortunately, this freakish bowling machinery was as dependable as a British Rail timetable. When the gods decided to throw a spanner into the works, Wright would bowl what batsmen refer to as cafeteria bowling: help yourself.

Barry Wood

Doug Wright

England's most capped leg-spinner since the War, Wright did not take his 109 Test wickets cheaply (average 39.11) but given the right day and the right conditions, he could win a Test on his own. On a helpful Sydney wicket in 1947 he claimed 7 for 102, yet a few weeks earlier on the same wicket he had been carted to the tune of 1 for 169. Later that year he ripped out the South Africans at Lord's with match figures of 10 for 175, the best of an England career which had started when, as a 23-year-old, he bowled Australian legend Jack Fingleton with his fourth ball. A gentle man, Wright left Kent in 1957 after a happy career which brought him 2,000 first-class wickets to become a successful coach at Charterhouse School.

D.V.P. WRIGHT born 21.8.14 (Sidcup, Kent). Tests 34 runs 289 average 11.11 wickets 108 average 39.11

BOB WOOLMER
Kent 19 Tests 1975-81

JUST when it appeared Bob Woolmer's calm, elegant batting was about to become a force in Test cricket, he was lured away by the rewards of Kerry Packer's World Series circus. Having taken two years to establish himself, floating around the order, Woolmer settled into the No. 3 position against the 1977 Australians with centuries in the first two Tests at Lord's and Old Trafford, and the comparisons with his Kent captain Colin Cowdrey duly followed.

Those comparisons with a cricketer whom he admired immensely were inevitable. Like Cowdrey, Woolmer was built for comfort, had an elegant air and plenty of patience. Bob even followed the same route to Canterbury, having been born in India and educated at a Kent public school.

Originally Woolmer made it into a strong Kent side principally for his medium-paced swing bowling and took a while to work his way up the order. In 1975 he stepped into the international arena and in his second Test against Australia took 394 minutes compiling his first century for England, which at the time was the slowest in Ashes cricket. The touch of class was evident even then but in 1977 Packer bought it up. When Woolmer did return after the truce with the Packer men three years later, he was never the same player. He appeared in four more Tests but needed little persuasion to join the 1982 rebel tour to South Africa.

Married to a South African, Woolmer played and coached with a multi-racial team in the Cape and emigrated there when back trouble ended his county career in 1984. He returned to Canterbury to help with coaching in 1987 and is currently coach with Warwickshire.

R.A. WOOLMER born 14.5.48 (Kanpur, India). Tests 19 runs 1059 average 33.09 100s 3 wickets 4 average 74.75

Bob Woolmer

BOB WILLIS

Surrey and Warwickshire 90 Tests 1971-84

JUST how Bob Willis got through 90 Test matches — a record for an English fast bowler — remains one of the mysteries of medical science. Willis' body was all wrong for the demands of fast bowling. His angular 6ft 6in frame looked like it might snap; his legs pumped and his arms flapped on his run-up, hence the nickname 'Goose'; his knees kept the surgeons busy but he refused to write off his career as others were doing. Willis came through it all to become England's leading wicket-taker of all time (until Ian Botham overtook him), and captain of his country for 18 Tests.

There was always a rebellious streak in Willis, driving him on. At Guildford Royal Grammar School he hated the rugby he had to play and became a goalkeeper with Guildford City. His hero was the American protest singer Bob Dylan, and he added Dylan to his own name in deference. And when his first England cap came at 21, it would never have fitted on top of his mop of unruly hair.

He had barely started playing for Surrey — he was not capped by the county — when the call came to replace the injured Alan Ward on the 1970-71 Australia tour. At the time Willis had not done much for Surrey, in fact he never did much in county cricket, but he was fast and he could make the ball take off.

Soon he left the Oval and moved to Edgbaston but, like John Snow, he did not relish breaking his back in a county game going nowhere. In his best summer he took only 65 wickets, and 25 of those were for England. The county and his colleagues became frustrated, Willis was disappointed himself, but he found motivation incredibly difficult after a draining Test match.

For England he played with an intensity that produced tunnel vision when he was bowling, and at night he listened to tapes supplied by a hypnotherapist to help him relax and sleep. Insomnia was another of the hurdles he had to clear. He served his England apprenticeship under Snow and Arnold, and in 1977 the Packer defections confirmed him as leader of the pack, a job he went on to share with the young bounding Botham. Knee trouble, which had flared in the mid-1970s, recurred again when he broke down in the Caribbean in 1981 before the series had started.

Yet the next summer he was back and producing the most spellbinding performance of his life. At Headingley, Australia, having made England follow on, needed only 131 to win but Willis, inspired by Botham's batting, was like a man possessed. Eyes fixed on some distant grail, he came in from the Kirkstall Lane end in manic flight and scattered the Australians with 8 for 43, the best by an English fast bowler in Ashes history. That ability to focus all his energies proved a drawback when, the next year, Peter May became chairman of selectors and installed him as captain. While Willis was no tactical slouch, when he wound himself up to do his job with the new ball the team was run by committee. Gower, Botham and Bob Taylor had to keep an eye on mundane matters such as field placings and who should bowl from the other end until Willis took his sweater and gathered his thoughts. Willis' appointment as Warwickshire skipper for five seasons was not the most successful arrangement, either. He was not the best communicator, believing professional cricketers should be able to get on with their own job very much as he had done.

In Pakistan in 1984 he fell ill and returned home, handing over the captaincy to Gower, a move that was made permanent that summer when Willis played the last three of his Tests. In his final match against the West Indians he recorded another curious Test landmark: two more 'not outs' took his tally to 55, a record in international cricket. A student of the windmill school of batsmanship, he was surprisingly effective — and often sent shock waves through his batting partner as well as the opposition. A friendly companion, he is still on the cricket scene as a commentator and boss of his own promotions company.

R.G.D. WILLIS born 30.5.49 (Sunderland, County Durham). Tests 90 runs 840 average 11.50 wickets 325 average 25.20

The Goose in flight... Bob Willis

England skipper Norman Yardley speaking at Don Bradman's farewell luncheon at the Savoy, 1948

NORMAN YARDLEY
Yorkshire 20 Tests 1938-50

IF THE selectors had not been besotted by the notion that only an amateur could captain England, Norman Yardley would have made a minimal impact on Test cricket after the War. A strong county all-rounder, Yardley struggled to make the step up to Test cricket as a player but he had the right pedigree as a skipper. He was captain in 14 of the 20 Tests in which he played, and was vice-captain to Wally Hammond in five others. The only time he played in a Test as one of the troops was in his first on tour in South Africa in 1938-39.

Yardley had excellent sporting credentials: a Cambridge Blue in cricket, hockey and squash, he was also North of England squash champion for six years. He became the natural successor to Hammond as England skipper in 1947 — a year before he took over at Yorkshire — and his enterprising, relaxed leadership made him a popular, if not always successful skipper.

His first summer against South Africa started with a 99 — his highest Test score — to save the first Test and victories in the next three followed. Business commitments, however, made him unavailable for tours and his next foray into Test cricket the following summer was a far less joyous occasion. Don Bradman's Australians whipped England 4-0 in a contest that was as unequal as the scoreline suggests. Work ruled him out in 1949 but in 1950, with good amateur captains thin on the ground, Yardley returned to lead England another three times, the West Indian spin wizards Ramadhin and Valentine ending his term in office with two more defeats. After his playing days he combined his work in the wine trade with stints on the troubled Yorkshire committee and as an England selector from 1951 to 1954.

N.W.D. YARDLEY born 19.3.15 (Gawber, Yorkshire). Died 4.10.89. Tests 20 runs 812 average 25.37 wickets 21 average 33.66

JACK YOUNG
Middlesex 8 Tests 1947-49

THE son of a music-hall comic, Jack Young was a theatrical performer and extremely popular with spectators. Only 5ft 7in with a low delivery, he could pin batsmen down for hours with his left-arm spin, and his 11 successive maidens to Don Bradman and Lindsay Hassett on his home Test debut was then a world record. He was not a big wicket-taker at Test level but his 1,182 wickets for Middlesex is bettered by only two players since the War, Fred Titmus and Jim Sims.

J.A. YOUNG born 14.10.12 (London). Died 5.2.93. Tests 8 runs 28 average 5.60 wickets 17 average 44.52

Jack Young

THE CAPTAINS' LOG

THIS section lists in chronological order the 33 men handed the honour of leading their country since cricket resumed after the War in 1946. It includes only players given the captaincy for a whole Test, not those who took over during the course of a game because of illness or injury to the official captain. The Test figure after each name indicates the number of matches as captain.

WALLY HAMMOND
20 Tests W4 L3 D13

Captain before the War, Hammond led England again when well past his best, at 43 against India, when cricket resumed and on an ill-starred tour of Australasia.

NORMAN YARDLEY
14 Tests W4 L7 D3

Hammond's vice-captain in Australia, Yardley never toured again because of business commitments, taking charge of home series only against South Africa, Australia and the West Indies.

KENNETH CRANSTON
1 Test D1

The Liverpool dentist went to the West Indies in 1947-48 as vice-captain but took over for the first Test when skipper Gubby Allen injured himself when skipping on the banana boat shipping the team out.

GUBBY ALLEN
11 Tests W4 L5 D2

In the absence of any leading amateur players, Gubby Allen, at 45, was asked to take the MCC team to the Caribbean in 1947 despite having played only one county match that summer. It was 10 years after his previous Test. It turned out to be a disappointing end to a Test career which saw Allen lead England eight times before the War.

GEORGE MANN
7 Tests W2 D5

George Mann, previously uncapped, took England to South Africa in 1948-49 when Yardley was unavailable, and, after a successful tour, he kept the job for two Tests the next summer before business commitments ended his tenure.

FREDDIE BROWN
15 Tests W5 L6 D4

Successful amateur captains were thin on the ground when Freddie Brown, at 38, took over in 1949. With Yardley unavailable for the 1950-51 Ashes tour, Brown stepped in again, this time keeping the job for the next 12 Tests.

NIGEL HOWARD
4 Tests W1 D3

Howard took a sub-standard party to India for an arduous tour in 1951-52 and proved to be a popular and successful leader.

DONALD CARR
1 Test L1

When Howard fell ill on the sub-continent, Donald Carr took over and collected the distinction of being the first international captain to lose to India.

SIR LEONARD HUTTON
23 Tests W11 L4 D8

The first professional to lead England since Arthur Shrewsbury in 1887, Hutton was regarded with grave suspicion by the Establishment but proved himself to be an excellent captain as well as a magnificent player during his three-year reign.

Rt. Rev. DAVID SHEPPARD
2 Tests W1 D1

Took over for two Tests against Pakistan in 1954 when Hutton fell ill.

PETER MAY
41 Tests W20 L10 D11

The Lord's lobby for a return to an amateur captain won the day and May, the outstanding batsman of his era, did not let them down when he took over from Hutton in 1955. Tough, astute and respected, May led England more often and to more victories than anyone else. His only great disappointment was losing 4-0 in Australia in 1958-59

SIR COLIN COWDREY
27 Tests W8 L4 D15

First led England as May's deputy in 1959 and '60 but never really convinced the selectors he was the man for the job. In all he had five periods in charge, the longest being a 12-match reign starting with a series victory in the Caribbean in 1968.

TED DEXTER
30 Tests W9 L7 D14

Like Cowdrey, Dexter was given the captaincy more for his outstanding batsmanship than his leadership qualities. His quixotic reign started with the 1961-62 tour of India and Pakistan and, after a head-to-head trial with Cowdrey in 1962 when they shared the job, he took over until 1964.

MIKE SMITH
25 Tests W5 L3 D17

There have been few more popular England skippers with the players than 'MJK'. He took over in India (1963-64) when Dexter was unavailable and again the next winter in South Africa when Dexter stood (unsuccessfully) as a prospective MP. Smith deservedly kept the job for the next two years.

BRIAN CLOSE
7 Tests W6 D1

Bristling with patriotic fervour, Brian Close took over for the last Test of 1966 and beat the West Indies. The next summer his team routed India and Pakistan. He was invited to lead the tour to the West Indies that winter but was then shabbily rejected after a time-wasting row at Edgbaston, Cowdrey being preferred.

TOM GRAVENEY
1 Test D1

Took over in 1968 for the fourth Test against Australia when Cowdrey was injured.

RAY ILLINGWORTH
31 Tests W12 L5 D14

Having been captain of a county side for only a few weeks, Ray Illingworth took over when Cowdrey was injured in 1969 and made such an impression with his aware leadership that he kept the job for four years, the highlight being an Ashes success in Australia (1970-71).

TONY LEWIS
8 Tests W1 L2 D5

When Illingworth was unavailable for the 1972-73 trip to India and Pakistan, Tony Lewis took charge, proving a tactful and popular leader.

MIKE DENNESS
19 Tests W6 L5 D8

Vice-captain to Lewis, Denness was chosen to lead England to the West Indies in 1974 after Illingworth stepped aside — much to the chagrin of Geoff Boycott. Denness enjoyed considerable success until his authority was undermined by the Australian pace bowlers the following winter.

JOHN EDRICH
1 Test L1

Took over for the fourth Test in Sydney in 1975 when skipper Denness dropped himself in grim circumstances.

TONY GREIG
14 Tests W3 L5 D6

The charismatic South African replaced Denness in 1975 and inspired much loyalty from his players until he caused a storm by linking up with Kerry Packer's cricket circus in 1977.

MIKE BREARLEY
31 Tests W18 L4 D9

Mike Brearley's winning ratio is the most impressive of all the leading post-War captains and he is generally regarded as one of the shrewdest skippers to set foot on a cricket field. Stepped down in 1980 but returned for a curtain call a year later to inspire a famous Ashes triumph. Also led England to the 1979 World Cup Final.

GEOFF BOYCOTT
4 Tests W1 L1 D2

Realised a long-standing ambition when he took charge on the 1977-78 Pakistan-New Zealand tour, after Brearley broke an arm, to the mixed feelings of the squad.

IAN BOTHAM
12 Tests L4 D8

Brearley's first choice to succeed him, but Ian Botham and the rigours of captaincy were not natural bedfellows. It did not help that his first two series were against the West Indies, and his own form suffered.

KEITH FLETCHER
7 Tests W1 L1 D5

Much-respected captain for the unforgiving 1981-82 tour of India and Sri Lanka, Keith Fletcher was summarily discarded when Peter May became chairman of selectors in 1982.

BOB WILLIS
18 Tests W7 L5 D6

Surprise choice to take over in 1982 as the rebels defected to South Africa, Bob Willis gave everything as a skipper and bowler for two years although communication was never his strongest suit.

DAVID GOWER
32 Tests W5 L18 D9

On first inspection David Gower's record looks pretty sickly but it should be noted that 10 defeats came in two 5-0 whitewashes by the West Indies which even Captain Scarlet would have had trouble averting. Gower's chivalrous style made him popular but his biggest mistake was coming back for a second term in office in what turned out to be a disastrous 1989 Ashes summer.

MIKE GATTING
23 Tests W2 L5 D16

After his first complete series in charge, which brought triumph in Australia (1986-87), Mike Gatting never won a Test as England skipper. More damaging to his reputation, however, was his notorious showdown with Pakistan umpire Shakoor Rana and a liaison with a Leicestershire barmaid which preceded his dismissal in 1988. Led England to the World Cup Final in 1987 and led a rebel team to South Africa in 1990.

JOHN EMBUREY
2 Tests L2

Took over in the wake of Gatting's controversial dismissal for the second and third Tests against the West Indies in 1988.

CHRIS COWDREY
1 Test L1

Shock appointment for two Tests to scrub up England's image in 1988, Chris Cowdrey lasted only one match before injury prompted a swift and shabby end to his captaincy.

GRAHAM GOOCH
30 Tests W10 L9 D11

Having become the fourth captain used in the summer of 1988, Graham Gooch took more permanent control when he led England to the Caribbean in 1990. Attaining the leadership late in his career brought out the best in him as a batsman and made him highly respected by his players. An inconsistent record was not helped by unfortunate injuries and illness on tour. Led England to the 1992 World Cup Final.

ALLAN LAMB
3 Tests L3

Took over when Gooch fractured a hand in the West Indies and was unfortunate to preside over two defeats which cost England the series. The following winter in Australia Lamb suffered his third defeat when Gooch was injured again.

ALEC STEWART
2 Test L2

Vice-captain since 1992, Stewart took over when Gooch was ill for the second Test in India in 1993. When Gooch returned home early from a disastrous tour, Stewart endured the ignominy of leading England to their first defeat by Sri Lanka.

THE CHAMPIONSHIP TABLE

THERE IS widespread conviction north of St John's Wood tube station that those in the Lord's committee room would have preferred it if Hadrian had built his wall somewhere along a line between Southend-on-Sea and Weston-super-Mare. In other words, if you are a northern cricketer who wants to be noticed by the England selectors, for every dour half-century scored by your counterparts at Canterbury and Uxbridge, you have to register dazzling hundreds at Worksop or Blackpool to arouse their interest. In the north they call it 'Southern Bias', in the south they call it 'Northern Paranoia'. The truth lies probably somewhere around Watford Gap — in between the two.

The table alongside shows the number of players each county has provided for the England Test team since the War. It is basically a bit of fun; it proves little except that Yorkshire, the most successful county in that period, provided the most players, as logic would suggest. The strugglers, meanwhile, such as Somerset and Glamorgan, provided the fewest. Some might point out that Middlesex, whose home is at Lord's, make a disproportionately high contribution to the Test team compared with, say, Worcestershire, who have won the Championship almost as frequently — five times to Middlesex's six. If that suggests southern bias how do you explain Lancashire's standing as the third highest contributor of Test players when the champions' pennant has flown over Old Trafford only once since the War — and that a shared affair? Derby, a supposedly 'unfashionable' county, have never won the championship in the post-War years yet they have supplied as many Test players as Essex, who have won it six times. And Hampshire, who could not go any further south without getting their feet wet, have built two championship-winning teams, yet had only seven Test players picked from their ranks, the lowest figure of all save newcomers Durham. In other words, the geographical argument is not stood up by the figures... but that will not convince anyone outside the Home Counties.

In the list, counties are credited only with Test players on their staff at the time of selection. For example, Mike Selvey appears under Middlesex, the county for whom he was playing when chosen by England, not under Surrey nor Glamorgan, for whom he also played during his career. Ian Botham, on the other hand, appears under Somerset, Worcestershire and Durham because he played for England while with those three counties.

YORKSHIRE 33

Bob Appleyard, Bill Athey, David Bairstow, Jimmy Binks, Richard Blakey, Bill Bowes, Geoff Boycott, Don Brennan, Brian Close, Geoff Cope, Alec Coxon, Paul Gibb, John Hampshire, Len Hutton, Richard Hutton, Ray Illingworth, Paul Jarvis, Eddie Leadbeater, Frank Lowson, Martyn Moxon, Chris Old, Doug Padgett, Phil Sharpe, Arnie Sidebottom, Frank Smailes, Gerald Smithson, Graham Stevenson, Ken Taylor, Fred Trueman, Johnny Wardle, Willie Watson, Don Wilson, Norman Yardley.

MIDDLESEX 29

Gubby Allen, Graham Barlow, Mike Brearley, Roland Butcher, Denis Compton, Norman Cowans, John Dewes, Paul Downton, Bill Edrich, Phil Edmonds, John Emburey, Angus Fraser, Mike Gatting, George Mann, Alan Moss, John Murray, Peter Parfitt, John Price, Clive Radley, Mark Ramprakash, Jack Robertson, Eric Russell, Mike Selvey, Wilf Slack, Fred Titmus, Phil Tufnell, John Warr, Neil Williams, Jack Young.

LANCASHIRE 25

Paul Allott, Mike Atherton, Bob Barber, Bob Berry, Ken Cranston, Phillip DeFreitas, Neil Fairbrother, Graeme Fowler, Tommy Greenhough, Frank Hayes, Ken Higgs, Malcolm Hilton, Nigel Howard, John Ikin, Peter Lever, David Lloyd, Winston Place, Dick Pollard, Geoff Pullar, Brian Statham, Ken Shuttleworth, Ray Tattersall, Cyril Washbrook, Alan Wharton, Barry Wood.

SURREY 21

Geoff Arnold, Ken Barrington, Alec Bedser, Freddie Brown, Alan Butcher, John Edrich, Laurie Fishlock, Alf Gover, Robin Jackman, Jim Laker, Peter Loader, Tony Lock, Peter May, Arthur McIntyre, Pat Pocock, Jack Richards, Graham Roope, Alec Stewart, Micky Stewart, Roy Swetman, Bob Willis.

WORCESTERSHIRE 19

Ian Botham, Len Coldwell, Tim Curtis, Graham Dilley, Basil D'Oliveira, Jack Flavell, Norman Gifford, Tom Graveney, Graeme Hick, Martin Horton, Dick Howorth, Richard Illingworth, Roland Jenkins, Don Kenyon, Phil Newport, Neal Radford, Dick Richardson, Peter Richardson, David Smith.

KENT 18

Mark Benson, Alan Brown, Chris Cowdrey, Colin Cowdrey, Mike Denness, Graham Dilley, Richard Ellison, Godfrey Evans, Alan Igglesden, Alan Knott, Brian Luckhurst, Jack Martin, Peter Richardson, Fred Ridgeway, Chris Tavare, Derek Underwood, Bob Woolmer, Doug Wright.

NORTHAMPTONSHIRE 18

Keith Andrew, Robert Bailey, Dennis Brookes, Freddie Brown, David Capel, Bob Cottam, Geoff Cook, Nick Cook, Allan Lamb, Wayne Larkins, David Larter, Colin Milburn, Roger Prideaux, David Steele, Raman Subba Row, Paul Taylor, Frank Tyson, Peter Willey.

LEICESTERSHIRE 16

Jon Agnew, Chris Balderstone, Jack Birkenshaw, Nick Cook, Phillip DeFreitas, David Gower, Ray Illingworth, Barry Knight, Chris Lewis, Tony Lock, Charles Palmer, Les Taylor, Roger Tolchard, Willie Watson, James Whitaker, Peter Willey.

SUSSEX 15

Ted Dexter, Hubert Doggart, Ian Greig, Tony Greig, Billy Griffith, Jim Langridge, Alan Oakman, Paul Parker, Jim Parks, Tony Pigott, Ian Salisbury, David Sheppard, Don Smith, John Snow, Ian Thomson.

WARWICKSHIRE 15

Dennis Amiss, Bob Barber, David Brown, Tom Cartwright, Tom Dollery, Eric Hollies, John Jameson, Andy Lloyd, Tim Munton, Dermot Reeve, Gladstone Small, Alan Smith, Mike Smith, Dick Spooner, Bob Willis.

DERBYSHIRE 13

Kim Barnett, Donald Carr, Bill Copson, Cliff Gladwin, Mike Hendrick, Les Jackson, Devon Malcolm, Geoff Miller, John Morris, George Pope, Harold Rhodes, Bob Taylor, Alan Ward.

ESSEX 13

Trevor Bailey, John Childs, Keith Fletcher, Neil Foster, Graham Gooch, Nasser Hussain, Robin Hobbs, Doug Insole, Barry Knight, John Lever, Derek Pringle, Peter Smith, John Stephenson.

GLOUCESTERSHIRE 13

David Allen, Bill Athey, Charlie Barnett, Sam Cook, Jack Crapp, George Emmett, Tom Graveney, Wally Hammond, David Lawrence, Arthur Milton, John Mortimore, Jack Russell, David Smith.

NOTTINGHAMSHIRE 13

Brian Bolus, Chris Broad, Harold Butler, Bruce French, Joe Hardstaff, Eddie Hemmings, Chris Lewis, Geoff Millman, Cyril Poole, Derek Randall, Tim Robinson, Reg Simpson, Bill Voce.

GLAMORGAN 10

Jeff Jones, Tony Lewis, Matthew Maynard, Jim McConnon, Hugh Morris, Gilbert Parkhouse, Greg Thomas, Peter Walker, Steve Watkin, Allan Watkins.

SOMERSET 9

Ian Botham, Brian Close, Neil Mallender, Vic Marks, Ken Palmer, Brian Rose, Fred Rumsey, Chris Tavare, Maurice Tremlett.

HAMPSHIRE 7

Bob Cottam, David Gower, Derek Shackleton, Chris Smith, Robin Smith, Paul Terry, David White.

DURHAM 1

Ian Botham.